CREATING SOCIAL ENTERPRISE

My story and what I learned

Creating Social Enterprise
My story and what I learned

Author

All rights reserved. No part of this book may be reproduced in any manner without written permission of the copyright owner except for the use of quotations in a book review.

First edition 2023

ISBN: 9-1-3996-1234-0

www.creatingsocialenterprise.co.uk

© 2023 Author Name

Published by

Enterprise...

Creating Social Enterprise

My story and what I learned

Written by Patrick Nash

First edition 2023

ISBN 978-1-3999-4733-6

www.creatingsocialenterprise.co.uk

© 2023 Patrick Nash

Published by
EnterpriseValues

For Amanda

Reviews

"If we are to succeed in building a fairer and greener economy, we have to create a new generation of social entrepreneurs. We need more people like Patrick Nash, who are ready to innovate and develop business models that prioritise people and planet. This book provides valuable insights and practical advice from a serial social entrepreneur that will inspire others".

Derek Walker
Future Generations Commissioner for Wales

"In this outstanding book Patrick tells of his life long journey as a social innovator. It details the highs and lows of creating social value from new ways of running helplines to environmental projects. It's an invaluable guide to those who would change the world through inspired social innovation".

Sir Stuart Etherington
Former CEO of National Council for Voluntary Organisations

"Like Patrick this book is funny, thoughtful and all about innovation, driven by an exceptional grasp on values. The story of unusual social enterprises told with warmth, honesty and pragmatism. Any reader will love this".

Rusty Livock
Co-founder Connect Assist

"If you believe that business should be a force for good, you will find this book not only an invaluable 'How To' guide, but also a well written and entertaining life story. Treat yourself and read Patrick's book".

Dirk Rohwedder
Associate Director – the School for Social Entrepreneurs

"Any community group that wants to set up a social enterprise will find this an inspiring introduction to the opportunities as well as the pitfalls"

Jane Foot
Researcher and author on asset based community development

About the author

Patrick Nash set up and led twelve successful social enterprises, including cooperatives, charities and companies..

In 1980, aged 22, he was part of the team that set up one of the UK's largest vegetarian food wholesale cooperatives. He went on to lead on the development of an eco-village in the North of Scotland, raising the funds and managing the construction of eco-homes, renewable energy and chemical free sewage treatment.

After a brief spell working for the Dalai Lama in the mid 1990s, Patrick set up the largest workplace counselling service in the UK, Teacherline, along with charities and social enterprises that worked in education to promote healthy working environments.

In 2005, while setting up a contact centre enterprise, he decided to locate in the Welsh Valleys, an area of high unemployment, in order to create jobs and growth opportunities. The company now employs close to 400 people who provide 24/7 support to many thousands of people each day facing challenging circumstances including mental health, poverty and debt, youth empowerment, seeking asylum and more.

This enterprise, Connect Assist, won the Institute of Welsh Affairs/ Western Mail Small Business of the Year Award in 2013 and Patrick won the Institute of Directors Director of the Year Award for Corporate Responsibility in 2017.

Patrick lives with his wife in Pembrokeshire, Wales and holds a number of non-executive positions, including trustee of Money and Mental Health Policy Institute. He is a volunteer founder of the St Davids Festival of Ideas and a trustee of the Solva Edge Festival. This is his first book.

Acknowledgements

Every time I have done something good in my life I have been fortunate to be surrounded by wonderful people. This was the same for this book so thank you all so much.

My wife Amanda Stone encouraged me to start writing, helped me every step of the way particularly when I got stuck. And then undertaking a final, essential review of the book.

I wrote every word of the first draft over multiple visits to a beautiful house in Devon thanks to Charlie at Urban Writers' Retreat.

The book was produced by a great team. Margaret Hunter at Daisy Editorial edited the book. Julia Sandford-Cooke at Wordfire Communications advised on the structure of the book. Christian Senior of Dead Sea Design drew the illustrations, designed the book and built the associated website. Brian Semple at Money and Mental Health took my photograph.

A few of my former colleagues read the text at certain points and were really helpful. Rusty Livock read the first draft and as ever came up with suggestions that improved the narrative. Paul Grassick, Alex Walker, John Talbott, Carol Lynch and Steve Thorp reviewed the sections where they were involved and were very encouraging as well as correcting some of my memories of events.

As well as encouragement from Amanda, my daughters Miriam Nash, Evie Nash and Treya Nash have enjoyed hearing many of my stories and encouraged me to write them. And thanks to my parents Norman and Mary Nash. My father died a few months before I finished the book so although he never got to read it, he enjoyed the parts of the book that I read to him.

Contents

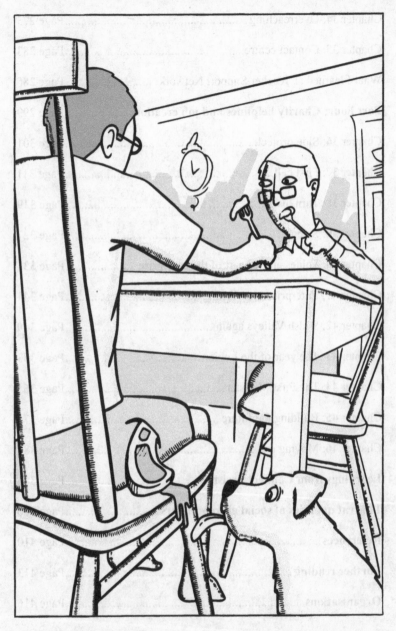

I would hide my piece of meat in a pocket or up a shirt sleeve

Introduction

I hate meat!

I never liked eating meat as a child. I hated it. The smell, the texture and the taste. It made me feel sick, and on occasions I was sick when I ate it. But I was born in 1957 and my Mum thought I wouldn't grow up unless I ate meat. And school only fed us meat, slices of slimy meat in hideous gravy served with vegetables cooked to slush.

My earliest memory of eating is of a plate of slices of meat (lamb, pork or chicken) with boiled potatoes and a green vegetable of some sort. I started by eating the potatoes and vegetables and then announced that I was full. But Mum was having none of that. I would have to eat my meat and was only allowed to eat my vegetables when I had finished it.

I got reasonably adept at disposing of meat. When no one was looking, I would hide a piece of meat in a pocket or up a shirt sleeve, depositing it in a bin after I had enjoyed a meal of potatoes and vegetables. I got really good at this and was sure that Mum had not found me out until one day she found a rotting piece of meat in my trouser pocket after she had done the washing. So now she was wise to my tricks.

It was easier to hide meat at school. I was a largely vegetarian, if hungry, child. I was not strong, did not really engage with team sports, wore glasses and was mostly solitary with a small number of friends. I felt that I was bottom of the pile.

However, as I got into my teenage years I started to eat meat. I never liked it, but I resigned myself to eating it, if nothing else because it avoided one of the many excuses for ridicule.

When it came time for me to leave school and home, I knew nothing about cooking and food and was not that interested.

At Bristol University I shared a small house with a fabulous group of friends and we took it in turns to cook for the group. In our first week together Andy, a veterinary student, brought back an off-cut of meat, left over from one of the experiments that vets do, and cooked up a pig's trotter stew.

This was the final straw. The next day Fiona, who also lived in the house, and I tracked down one of Bristol's first wholefoods shops and returned laden with beans, rice, soya sauce, herbs, spices and the Cranks vegetarian cookbook. I became a vegetarian and discovered a lifelong love of cooking for people. I have cooked for well over 45 years now but have never once cooked meat.

I also began to educate myself about the impact of the meat industry on land use, on methane and carbon production and therefore on climate. In the late 1970s there was a beginning of an understanding of the impact of our way of life on the environment. Fiona and I started to write about this and produced a magazine on environmental and related political issues, which we sold at our environmental bookstall at the students' union twice a week.

I still hate meat, but I love that my hatred of it was at the heart of how I became a social entrepreneur.

What do you want to do with your life?

Somehow the whole 'what do you want to do with your life' conversation passed me by. I never engaged with the notion of 'having a career'. Once I'd left school, I worked my passage by sea to Australia and travelled there for a year, working to pay my way and living on a shoestring. By the time I got to university, I had learned to live reasonably well on very little.

I did an economics degree at Bristol University in the second half of the 1970s. At least that was what I was studying. What I was mostly doing was becoming a person for the first time and finding out what I

'Campaign for Nuclear Disarmament' demonstrations

was interested in, principally politics and music. I got involved with the environmental, anti-nuclear and peace movements, and by the second year Fiona and I were organising benefit concerts and lectures (we put on the first ever Schumacher Lecture, a series concerning the environment and society) and booking buses to go to demonstrations in London and various nuclear power station construction sites around the country.

This did mean that I got comfortable with managing what felt at the time like large sums of money. On one occasion we sold £10,000-worth of tickets for a benefit concert, which we counted from a large pile of notes and coins on a table while up-and-coming punk group The Pop Group played a sell-out gig. The local Greenpeace and Friends of the Earth groups could not quite believe it when we gave them half each. The band played for free as they were keen to have a large concert as a showcase for London agents, after they had previously been fobbed off by the students' union events committee. Their loss, our gain.

Towards the end of my time at university, I noticed that friends and fellow students were going off to interviews with companies, the civil service and other employers. My Dad was a chartered accountant and had gone to work for his father after he had qualified. I was vaguely aware of comments like 'If you get an accountancy qualification you'll be able to work anywhere', which I ignored.

All thoughts of career passed me by and all I knew was that I wanted to travel, so after graduating I started planning my next travelling adventure, this time to Africa.

That's a story in itself and not one to be told here. But in some ways my social enterprise career did start there. I had travelled overland on top of a lorry from Khartoum in the north of Sudan to Juba in the south, a rough journey. I was tired and hungry, and vegetarians were certainly not catered for. In the one backpacker hotel in Juba I met a fellow traveller.

"Do you know where you can get anything vegetarian to eat?" I asked him.

"Sure," he said. "There's a great bean stall in the market. Let's go."

We went to the noisy, hot and dusty market and sure enough there was a stand with two brothers serving a sludgy bean dish wrapped in a flat bread. It was the nicest food I had eaten in weeks.

We spent a week together in Juba. He had lived in a community in Yorkshire and worked at a wholesale vegetarian food business in Leeds named Suma.

After nine months of walking and hitch-hiking across 11 countries in the north and centre of Africa, I was tired and ill. I got back to my parents' home in London only to be admitted to the tropical medicine hospital with a bout of hepatitis A.

I came back a more confident person, having dealt with a number of difficult situations, changing my plans regularly according to circumstances and having to make quick decisions. All useful entrepreneur skills.

Why this book now

We live in a time of uncertainty. What's the future for the climate, the economy, our politics, our health, our communities? Most of us don't know and many of us, including me, are having to face real anxieties, not just about our future, but about our present. We are going to have to make changes to survive and thrive as people, but how do we know what to do to respond to this?

5

As a young person growing up in the 1960s I was terrified about nuclear weapons. In the 1970s I marched in protest. It was scary, with rows of police and their horses charging at us. But it gave confidence to a young, shy boy and I started to find out what was important to me.

I decided not to take the easy course and start a traditional career. I know that not everyone can do that, but I felt that I could and had to take the risk. My first job wasn't a job, it was setting up and scaling a social enterprise, a workers' cooperative. And our strategy wasn't to make money, it was to change the world. Or at least the bit of the world that we felt we could change, which was vegetarian food and the positive impact that this had on our health and the climate. Yes, we knew the science of this 45 years ago.

I didn't hear the term 'social enterprise' until I was well into my 40s. Despite studying economics at university, I had no understanding that business could be such a force for good. The best definition of social enterprise that I have found comes from Social Enterprise UK and I summarise it here:

Social enterprises are businesses that are changing the world for the better.

My early start with a workers' cooperative led me to a lifetime of setting up and running a number of social enterprises and projects based on values, not just profit. Don't get me wrong, I am not against profit. It fuels growth, helps pay people better salaries to live better lives and allows an enterprise to invest and take risks. But any social enterprise has to have a desire to change the world for the better and support people's lives while doing that.

Looking back, the key feature of these social enterprises has been that they have experimented with doing something new, doing something better or bringing something to a community they haven't had before. All in the service of positive social or environmental change. I have

6

built enterprises working in vegetarian food, ecological building, schools, teachers' mental health and support for people in challenging circumstances. Social enterprises are mainstream now and in many cases are being done bigger and better than I was able to do. I was fortunate to be in at the beginning of these and I hope help shape their acceptance into the broader economy and society.

And along the way I was able to learn from and experiment with certain new ideas and concepts, implementing them within a business model to create change and impact. These enterprises were new, and in some cases ahead of the curve, working with climate and food, community assets and ownership, wellbeing, values-based business, kindness and empathy.

Social enterprise is about finding ways to get your values aligned to the commercial mission of the company. Don't make the mistake of thinking that the social or environmental values of a company are somehow more important than the commercial interests.
They are the same.

Business still has a bad name, and I can see why. There has been too much greed, excess, pollution and exploitation in the name of a strong economy. That's no longer OK. What the world needs now is a new generation of socially motivated entrepreneurs who are prepared to change the status quo and take on the big challenges. Doing this in an enterprise context is difficult, and I've had my fair share of challenges and failures. But picking yourself up and learning the lessons means that the next venture will be more successful and have greater impact.

Some years ago a colleague kindly wrote:

> *Patrick's innovative approach to managing social ventures dates back to a period long before it became fashionable. If he ever retires, which I doubt, he needs to write a book to share his vast experience and perspective with the next generation that can help build on his legacy.*

7

This is that book. I'm not quite retired but decided it was time to write. I've included almost everything I have learned and the mistakes I have made. If you are reading this, I hope that my story will encourage you to think about what you want to do in this uncertain world and perhaps have a go at social enterprise. It's worth it – for you, for what you believe in, for the people around you and for the world that we share.

About the book

I was fortunate to stumble into social enterprise just after my 22nd birthday. I did not come across the term for at least 20 years after that, but social enterprise is what I have done.

The book focuses on the four key stages of my social enterprise journey:

- as a vegetarian wholefoods wholesaler

- building an eco-village

- promoting teachers' wellbeing and mental health, and finally

- delivering charity helplines and creating jobs in the Welsh Valleys.

I have left out masses of other experience that is not so relevant to a book about social enterprise. It's not a history, so please forgive me if you feel that you have been left out of your part of the story.

For this reason, I have decided to leave out my personal and family life. Of course family and friends have had a huge impact on what I have done and how I have done it, but I have taken a decision that writing about my personal life would be a distraction from the subject. So, apologies to all of you who I know and love. You know who you are, and I thank you.

I have drawn out 44 'Learnings' from my social enterprise journey. These appear throughout the story and are also gathered together (and in some cases expanded upon) in sections at the end of each of the four parts. This means you can just read, or re-read, these and skip the story if you wish. They were key factors in the success of my enterprises. I've shared many of these at talks I have given and workshops I have facilitated.

Like anyone who has had some success as an entrepreneur, perhaps especially a social entrepreneur, the achievements are not solely mine but also those of the many wonderful and talented people I've worked with. Some of these people are mentioned by name, although typically only by their first name, unless they are or were a public figure.

For those of you I worked with, I expect that you may have some different memories of the events where we intersected and worked together. If you are reading this, I hope you won't mind reading my side of the story even if our memories don't exactly converge. I hope you feel that I have captured some of the spirit of the times in which we worked together.

Part One: Nova Wholefoods

I went down to the local job centre and looked for work

Chapter 1

Jobcentre

When I came out of hospital after my trip to Africa in 1980, I had a week's recovery at my parents' house in south London. I woke up one morning realising I needed to do something, so I went down to the local job centre and looked for work. As I looked at the cards on the noticeboards my eyes blurred and I couldn't really read them. And then I had this thought.

"Go back to Bristol and set up a wholefoods wholesale company."

Where did that come from? I stood gazing at the job cards but not reading them. Then I remembered the conversation in Juba.

I still knew a few people in Bristol so I made some calls and was offered somewhere to stay for a short time by a friend. I packed a bag, got the bus to Hammersmith and hitch-hiked down to Bristol.

My friend was a vegetarian and told me where there were wholefoods shops and cafes nearby in Montpelier, which has always been an alternative area and a hub for vegetarian food.

These shops were different from today, with not a plastic bag in sight. Much of the food staples, such as beans, lentils, rice and flour, were stored in their original sacks sitting on the floor around the shop, with a large stainless-steel scoop in each. There were large tubs of jams, peanut butter and tahini, similarly with scoops. And large tins (often the size of a small dustbin) with oils, soya sauce and other liquids. Fortunately, now that we realise the damage caused by plastic pollution, this approach is coming back. It should never have been dropped.

13

Customers would arrive with their own jars, paper bags and bottles, weigh out their purchases on one of the many sets of scales and pay for them. The shops had a social element to them, political too. The windows and any spare wall space had small cards and posters advertising a wide variety of groups and events: meetings and demonstrations against nuclear power; Buddhist meditation groups; flats and squats to share; and much more. People would meet friends and discuss their lives; recipes were shared.

I was familiar with wholefoods shops. I had frequented them regularly when at university. But this time I was on a mission. I went to the first one and approached the person serving.

"Hello, I'm Patrick. I hope you don't mind, but I wondered where you buy your stock from."

"That's OK," she replied. "We typically drive up to London every other week. We go to a few places there. The main place is Community Foods in Southgate. And we sometimes go to Whole Earth in Neasden and Sunwheel at London Bridge."

"Isn't there anywhere closer you can buy wholefoods supplies?" I asked, feeling optimistic.

"No, there isn't," she replied, "but there is a guy called Paul who is starting something up in Bristol. I have heard about him but we haven't met. Anyway, why are you asking?"

"I'm keen to set up a wholefoods wholesale operation in Bristol. I'm sure there are enough shops in the city, and it would save everyone driving to London."

"So, you should find this guy Paul," she said. "Ask around. I'm sure you will find him."

I did ask around. It took visiting two more shops and a vegetarian cafe but by the late afternoon I had found out that Paul had started a small wholesale operation very recently and was already delivering to some of the shops in Bristol. I was excited but also a bit nervous. What if he didn't want to talk to me? Would my idea be over before it had started?

I walked up the steep hill up to Totterdown Community Centre on Wells Road that looks down over the Temple Meads area of Bristol and the railway station. I gingerly went into the centre, walking past a lorry parked outside on the road.

As I went in I heard an enormous argument between two men. One was speaking in a firm, measured voice with a Scottish accent. The other was screaming back at him. The temperature was rising, and I walked right in.

"I'm looking for Paul," I said.

The Scottish accent stopped mid flow. "What do you want?" he said brusquely. "Can't you see I'm busy?"

"Yes, its fine, I'll wait," I said, retreating to a small room filled with sacks of flour.

The argument continued where it had left off, getting more and more heated, and although I could not hear what was being said, it was clearly not going to end well. And sure enough after about ten minutes there was a loud crash of a door slamming and all was suddenly quiet.

The Scottish man came back in. He was flushed but calm.

"Sorry about that," he said. "What did you want to talk about?"

I hadn't prepared what I would say, so I just blurted out "I'm Patrick. I have had this idea to set up a wholefoods wholesaler in Bristol. I was at university here for three years and have just returned from a year travelling in Africa."

"Great," he said. "We need someone now. Can you drive a truck?"

15

There were large tubs of jams, peanut butter and tahini

"Yes," I said. This wasn't a complete lie, as I had worked a temporary job in London as a lorry driver for two days until I had nearly written the lorry off mounting the pavement at a pedestrian crossing in Battersea.

"Good, can you start tomorrow?"

"Sure."

And that was it. I was a member of Nova Wholefoods. It was and still is the shortest interview or pitch I have ever done, all over with both sides making their decisions in a couple of minutes. I have spent the following 40 years wondering why people take so long to make decisions, needing second, third and more meetings to finally come to a decision that they are still unsure of. This was all over in 120 seconds and yet it's arguably the most significant career decision I have ever made. It set the course for the rest of my working life.

We then had a longer conversation. Paul had previously set up a shop in Durham called Durham Wholefoods. He met his wife Annie and moved to Bristol to live with her. When we spoke, he had just started this small wholesale business with Graham, who previously worked in Glasgow for a cooperative called Green City Wholefoods, as well as the person who had just left.

At 5.30 the next morning I left my room in Montpelier and walked to where Paul lived in nearby St. Paul's. Graham drove the lorry half way up the M4 to London and I drove from there. I was anxious about the driving but by the time we arrived in London I was more confident behind the wheel. We talked the whole way, with Graham explaining how the day ahead would work.

It was a long and fascinating day and how I would spend every Friday for the next year.

17

Once we arrived at the Hammersmith fly-over we drove across south London to the warehouse of Sunwheel Foods, which was in a railway arch near London Bridge. Sunwheel were the first UK importer of Japanese macrobiotic foods such as miso and seaweeds.

Sunwheel Foods were a company spun out of Erewhon, the US-based natural foods pioneer company founded in 1966. One of the founding entrepreneurs of Erewhon was Paul Hawken, whose highly successful book The Magic of Findhorn introduced a whole generation of spiritual and environmental seekers to the Findhorn Community, more of which later. This was the first of many ways in which my entrepreneur journey has followed similar journeys of others.

We collected our order that had been phoned through that morning and headed off to our next stop, Harmony Foods, who had a warehouse at Neasden, just off the North Circular Road. Harmony stocked much of what we needed to fulfil the next week's orders, including their famous Whole Earth brand of jams, fruit concentrates and peanut butters.

Harmony was founded and led by brothers Greg and Craig Sams, and in many ways they were the UK's pioneers of wholefoods. Greg and Craig catered the first ever Glastonbury Festival. Craig and Josephine Fairley, his wife, went on to establish Green and Black's, the organic chocolate brand, and Craig is still a leading light of such organisations as The Soil Association and the Green Party.

From Harmony it was off to the last and most important stop of the day, Community Foods. Community was founded in the early 1970s from a squat in Camden and by 1980 had a large warehouse in New Southgate, north London. In the early days we bought the majority of our food from Community – rice, beans and pulses, oats, flour, dried fruit, nuts, juices and much more. Their warehouse was designed as a cash and carry, so we would rush around collecting all we needed to fulfil our customer orders and load these onto the truck. By the time we left Community, the lorry was full. It was time to get onto the M4 and head back to Bristol.

Learning #1: Intuition

Intuition is the ability to understand something instinctively, without the need for conscious reasoning.

Sometimes intuition comes in the form of words, but mostly it is a clarity of thought that 'just knows what to do'. I have found believing and trusting in my intuition really helpful when faced with the many decisions that have to be made on a daily basis. But that doesn't mean that every decision I made with intuition was necessarily a good decision. My best intuitive decisions were ones that I then developed, elaborated on and discussed. For me, it's often been the starting point for a decision, but there are moments where it is the decision, such as the thought in the Jobcentre.

Most of the social entrepreneurs that I have met use their intuition from time to time.

I quickly discovered one of the delights of driving a 7.5 tonne truck

Chapter 2

The business model

The business model at Nova Wholefoods was fairly straightforward, which Paul had developed from the start. It was a week-at-a-time process, with Thursday as new orders day, the first day of a weekly cycle of activity.

As there were only three of us (Paul, Graham and me) we each did everything. There was no one to delegate anything to. Each of us at some time was truck driver, sales director, customer service adviser, operations manager, warehouse worker and more. We checked stock, took orders, mixed muesli, loaded lorries and fulfilled deliveries. I could not have asked for a better way to learn about enterprise.

I quickly discovered one of the delights of driving a 7.5 tonne truck, that cars tend to get out of your way. It's an obvious metaphor that driving forward with confidence removes obstacles. This has been my approach to much of what I have done in my life ever since. And learned while driving a truck!

Thursdays

On Thursday morning we would start the weekly stocktake. In the early days this took no more than an hour, as we had a rudimentary version of what is nowadays called a just-in-time supply chain, ensuring there was as little stock as possible left over at the beginning of the weekly cycle. Later on this took all day.

These days most operational models are digital, using stock and order systems, barcodes and with invoicing as part of the accounting system. But this was the early 1980s. There were no computers (at least they were not affordable for a small business such as ours), no barcodes, no mobile phones, no satnav in the lorries. The whole operational model was based on pen and paper, landline telephony and A to Z map books of Bristol, Bath, Cardiff, London and other cities we operated in.

All our customers knew that they had to call us with their orders on a Thursday. We hand wrote them straight onto pre-printed invoices made for us by a local printing cooperative, with carbon paper underneath to produce a copy of the invoice. We wrote the customer's name at the top and then below we listed what they ordered, using a range of shortcuts and acronyms. Among some of our top-selling items, crunchy peanut butter was CPNB and the smooth variety was SPNB. Long-grain brown rice was LGBR and the short-grain variety SGBR. P Oats was porridge oats and J Oats the larger jumbo variety. So far so good.

It is so long since I used carbon paper that I could not remember its name as I was writing this. Carbon paper was paper coated on one side with a layer of a dry ink, loosely bound with wax, and used for making one or more copies simultaneously when using a typewriter or a ballpoint pen to write on the paper.

At around 6pm, the phone lines would dry up and we would drive the two trucks back to Paul and Annie's house in St. Paul's where we would complete what we called 'the lists'. These were sheets of paper with as many rows and columns as could fit on, a paper version of a spreadsheet. We wrote products down the left-hand side, with a row per product, and we wrote the customer name at the top of each column. One of us then read out the invoices and the other filled in the relevant list. This exercise took us long into the evening, rarely finishing much before midnight. Even as we grew, we used this system, the only change being that more of us worked on the lists on a Thursday night.

Fridays

The next morning we were up very early. Typically, Paul would stay in Bristol and phone orders through to our London suppliers, while

22

Graham and I would take a truck each and head off to collect the goods. Either the supplier would be called with an order to have ready for us to collect or in some cases we would arrive, call Paul at the office, who would read us the order and we would collect it ourselves. The potential for human error was really high and yet we very rarely made a mistake. Our reputation depended on every customer receiving all the items they had ordered.

It is hard to remember the time without smartphones and personal computers. Today we rely on these for so many processes and they play a major part in the efficiency of businesses. We had only ourselves to rely on to run an efficient operation, and although I later embraced digital technology, I'm happy that I learned my business and operational skills in the pre-digital days.

We would collect from Sunwheel, Harmony and Community Foods, as I had on my first day, who gave us a few days' credit, so we could leave them post-dated cheques until the following Wednesday. In no time at all we found new producers, importers and suppliers. These included Doves Farm (flours), TRS (poppadoms, chutneys, specialist rice), Katsouris Brothers (olive oil, olives, tahini, halva, pitta bread), Baldwins (sarsaparilla), and a nut-roasting company in Stoke Newington. Some of these were well-established companies and they kindly took us three young people from Bristol under their wing and on many occasions helped us out.

We would get back late, typically around 9pm. We would often be tired on the drive back down the M4, so would stop the trucks at Membury Services for a break and to play Space Invaders as a way of getting our energy up for the final hour back to Bristol.

Saturdays

One of the things our customers liked was that we would deliver fresh pitta bread on a Saturday. Many of the small shops and cafes we

23

supplied sold take-away food and in those days the supermarkets did not sell pitta. This was what I later learned was called a 'loss leader'. We didn't make money on it, but it was really popular and helped us find new customers, as those days pitta bread was not easy to find.

Pitta bread deliveries involved just one truck covering Bristol, Bath and nearby, but after six months this was already over 15 shops, so it took the best part of the day for one of us, with the others starting to sort out what we had collected the day before. Saturday was an early finish, typically around 3pm.

Sundays

Sundays was lie-in day. We gathered at our 'warehouse' in the Totterdown Community Centre around midday and we would make up the orders for delivery on Monday and load the trucks.

We had only a small corner of the community centre and needed more space to organise the deliveries. Much of this took place on the pavement outside, but when it rained, which was often as Bristol is a wet city, we would take over the rest of the centre, hoping that rogue raisins and accidental spillages of flour weren't found by the other tenants on Monday morning. We would then complete the invoices and get as much as we could of Tuesday's deliveries organised.

Mondays

In the early days one truck covered both Bristol and Bath on a Monday. But soon we had outgrown this in terms of carrying capacity and the time it took to get the deliveries done in a day. From early on, one truck concentrated on the Bristol deliveries. These were our original customers and at the start we had promised to get their orders delivered right after the weekend. As we grew, it would have been more convenient to deliver elsewhere, but we kept to our original promise and they always got Monday.

We had about 15 customers in Bristol. Some were fully-fledged wholefoods shops, others were shops that stocked wholefoods but had other products as well. Some, like Wild Oats founded and led by Mike Abrahams, still exist, but many are sadly no longer, although there is still a thriving wholefoods scene and the city has a number of great vegan and vegetarian restaurants.

The other truck delivered to Bath, Frome, Westbury, Weston-Super-Mare, Chippenham and beyond. We delivered to shops, cafes, small regional wholesalers and food co-ops. Food co-ops were groups of people who would bulk buy together, often residents of a village or a group of school parents. There were a lot of food co-ops in the villages of Wiltshire and North Somerset, as well as some based out of squatted houses in Bristol. Some of the most interesting deliveries were to food co-ops, as it often meant finding someone's house in a remote village, to be welcomed with a cup of herbal tea and piece of home-made carrot cake.

We were very keen on the principle of food co-ops, being fans of collective action. But we had to be careful as they potentially competed with their local wholefoods shop, who would invariably also be one of our customers. We soon introduced rules on a minimum order size. This excluded some of the smaller co-ops, who weren't happy, but it was the right thing to do.

Most of the shops we delivered to were small, and access was often poor. There were many tiny storerooms in basements down treacherous stairs. We would park the truck as close as possible and carry boxes and sacks, the latter on our shoulders. The sacks could be heavy – 50kg for rice and on occasion 80kg for hazelnuts. I've never been physically strong and it wasn't long before I put my back out. Luckily Bristol was the capital city of alternative medicine at the time, and I saw an acupuncturist who sorted me out in one session. I have been going for acupuncture and osteopathy ever since.

Finding someone's house in a remote village, to be welcomed with a
cup of herbal tea and piece of home-made carrot cake

Every week we were acquiring new customers, entirely by word of mouth. We never did any marketing; it was years before websites and the internet, and the founders of Facebook and Instagram weren't yet born. We traded entirely on our reputation for quality food, for always making deliveries on time and for always taking responsibility for mistakes and fixing them immediately. And I like to think our customers, most of whom were a good bit older than us, liked leaving the heavy lifting of deliveries to these young, enthusiastic, energetic newcomers. In the early days we added 15% to the cost prices we paid in London, making us much cheaper for our customers than their alternative of driving a small van to and from London weekly.

Tuesdays

On Tuesdays two trucks went to South Wales, where our growth was the most rapid in the early 1980s.

Tuesday was an early start, as the trucks had to be at their first delivery by 8am. Getting to Swansea on time meant being on the road before 6am. Most weeks we delivered a full truckload to a great shop there called Ear to the Ground. They had a sizeable shop on one of the city's many high streets, plus a stall in the central covered market. They also had a small wholesale business, so Nova supplied as far as Swansea, with Ear to the Ground delivering to shops in West Wales, such as Carmarthen, Llanelli and St. David's.

The early start on Tuesday was due to our bank deadline. We had to pay our customers' cheques for the deliveries into our bank before it closed at 3.30pm. This was vital. In the early days we had very little cash as almost everything we earned was spent on stock. We therefore had to get the cheques paid in on Monday and Tuesday, before the post-dated cheques we had paid to our London suppliers the previous Friday cleared. If we had missed getting customer cheques in the bank, we would have let our suppliers down and put the post-dated cheque arrangement at risk. The business carried on like this for at least the first two years. I have taken cashflow seriously ever since.

Nothing was allowed to get in the way of getting the cheques in on time. If a truck broke down, someone would drive a car out, collect the cheques and drive at high speed back to the bank, leaving the truck driver behind. On one occasion I was driving back over the Severn Bridge and saw Graham in our other truck broken down on the hard shoulder. I stopped briefly to collect the cheques and raced back to the bank in Bristol, leaving him to sort the truck out. We had to be ruthless – the survival of the business was our priority.

Wednesdays

As we grew, Wednesdays became a delivery day, but in the early days it was a catch-up day. We had plenty to do at our tiny warehouse, including mixing muesli and trail mix, splitting down sacks of rice, nuts, etc into 5kg and 10kg bags for smaller customers and keeping the space tidy. And it was the only day of the week apart from Sunday afternoons that the three of us would be together.

Learning #2: Reputation is everything

I've always made it a priority to find out what customers really value about the enterprise. And didn't ever stop doing that. At Nova we traded entirely on our reputation – for quality food, for always making deliveries on time and for always taking responsibility for mistakes and fixing them immediately.

I've always found that taking responsibility for mistakes and fixing them immediately is one of the best ways to build a positive reputation. Customers, staff and suppliers will forgive you if you offer an immediate apology and make a genuine attempt to rectify the problem or complaint. Frequently I have been told by customers and employees that this is a quality they value and respect about the enterprise.

28

A month later we made our first delivery to their shop

A month later we made our first delivery to their shop

Chapter 3

Welsh Valleys

The early 1980s was a tough time for South Wales. Margaret Thatcher had recently become prime minister and, although it was not until 1984 that the miners went on strike, miners were being made redundant and pits were starting to be closed. This accelerated throughout the 1980s, putting thousands of miners out of work, typically for the first time in generations of their family.

We had customers at Nova who ran established wholefoods shops in the main cities of Newport, Cardiff and Swansea as well as some of the larger towns in South Wales. Then one day an enterprising recently redundant miner called us.

"Are you the company that sells cheap vegetarian food?"

"Yes," I said, and started to explain what we did.

He quickly interrupted me. "I've heard that it's cheaper to feed a family if we stop eating meat, is that right?"

"Yes, it is," I said, intrigued.

"I'm thinking of setting up a shop to sell this vegetarian food, so can you come and tell me how to do this?"

"Of course," I said and arranged to go the next Tuesday.

After my regular Tuesday deliveries in Newport, Cwmbran, Pontypool and Cardiff, I headed up the Valleys. This miner had been given his redundancy notice the week before and there were rumours that the pit would soon be closed.

I was there for a couple of hours. The family had eaten meat and two veg for dinner most evenings their entire lives. They had never set up or run a business. We talked about vegetarian food, we discussed the financial dynamics of a small shop and they were open about their family finances. These days I would have created a spreadsheet, but this was the 1980s so we worked out a financial plan for their shop on the back of an actual envelope.

The redundancy payment he was to receive was small, but it was enough for them to feed the family for six months as well as pay a deposit and three months' rent on a small shop premises they had found in the town. I helped them work out what their initial stock would be and what it would cost. They couldn't afford it.

I took a gamble and hoped that Paul would be OK with it. He was. We would loan them the initial stock and they could pay us off each month over a year. I promised to support them with recipe suggestions to share with their customers.

They agreed and a month later we made our first delivery to their shop, which was beautifully shelved out with a fresh coat of paint. They had decorated it all themselves. It was a great moment.

The shop did well but it was only the beginning. Word got around and one by one mining towns saw a wholefood shop open, all by miners' families who were being made redundant and all supplied by us. We often took calls asking for recipes because they had been asked by their customers, most of whom were new to vegetarian cooking.

By the time I left Nova we had many customers in the Welsh Valleys, and a truck load of deliveries went there every Tuesday. They were the customers who proved to be most loyal to us when the inevitable competition arrived.

After 1984 it was a long time before I went to South Wales again, but that experience never left me. And if you keep reading this book, you'll see that over 20 years later I returned to the Valleys and it became the home of my most successful enterprise.

Learning #3: Align values and commercial interests

Nova Wholefoods was a start-up that grew fast. We had little time to discuss strategy or articulate values. These just emerged as we went along. But it became clear quite quickly that we held values that the majority of our customers shared.

This became obvious when we supported our first former miner's family to set up a wholefood shop in their village. Miners were losing their jobs and livelihoods and it was absolutely core to the values of a workers' co-operative to find a way to help mine-workers to support themselves and their neighbours with cheaper ways to eat. And this was aligned to the commercial interests of the company.

Social enterprise is about finding ways to get your values aligned to the commercial mission of the company. My early years at Nova taught me never to make the mistake of thinking that the social or environmental values of the enterprise are more important than the commercial interests. They are the same.

For me, the whole point of social enterprise is to show that changing the world for the better can be done successfully by commercial enterprises. It definitely can.

If the loaded pallet wasn't perfectly placed in the middle of the lift, the pallet would lose its balance

Chapter 4

Growing fast and growing up

We were growing fast, gaining new customers most weeks and delivering further afield. So fast was the growth that Nova Wholefoods often felt like a very different enterprise from one week to the next.

Our own warehouse

Early in 1981 we outgrew Totterdown Community Centre and temporarily rented a corner of a large warehouse down in the old docks in the centre of Bristol, opposite what is now the Arnolfini Arts Centre. We were on the first floor so we had to use forklift trucks to load pallets of food onto a large mechanical lift, press a button to raise this to the first floor and then use another forklift truck to move it off the lift and take it to our corner of the warehouse.

It sounds easy but it wasn't. None of us had ever used forklift trucks for moving pallet loads of food before. If the loaded pallet wasn't perfectly placed in the middle of the lift, the pallet would lose its balance as it was lifted and items would fall off the top. We lost quite a few items before we got the hang of it, and I was never wholly comfortable with this.

This warehouse wasn't an ideal solution, not just because of the pallet lift, and it spurred us on to start searching for a larger warehouse of our own. Paul found a 10,000 square foot warehouse on St. Thomas Street near Temple Meads station. It was enormous, far larger than we needed at the time. And it was tall, enough for four storeys of pallet racking.

"Are you sure this isn't too big?" I asked, the day in spring 1981 that we moved in with what we thought was a lot of stock, until we unloaded the trucks and surveyed our tiny pile of food in this huge empty space. The new warehouse was enormous and so was the rent. Little did we know how quickly we would fill it up.

Trail mix

The engine room of our growth was trail mix. I honestly cannot
remember how we managed to corner the market for this, but we
did. Trail mix was an idea that came from the USA. It was a simple,
relatively healthy, sweet snack, initially designed for trekkers and
climbers. Our recipe was simple: banana chips, coconut flakes, raisins
and almonds – mixed in a secret combination of the four. And it was
really popular. There wasn't a single customer who didn't order it
every week, and they all reported that it brought new customers into
their shops.

Paul knew a builder, who constructed a mixer made of a hexagonal
drum with a bar across the middle resting on the outside frame. One
of the panels had a sliding door and there were handles on the outside.
We poured the ingredients in, turned the handle for a while and then
poured the mix out into sacks. Simple. Except with just three of us we
struggled to keep up with demand and every spare moment was being
spent at the mixer making trail mix and various types of muesli. We
needed to start hiring people.

Trail mix was our highest gross margin product. We could mark up the
ingredients at a higher price than selling them individually. We were
onto something. I'm convinced that if we hadn't had the additional
profit that trail mix brought us, we would have struggled to make the
money we needed to finance the growth of the business.

Ever since then I have looked for the high-margin product or service
to support business growth, and when I have found it, up has gone the
profit and the cash balances.

Hiring people

We were growing fast, and with hindsight we didn't manage it that
well. We were managing the logistics of the business fairly well, but

relationships could be strained. Paul and I were driven, hardworking and in my case intolerant of others who were not like us. In addition, we were paying ourselves very little money. In retrospect, I expect that this was too much for Graham and it wasn't long before he announced that he was leaving.

We started by hiring people we knew. Rob, who I had met in Sudan, joined us. He was an ideal choice as he had worked in wholefoods already. Gordon and Jill were a couple who both came to work with us. A bit later Tim, a university colleague of mine, joined us, and he still works with the cooperative today. We had no induction process; we just expected people to start work and learn on the job, as we had. By the time we moved to St. Thomas Street we were six people.

I spent more and more time in the tiny office and less time on the road. We had created a small office in a corner of the warehouse where Paul worked, and over time I joined him, taking on the stock-buying function along with managing the logistics. Paul focused more on the financial management, which was becoming more complex. The newer people took on doing the bulk of the deliveries and collections.

I had been a rather shy teenager, lacking in confidence. Being part of the team that grew Nova Wholefoods had taught me a lot, but I had become confident without wisdom and empathy. I was by now 23 years old, which is young to be a leader of a business. If I was unhappy about anything, people knew about it. I don't think I was easy to work with and I'm certain that was partly why Graham chose to leave.

I assumed that having more people would make life easier. In some ways it did as we had more drivers, more people to share the mixing tasks and do the warehouse work. But we had new people-related challenges to deal with, which at the time I felt completely unqualified for.

Pay and working hours were two such challenges. In the early days we had earned very little, depending on what we each needed and what the business could afford. I was earning £25 a week plus all the food I needed, much of which was sweeping spillages from the floors of the trucks at the end of the day. Paul earned more as he was married with three young children, but it was very little for a family of five. We were focused on the growth of the business and for us that came first. We would work every hour that was needed.

While our first co-workers were people a bit like us, with alternative values and prepared to work hard for little money in pursuit of a vision, we started to hire people to do specific jobs. This was partly because not everyone is prepared to do or capable of doing every task in a business. It took me some time to accept this reality. They also expected to earn enough to support themselves and their families, a fact that of course is wholly reasonable but one that at the time I found tricky. Not for the first time in my career I was among the lowest-paid workers yet shouldering much of the responsibility, a fact that I now accept as an element of start-up entrepreneurship, but at the time I think I acted out my frustration at this by making excessive demands on some of our new co-workers.

Although I had passion and enthusiasm for our work, I lacked basic empathy towards my colleagues. I learned a bot more about empathy later, but at that stage I had little understanding of this.

Customers further afield

Paul's former colleague John ran a bakery in Buxton and a shop and small wholesale operation in Sheffield. We started delivering there once a fortnight and en route delivering to a smaller wholesale co-operative in Birmingham. At first we took the smallest truck that we had, but then Rob had the bright idea to take some trail mix to Suma in Leeds.

Suma Wholefoods were older and more established than Nova.

They had been set up in 1977, just before us, and like us were growing fast. They were a workers' cooperative, like so many of the wholefoods businesses of the time. We had had some contact with them, but nothing had come of it.

Rob contacted his former colleague Rick, who was the main buyer, a role I was slowly taking on for Nova. Rob and I took a few sacks of trail mix and went up to Leeds after dropping off a delivery with John in Sheffield. We stayed the night with Rick in Leeds and he liked the trail mix. We went to the Suma warehouse, which was based in a very old four-storey building.

The next week Suma ordered a tonne of trail mix. It was our biggest order ever of a single product and thankfully we had recently hired 'Mike the Mixer', who spent his days mixing trail mix and muesli. He liked the slow, meditative pace to mixing, although he perhaps hadn't realised that at Nova nothing was slow for long. Mike had his work cut out producing an additional tonne of trail mix in a week, along with growing orders of muesli and other snacks we were developing (the chocolate trail mix was hard to stop snacking on).

Two weeks later Suma ordered two tonnes, and it wasn't long before we were taking them two tonnes every fortnight. One of our customers came up with an idea for a larger motorised mixer that could mix 100kg at a time and his engineer son built it for us. Mike was happy and so were we all.

Diversifying our supply chain

For the first period of the business we basically had about six suppliers and over 80% of our products came from Sunwheel, Harmony and Community Foods, the established wholefoods suppliers in London. But by the end of 1981 this was changing fast. We still ran the lists operation every Thursday to minimise stock and maximise cash in the business, but increasingly we needed to purchase at least a tonne of many items each week. Rather than buy by the sack or box, we started buying by the tonne of sacks or boxes.

This took us up the supply chain to larger wholesale suppliers and in many cases direct importers. Paul researched suppliers, which in those days involved making lots of phone calls. He found a dried fruit importer in Liverpool who would sell us a tonne at a time of raisins, sultanas, figs, dates and prunes and started going there with an empty truck after we had dropped Suma's trail mix in Leeds. We would make the beautiful drive over the Pennines, collect four tonnes of dried fruit and head back to Bristol.

We found other importers that would let us buy a tonne or two at a time. We found a rice importer on the Isle of Dogs in London's East End. The first time we went there I was driving as Paul and I liked one of us to meet suppliers the first time. I've done this ever since and have sometimes rejected potential suppliers at that first meeting, often based on intuition.

The Isle of Dogs is now better known as Canary Wharf, with its skyscrapers, sharp suits and banking headquarters, but in those days there was a road that went around the perimeter of this huge bend in the River Thames with long, low warehouses leading to the water's edge. It took me a while to find our new supplier but I eventually found this delightful Anglo-Italian family business, who imported the same Italian brown rice we had been buying from Community Foods but could sell it to us at a significant discount. This allowed us to offer better prices to our customers as well as increase our gross margins, creating more cash that we needed to fuel our growth.

We still bought about half what we needed from our original suppliers and still had their five days' credit terms, but the importers gave us 30 days' credit once we had paid our first order in advance. This had a huge impact on cashflow and allowed us to fund the next phase of growth.

Learning #4: Risk-taking

Every entrepreneur has to take risks.

On the one hand there is the 'buccaneer' image of an entrepreneur who takes risks with little or no thought to the future. On the other hand is the person who takes a long time to take a risky decision, going through detailed risk assessments all along the way.

I've found that successful risk-taking lies at neither of these extremes. The trick is to develop an ability to see the risks of every decision and every action all the time, so that having an overview of risk is simply a part of the day-to-day of leading an enterprise. Doing that I found that when bigger and a more significant decision came along I had analysed much of the risk already and could make a decision quickly. This was really helpful as on many occasions if I didn't move fast, I would probably lose the opportunity.

A typical portacabin co-op meeting

Chapter 5

Workers' co-op

In the 1980s the social enterprise label was not a thing. And we were all too busy to really think about the detail of our social or environmental mission. For me that narrative came later. But although we did not really market Nova's social mission or set-up, it was obvious to everyone who knew us. We were passionate about the impact that vegetarian and vegan diets would play in some of the big global issues, such as health, pollution, climate change (yes, we knew about that in the early 1980s) and global inequality. We supplied pamphlets on cooperative working, climate change, plant-based diets and more that many of our customers sold on in their shops. I like to think that we were political vegetarians.

Despite the lack of marketing (although we did start producing a quarterly price list in 1981), I am now convinced that our passion and enthusiasm for the products we sold and the context for doing so shone through, and this was the primary factor in our rapid growth.

There was a severe global recession in the early 1980s, which in the UK followed a string of crises that had plagued the British economy for most of the 1970s. Unemployment reached three million (12.5% of the workforce) in 1982 and stayed at that level until after 1986. Inflation was around 10% per year. We grew the business through a recession, for the first but not the last time in my social enterprise career.

But I was too busy to read newspapers, and did not own a TV. As we were growing fast, we were largely insulated from and unaware of the devastation in much of the economy around us. The experience of our new customers in the Welsh Valleys was probably the closest I came to understanding what was going on all around us. It took some years after leaving Nova to realise how significant it was to set up and grow this enterprise during this time, and although we had created about 20 jobs by the time I left, I am perhaps most proud of the fact that we helped so many people who were struggling financially to set up wholefoods shops in their towns and communities.

I had paid no attention to the corporate structure of Nova. In the early days it was just three of us – Graham, Paul and me. We made most decisions together, but it was clear that Paul was the senior partner. He managed the finances and did most of the stock ordering. We discussed decisions but it was Paul who typically had the final say. I was good with that. I was really enjoying the business and honestly had never felt so alive in my life.

But once we were established in the warehouse, and the 10,000 square feet of floor space was starting to fill up, we started to talk about the structure of the business, something we had not really done before. It was at the time a private company wholly owned by Paul and, to his credit, he had the ambition to turn it into a workers' cooperative.

Cooperatives had been around in the UK since 1844 and started in food. According to Co-operatives UK, the first UK cooperative

> started when 28 workers in the north of England called time on the expensive and poor-quality food the mill owner sold them. They clubbed together to buy basic foods (flour, butter and sugar) in bulk and opened a small shop.

> As the generation of the 1960s came of age, there emerged a rush of more radical co-operatives, owned and controlled by their workers. They were often trading in wholefoods, books and bikes, with equal pay and no hierarchy. And, quite remarkably and ahead of their time, they pioneered a different way of doing business, pre-empting the participative management style now favoured by some of the world's most successful businesses.

In 1981 we applied to become a workers' co-operative. This meant registering with The Registrar of Friendly Societies, though these days it is easier to do this with Co-operatives UK. Paul took care of this and on 10 April 1981 Nova Wholefoods Cooperative Limited was registered.

There was some celebration when we became a cooperative, which I joined with, although for some reason there was a little part of me that felt some trepidation. This did change things somewhat as legally all of us were co-workers. We paid everyone the same amount, although there was an additional salary paid per child to those who were parents. I was still the lowest paid member of the cooperative.

We started having weekly cooperative meetings where all of us got together to discuss business issues. A couple of people who ran a catering operation came and cooked us a hot meal at the warehouse, so we ate lunch together and discussed business issues.

It's fair to say that for a while Paul and I were still dominant. By mid 1981 we were both working much of the time in the tiny office we shared, me focusing on buying and logistics and him on finance and finding suppliers, and both of us sharing the stocktake and order process on a Thursday. We discussed business issues together as we had done for some time, which of course was a source of tension with those who were very attached to the principles of collective decision-making down to every minute detail.

I was not against the principle of collective decision-making, but even back then I developed a view that this was for significant strategic and business decisions (in the same way as with a charity trustee board) and that most day-to-day decisions should be taken by the people responsible for those areas of work, which of course often meant Paul and me.

However, as we grew this did change, and in time we found an equilibrium. As other co-op members took responsibility for different areas of the business, they found that they had decisions of their own to make, and in general Paul and I were delighted to let them make these without the need for a collective discussion.

Mike the Mixer made decisions about recipes and production schedules, while Pete (one of our drivers) looked after the welfare and servicing of the trucks and he and I worked on the logistics of the various collection and delivery runs together.

Learning #5: Decision-making

My experience is that decisions are best made by the people closest to managing that decision. This is a view widely held within many businesses, not just social enterprises and co-operatives. And it makes common sense.

Large groups struggle to make small decisions. It's painful, inefficient and takes a lot of time. There are times when a large group needs to come together to discuss strategy, culture and values, and that is healthy from time to time.

I have heard it said by members of cooperatives that I have worked with over the years that they need to spend more time in meetings. I disagree. My experience is that far too much time is spent in inefficient meetings and that good communication and decisions are best made in shorter meetings

I found that the trick was to find ways to streamline decision-making so that it is transparent and efficient and that there is a mechanism to question decisions. It's entirely possible.

The two of us decided to try to slide the barrel to the side.

The five of us decided to try to slide the 'artic' to the side

Chapter 6

Broken laws and broken glass

The trucks

Nova Wholefoods is largely a story about wholefoods and co-operative working. But the business was fundamentally a distribution business. Much of the day-to-day operation was about logistics, and that meant the trucks.

We started with hired trucks, but early on we lease-purchased two 7.5 tonne gross weight Iveco trucks, each with a carrying capacity of four tonnes each. Both models are discontinued now: one was a traditional box truck design with a roller shutter door at the rear and a separate cabin; the other was like an elongated van (known as a panel van), lower but longer than the box truck, with two opening doors at the rear.

Both were painted in deep yellow (our colour) and decorated with the Nova Wholefoods logo, a sun with a smiling face in the middle. A logo very much of its time.

While we were taking the customer orders on a Thursday, we would start planning the collection and delivery routes. This was dependent on minimising distance travelled and time taken, allowing for potential traffic hold-ups and ensuring that we would be carrying no more than four tonnes of food at any one time. There were no computers or satnav to help. Distances were measured on map books, and weights were calculated manually on each customer invoice.

The transport stories are some of the most memorable.

Blocked motorway

The first Friday in January 1982 our two trucks set off to London on

49

the first collection run of the new year. We left around 5.30am. I was in the box truck and Gordon was a few minutes behind me in the panel van.

There was a lot of snow falling as I made my way out of Bristol up the M32, and by the time I got onto the M4 heading east towards London the snow was deep, with track marks of the vehicles that had made it so far. I carried on slowly, determined to get to London. It was the first week after the Christmas break and, as we had one week a year off deliveries between Christmas and New Year, it was vital we got to collect the order requirements that day and get them back to Bristol.

A couple of miles up the motorway I slid to a slow stop behind another truck. Up ahead an articulated lorry had jack-knifed. The way ahead was blocked. The snow had eased off, but it was not yet 6am on a January morning and it turned to ice as soon as it fell.

The drivers of the first five lorries got out of their cabs and surveyed the scene. I looked back but could see no sign of Gordon in the other truck. The five of us decided to try to slide the 'artic' to the side. It took a while of hard pushing, but it started to skid on the ice and soon enough we had cleared enough space for the five of us to squeeze past.

We were all heading to London and agreed to drive in convoy, with an 'all for one and one for all' mentality that I always loved about being a lorry driver. It took hours, and around midday we approached the Hammersmith fly-over having barely seen another vehicle. With much hooting of horns as a goodbye and good luck, I headed off to the first collection.

My first pick-up was at Sunwheel at London Bridge, then to Katsouris in Drayton Park and the nut roasting factory in Stoke Newington, finally heading to Community in New Southgate. When I got to Katsouris there was a message to call Paul. Gordon was still stuck on the M4 and the emergency services were digging trucks out of the snow one by one. He suggested I complete my collections and go to my parents' home in south

London for the night, before heading back to Bristol the next morning.

I called Mum and Dad and explained the situation – they were thrilled that I was going to stay the night, and about 8pm I finally parked the loaded box truck outside their house.

In the morning the snow had stopped falling in London but there was plenty still on the road. I called Paul, who told me to set off back. I went to the petrol station just before the M4 starts, filled up with diesel and used their payphone to call again.

"We can't get the trucks out of Bristol," Paul said. "I've called all the companies for Gordon's collection run and they will stay open until 2pm for you."

I called Dad. "Can you clear the garage and be ready to help me empty the truck into it? I'll be back in 30 minutes." He agreed, and I put down the phone and raced back.

My parents had a student from the USA visiting and, when I returned, he and Dad had cleared the garage. Then came the fastest unloading of a truck ever, and in under 10 minutes Dad's garage was full. I set off to make the other collections.

There was still quite a bit of snow on the roads in London and all our suppliers had very kindly stayed open. It was after 5pm by the time I left Harmony in Neasden, where Craig Sams had very generously helped me load the order. I got back home around 7pm and collapsed exhausted.

The next day Paul and Pete arrived at my parents' house at midday. They said the roads were clearing. Mum cooked lunch for us all and then we loaded up their truck with the contents of the garage and headed back to Bristol. It was slow, but we made it, and most importantly we ensured that we never missed a delivery.

Broken laws

New regulations had been introduced requiring the fitting of tachographs to all commercial vehicles and our new trucks were fitted with them. Tachographs are machines that record how long each driver drives a day, whether they have the right number of breaks of the right length and the time since the last break. For good road safety reasons, the laws on their use are strict, and from 1982 there were roadside checks by police and transport department officials.

We were young and inexperienced, and we had not implemented tachograph recording, despite having the equipment fitted. We were so busy growing the business that we were lax about implementing this change. This was a mistake.

Early in 1982 I was driving along a road and saw a road-block up ahead. I pulled to a halt and a Department of Transport official asked me to hand over my tachograph disc. It was unused. I was caught.

"I'm very sorry, we are a young company and we are just getting to grips with the new regulations," I said. "I promise that it won't happen again."

"Sorry, sir, that's not good enough." He climbed into the cab seat next to me and proceeded to take my details and those of the company. He then read me a statement basically saying that the company would be prosecuted for my misdemeanour.

"Can I have the names of the company directors?" he asked.

"We don't have any directors. We are a workers' co-operative," I replied.

"You must have directors if you're a company."

I tried a charm offensive "We don't have directors because we are a

52

Friendly Society." I was sure that this approach would, if not get me off, awaken some sympathy on his part.

I was wrong. He watched me load up the tachograph disc in the truck and sent me on my way. A week later we received a letter with a date for a hearing at the Bristol transport tribunal in a month's time, with a suggestion that we get legal advice.

For the first, and the last, time in my working life I did not have a lawyer to turn to. We called the local lawyer who had done the lease on the warehouse for us, and he didn't know what on earth we were talking about. He found a colleague, who he put on the phone.

"Call the Freight Transport Association," he said.

We did. They were amazing. They immediately sent around the Bristol representative of what I later discovered is one of the biggest business groups in the UK. He signed us up as members, finding some obscure cheap subscription rate for businesses run by under 30-year-olds, and then went through the summons from the transport department. He then wanted to know all about the business, took copious notes and told us their lawyer would represent us at the tribunal.

The day of the tribunal came. I had on an old suit I had last used at my university graduation, putting on a tie for the first time in years, and Paul and I went down to the tribunal. We met the FTA lawyer and the representative, who had also come. They were so supportive.

"Leave this to me," said the lawyer. "Best you both say as little as possible." We sheepishly but enthusiastically nodded agreement.

When our case came up, the transport department 'prosecutor' made a strong case against us. He went on for a while and ended by addressing the chair of the tribunal with the words "We recommend a fine and a two-week ban on the company driving on the roads. In conclusion, it is the department's view that these young people should be made an example of."

Our hearts sank. Two weeks would bankrupt us. But it was a mistake by the prosecutor. The FTA lawyer got up and made mincemeat of their case. I can't remember all that he said, but by the end the transport department officials were not looking so pleased with themselves. Finally, the tribunal chair consulted with his two colleagues and then spoke.

"I completely understand the need to enforce this new law, but today we have heard of two young men who have set up a new company, created jobs in the city at a time we need them and supported enterprise across the region. They have made an error of youth, accepted their mistake and promised to comply with the law."

And then came his ruling.

"We completely disagree with the view of the department; indeed, I am surprised that you even brought this case for us to hear. In case you hadn't noticed, there is a recession, and this city needs young people like these to get our economy back on its feet." And with that he said "Case dismissed", got up and walked out.

I've been committed to job creation ever since.

Broken glass

Given that we had two trucks on the road six days a week, we had surprisingly few breakdowns. The FTA got us on their regular safety check system, and we found a new and much better Iveco dealership in Newport, across the Severn Bridge in Wales. We had a good team of drivers, and although Paul and I were largely office-bound now, we still got to go out on delivery runs once a month to stay in touch with our long-standing customers and suppliers.

As the company grew, we increased our buying power. We purchased more and more products by the pallet load or tonne rather than a few boxes or sacks at a time, and although we kept going to Community Foods in London, we were less dependent on them as we were buying many products from the same suppliers as them. To their credit, they were as supportive of us as ever, celebrating our success rather than seeing us as a competitor. The wholefoods trade felt more like a community than a competitive industry.

It was always a big day when we went to a new supplier for the first time. We sold a lot of honey, and the main supplier was Rowse Honey, a lovely family business in Wallingford, Oxfordshire. They had what was for us a large minimum order to get a decent wholesale price, so it was a big day when we placed a four-pallet order of honey in jars. Pete took the box truck to do the collection.

It was late afternoon on a busy day, and I took a call from Pete, who sounded shaken. He was at Membury Services, half way between London and Bristol on the M4. The accelerator on the truck had stuck and he had managed to do an emergency stop in the Membury slip road, which luckily is long and straight. Could we come and rescue him?

I called the garage at Newport and one of their mechanics drove over and met me. We took the other truck and I drove us to Membury, not knowing what we would encounter. I had a bad feeling about it all the way.

When we got there, Pete was parked at the side of the slip road waiting in the cab. Luckily, he hadn't tried to open the roller shutter door, which was bulging outward and jammed shut. We took a couple of crowbars and the mechanic and I forced the door open, jumping to either side of the door as four tonnes of honey and broken glass slid slowly onto the tarmac.

We had to laugh; and then we had to clean it up. We caused such a commotion that we ended up with staff from the services, two RAC patrolmen and a policeman helping us clean up. It was dark before we

55

As four tonnes of honey and broken glass slid slowly onto the tarmac

got away, and we had lost the lot. It was the largest loss of stock we ever incurred, but I have never forgotten the sight of the slow-moving cascade of glass and honey emerging from the truck onto the road.

Learning #6: Say sorry and ask for help

I learned early on that saying sorry is helpful. The truth is that every entrepreneur makes mistakes, and at the start of my career I made quite a lot.

I believe in the power of a sincere apology. When Paul and I apologised to the transport tribunal for non-use of tachographs, we were genuinely sorry and realised we had broken the law.

Asking for help is again something I learned early on, but often in quite random situations. The day that four tonnes of honey and broken glass ended up on a motorway slip road required me to ask for help. My experience is that people enjoy helping people who ask for help.

I'm glad that at an early stage I learned to say sorry and ask for help. Both have served me well.

We ended up with a group of Sannyasins, followers of Bhagwan Shree Rajneesh, who wore light orange robes whatever the weather

Chapter 7

Fast growth and leadership challenges

By 1982 Nova Wholefoods was turning over well above £1m a year.
The warehouse was filling up fast, our trucks were full of deliveries
or collections most all the time, and more people were joining the
cooperative and working with us. We were growing very fast.

With fast growth came new experiences and situations that required
us to learn quickly and on our feet. There were so many that it could
be hard to keep up, but six experiences remain memorable. These are
stories of the impact of the media, how hard it was to raise finance,
rapid scaling up, providing opportunities for young people, supporting
our supply chain and scary leadership challenges. All issues and
situations that I had to deal with for the whole of my career. Like so
much of what happened later, I learned it first at Nova.

Media impact

In 1982 Audrey Eyton's international bestseller book The F-Plan Diet
was first published. The book was serialised in the Daily Express and
the first we heard about it was that one Thursday we had off-the-scale
orders for dried apricots and bran flakes. Shops that ordered at best a
box of apricots a week ordered ten boxes, with similar volumes for
sacks of bran.

We figured out what was going on by mid-morning so by the afternoon
we were on the phones trying to buy up as much apricots and bran as
we could. By the following week we went from selling ten boxes of
apricots a week to 160.

It was the start of a step change with all sorts of consequences,
and plenty of problems to solve quickly. Problems that I now call
'problems of success'.

59

We don't fund cooperatives

In a matter of weeks we ran out of floor space. We were desperate for pallet racking. Given that the economy was still in recession, getting hold of good-quality pallet racking second-hand wasn't too difficult. We sourced enough for us to rack out most of our floor space with four storeys of pallets, effectively increasing our stock capacity four-fold.

We bargained the price and agreed on £5,000. This was a lot for us, and cash that we didn't have as all our cash was tied up in stock and forward orders of containers of imported food. We had banked with the Co-op Bank in Bristol since we started and were confident that they would lend to us. Paul prepared a simple business plan and set of numbers.

He and I arranged a meeting and went to the bank. They listened patiently to our pitch and then asked us whether the shareholders would guarantee a loan.

"We are a cooperative, so we don't have shareholders," said Paul.

"What, you mean you don't have any shareholders?" asked the bank manager.

"That's right," said Paul. I could see he was in disbelief. This was the bank with 'cooperative' in its name, for goodness' sake. He kept it together and I followed his lead.

We then had to explain our corporate structure, our registration as a Friendly Society and so on. Paul had shown that we could afford to repay a loan with interest over four years. The bank manager listened and then finally said, "We don't fund cooperatives."

We got outside and Paul exploded with uncontrolled rage on the pavement. "It's the **** Co-op Bank for **** sake!" He was right. I've never banked with the Co-op Bank again.

We did something we never did and went into a local pub in the middle of the afternoon and had a couple of drinks.

That evening I called Dad. I felt really uncomfortable doing this. He had lent me money for a car when I was at university and I had paid him back by working hard the following summer in the Netherlands and living in a tent. But he was the only lender that I had a credit track record with.

Today five grand for a business loan doesn't sound so much. But you could buy a small house in St. Paul's in Bristol for ten grand in those days. It was a lot, not just for us, but for Mum and Dad too.

I made the call and explained the situation and how we proposed to pay them back. Dad was amazing and agreed immediately. I've set up a lot of enterprises since, but that was the first and last time I borrowed from my parents. I have taken out personal loans to fund businesses, I even maxed out two credit cards, but I didn't ever want to borrow from family again.

The pallet racking was delivered two days later and three of us spent the weekend erecting it ourselves. And just in the nick of time as three containers of stock arrived the following week.

Scaling from pallets to containers

In no time demand went through the roof. We were buying 20-tonne containers of raisins, sultanas, apricots, figs, prunes, dates and more. The F-plan diet had introduced millions of people to products they had never bought before, such as brown rice, wholemeal flour, bran flakes, muesli and porridge oats. Basically, all the staples we sold.

At first it was hard to order containers direct from importing companies. The up-front costs were high, we had to start paying in US dollars, we had to deal with import duties and deal with the risk of products turning up damaged or infested. We started sharing orders with Suma Wholefoods, who thankfully were up for this as they were undergoing the same quantum leap in demand as we were. We could buy four containers of Italian brown rice and have two of them delivered to Leeds and two to Bristol.

By the middle of 1982 we would have a container or flatbed lorry arrive once or twice most weekdays. Time was money with the deliveries, so when one arrived almost everyone would stop what they were doing and we would all get to unloading. We had a flatbed come from Kirriemuir in Scotland once a week laden with porridge and jumbo oats. This was easy to unload as it came on pallets, which were lifted off with the forklift truck.

Containers were another matter. The container would be packed floor to ceiling with sacks of rice or boxes of fruit or nuts. I would have to climb up and open a few sacks or boxes to check for infestation before we could accept delivery.

I was the buyer, but Paul and I had to work really closely to ensure that we could manage the cashflow. We typically had to make decisions on how much of a particular product to order months in advance. The business model had completely changed.

It was very exciting because as ever we were learning on the job. I was working late into the evenings and starting early, just to keep up with the new demands of the job.

Youth opportunity

We recruited largely by word of mouth, mostly from the alternative community in the city. We didn't really have much to do with the mainstream business community in Bristol. We were a good 20 years younger than the average business owner in the city. We were of course very much part of the wholefoods scene and known within the industry across the UK.

We were creative about recruitment and after one individual joined us we ended up with a group of Sannyasins, followers of Bhagwan Shree Rajneesh, who wore light orange robes whatever the weather. There was a small group of them who took over mixing muesli and trail mix, as well as breaking down sacks into smaller bags of rice, oats and so on for smaller shops and food co-ops. They would typically work with us for six months to save enough to go back to their Ashram in Poona, India, but about a week before they left they would replace themselves with Sannyasins who had just returned and needed work. It was our own self-sustaining recruitment agency, and with no fees to pay.

It was a genuine surprise when one day we got a visit from the head of the Youth Opportunities Scheme (YOPS) in Bristol. We had not heard of YOPS, or indeed any government employment scheme.

YOPS was a UK government scheme for helping 16–18-year-olds into employment. It was introduced in 1978 and ran until 1983. The local YOPS officer came and explained that basically we could take a young person, typically straight out of school, give them a job and the government would pay their salary for six months and provide training.

If we said yes, what did we need to do?

"What job do you need filling?" he asked.

This was not a question we were used to being asked. People just came to work and somehow found their place.

"I see you have all this pallet racking," he said. "Do you need a forklift driver?"

We did. We had recently taken a lease on a new reach truck, a type of forklift truck that could place and remove pallets on racking up to 10 metres high, which we now needed.

He explained that the scheme worked by us identifying a business need

63

and training a young person to fill it. He said that typically employers took a young person for six months for free and then replaced them with a new young person funded by the scheme.

"We would never do that," we both said.

He said nothing, but his face said "We'll see".

So Wilton joined us. He was a young man from St. Paul's who had recently left school. He took to the reach truck really quickly. He went off on training courses and got really proficient. He was miles better than the rest of us and after six months we gave him a permanent job and pay rise to the same level as the rest of us. The YOPS man couldn't believe it. We were the first company in Bristol ever to do this. And then we took on our next YOPS person.

As far as I know, Wilton worked there for his whole career. And I have been giving permanent jobs to apprentices and people on job creation programmes ever since.

Supporting our supply chain

Quite a few wholefoods start-ups would approach us for help. We listened to them all and did our best to help out. Typically, we would offer loans of stock if they were a shop, or agree to stock and supply their goods if a supplier. There were quite a few of these but the one that stands out was Cauldron Foods.

Pete and Phil were setting up a tofu-making business. We loaned them two tonnes of soya beans and gave them a year to pay it off. We bought a second-hand walk-in refrigeration unit and put it in our warehouse so we could store their tofu and other perishable foods. We bought insulated boxes, like glorified picnic boxes, so we could include their tofu on our delivery runs.

I don't know what happened to Pete and Phil as I lost touch with them after I left Nova. But I didn't lose touch with Cauldron Foods' products. I've been eating their tofu and vegetarian sausages my whole adult life. I do know that Cauldron was bought by Premier Foods in 2005. I hope Pete and Phil did well out of the deal, and I hope they still remember how we helped them out at the start.

We helped out a lot of wholefoods and related companies. We supported another wholefood cooperative business in Brighton when they had cashflow problems, again loaning stock. We saw it as part of our mission and responsibility to help the expansion of wholefoods as both an industry and a way of life.

Scary leadership challenges

Leadership was not a word that we used. We were a cooperative and in theory leadership was shared. Of course, it wasn't exactly like that. By then we were over 15 people working in the business and each had their own jobs and areas of responsibility. There were times when we had to just join in, like unloading containers or getting trucks loaded in a hurry. But we had organised into four distinct teams: the warehouse team, the muesli/trail mix mixing team, the drivers and the office.

We needed more office space and purchased a second-hand Portakabin and had it put above our existing small office and tea room. We had an office that could comfortably fit four people. I had a desk in the corner with a view of the warehouse, two telephones on the desk and a fax machine. This was really important since we were buying food directly from producers and exporters in countries like Italy for rice, Turkey for dried fruit and nuts and the Philippines, where we purchased a whole island's annual production of banana chips, the key ingredient of trail mix.

Our success brought us more attention, most of it really positive, but not always. We needed to keep some cash in the upstairs office, which was locked, but not alarmed. There was a side door from the street into the warehouse, the main door being an enormous roller-shutter door big enough for three lorries to reverse in side by side.

One day I arrived early at the warehouse. The street door had been forced, but not broken, and the upstairs office door was open. I went in and found that our cash had gone from the locked drawer it was left in overnight. It was £300, a large amount of money. We had been burgled.

I was shocked. Nothing like this had happened before. We were a co-operative that was founded on and traded on goodwill and trust. When everyone else had arrived, we met in the downstairs staff room. Some wanted to call the police, others disagreed. As was often the cooperative way, there was no easy consensus.

During the meeting I noticed one of the co-op members looked uncomfortable. Afterwards I sought him out.

"There were some new guys asking me about Nova at the cafe," he said. "I didn't tell them anything about the money, but they were saying that we must all be really rich. I was anxious that they might try and rob me."

The cafe was just around the corner from where Paul and the family lived. We often parked the trucks there overnight. We were generally respected there for employing a couple of the regulars.

"You'll have to go there," said the co-op member. I was terrified. I was a young, rather skinny young man. I had never been to the cafe. And Paul was away.

We agreed on a plan and later that afternoon I walked into the cafe. The room went completely silent and all eyes looked at me.

"I think most of you know that I'm from Nova. Someone stole cash from us last night and some of your regulars who work with us are upset about this."

The room was still silent.

"If the cash is all back there by the morning, that is the last we will say anything about this. Otherwise, we will have to go to the police."

As I said the dreaded word 'police' I turned and walked out, shaking.

The money was returned, we changed the locks and got an alarm connected to the local police station.

Learning #7: Difficult conversations

Leadership means that you sometimes have to do the scary stuff.

My first experience of this was walking into the cafe in Bristol following the theft of cash from our warehouse. I was shaking when I came out, but this intervention worked, and I learned that difficult conversations are part of being an entrepreneur, and indeed of any leadership role.

I have had to have a lot of difficult conversations over the past 40 years. Some of these are covered later in this book and you can read about these in Chapters 18 and 29.

My employment solicitor, who I respect very highly, once told me that there are few problems that can't be solved by a straightforward conversation. It's one of the most helpful pieces of advice I've ever received.

The sack was infested with weevils, a small herbivorous
(so vegetarian) beetle

Chapter 8

Christmas comes early

Christmas at Nova always started in September. After the summer was when people started to think about Christmas and make cakes and puddings in preparation. We knew that in the month of September we would sell between 40% and 50% of our entire dried fruit sales of the year.

From about May or June I had been buying up containers of raisins, sultanas and currants for shipping to Bristol by the end of August. I assumed that we would have room in the warehouse for everything as around five containers with 100 tonnes of fruit would be arriving then, on top of the regular orders of bulk products such as rice, oats, banana chips and nuts.

We had already expanded our storage by getting some more pallet racking and creating two mezzanine floors at the rear of the warehouse. One of these was storage for mixing ingredients and the other floor was our new mixing area, with two large stainless-steel mixing machines. This was run by our orange-robed Sannyasins, who were thrilled as they could have a small unobtrusive shrine to Bhagwan Shree Rajneesh.

We had also created a front desk out in the warehouse, which was where our increasing numbers of cash-and-carry customers would come to pay for their goods and where customers' phone orders were taken and invoices processed. While Paul and I still ran the lists operation on a Thursday, the rest of the customer process was taken care of by co-workers here, led by Sanjoy. This was a great innovation and very popular with customers, especially the Bristol and nearby ones, who would come and browse what we had, try out new products and have a chat, as well as benefit from the cash-and-carry discount.

It was great too as it allowed Paul to focus on managing our more complex finances, and in particular ensuring we had sufficient cash. And I could focus on sourcing products, buying and selling and logistics. Much of what we bought we never saw as we now shared large orders with Suma and a few other companies, including some of our original suppliers from the early days.

We soon ran out of warehouse space and had to rent more in other warehouses nearby. This was challenging as quality control was key now that we were importing. Most container delivery contracts allowed us to send the container back within a half hour of delivery if there was a problem such as mould or infestation.

Typically, we would have the containers stop at our warehouse at St. Thomas Street and I would pop down, break the seal on the container door and climb up inside, opening a few sacks or boxes to check them, and then send them off to one of the warehouse spaces we were renting. For a long while everything was absolutely fine, but on one occasion I clambered up into the back of a container piled high with 50kg sacks of organic brown rice. I had a small knife and cut into one of the hessian sacks. I moved along, crawling at the top of the pile of sacks and cut into another. It was moving. The sack was infested with weevils, a small herbivorous (so vegetarian) beetle. I got out quick, shut the doors, ran up to the office and called the shipping agent, cancelled the bank payment and told the driver to take the container back to the docks.

Always check the quality of what you are buying before paying.

December 1982

Despite the early run on dried fruit in September, it was December that was always the busiest month. We worked up until the day before Christmas Eve, as some of our larger wholefoods shop customers

70

needed two deliveries in the week before Christmas. By then we had our first heavy goods vehicle (HGV) truck, complete with two HGV licensed drivers, plus two 7.5 tonne trucks and a smaller Iveco Daily van, which was used for smaller deliveries and was really useful.

In the final two weeks before Christmas the two lorries were in and out of our warehouse all day and every day. We had grown so much in the previous year and even did Sunday deliveries that December, such was the demand. From our initial Bristol and Bath base, we had customers all across Somerset, Devon and Cornwall, across Dorset, Wiltshire and as far as Brighton. We delivered to Gloucestershire, Worcestershire, Oxfordshire, Herefordshire and up to Birmingham. We had the Derbyshire, Sheffield and Leeds delivery run. And South Wales took at least two delivery runs a week, covering as far as Swansea, the whole of the Valleys, the Wye Valley and parts of mid Wales such as Llandrindod Wells and Builth Wells.

December 1982 was the busiest month in the history of the company and that year we booked a turnover of around £3 million, a stunning achievement. The UK was going through a significant economic recession. We were supporting lots of new businesses, shops, cafes and food co-ops and seeing the vegetarian revolution take place. It was an exciting time to be alive and doing this thing. Apart from temporary jobs while at school, university or travelling, I had never worked before. I loved it. I had boundless energy. I had found what I wanted to do for the rest of my life. Paul and I had ambitious plans for things like setting up and supporting producer cooperatives overseas, which were shared by most of our co-workers. I was the happiest I had ever been.

Well, it didn't turn out quite like that.

That weekend Dad taught me double-entry book-keeping

Chapter 9

I learn accounting

Paul had been off for a couple of days. As far as I knew, he was visiting a friend in Cambridge having a rare and well-earned break. It was a Friday and he was due back in the following Monday. In the middle of the afternoon he unexpectedly came into the office.

"Hi, Paul, what's up?" I was in the office on my own.

"We need to talk," he said. He went on to tell me that he had a rare and dangerous ear infection. I knew that he had been having tests, but this was serious. "I have found a consultant who will operate next week, and I need to go to the Addenbrooke's Hospital in Cambridge. I will be away for a while, maybe a couple of months."

"A couple of months!" I wanted to shout out, but wisely didn't. For once it was time for him to put himself before the business.

"Here is the Simplex D," he said. "I can give you a quick lesson in how it works."

The Simplex D was an accounts book that many small businesses used at the time to manage their weekly finances. It was basically a cash book and Paul had used it to skilfully ensure we had stayed cash positive all this time, despite our rapid growth. Paul gave me a quick tour of this and his accounts system and then left.

I was terrified. I had no experience of accounting. Paul had always run the finances at Nova, and every financial question I had or decision we needed was answered or made by Paul. He had a forensic understanding of the business as a whole and, mixed with an extraordinary intuition, he always made good financial decisions quickly. Despite us being a workers' cooperative, all of us deferred to Paul's financial genius.

I sat at the desk staring at the Simplex D. I suddenly regretted dismissing Dad's "If you get an accountancy qualification, you'll be able to work anywhere" comments. And then I picked up the phone to Dad's office.

I was put through to him, and if he was surprised that I had called him at the office, he didn't let on. I burbled out what had just happened with Paul's operation, the Simplex D book and the fact that I was now the least-qualified or experienced accountant ever of a £3 million turnover business.

I ended with "What are you doing this weekend?"

Dad was smart so he had figured this was coming. "Not much," he said. I knew that wasn't true. Mum and Dad were always furiously busy with their social and family life. "Why don't you come up and we can have a look?"

He sounded proud.

The next morning I took the train to London. Dad picked me up from the local underground station. When we got to the house, the dining room was cleared and in the middle of the table was a large, deep-red ledger book.

That weekend Dad taught me double-entry book-keeping, which is the fundamental principle behind all accountancy and all the accounting software packages that I have subsequently used, including Sage, QuickBooks and now Xero. Once he had taken me through the principles, we recreated the previous few months of Nova's accounts back to the start of the financial year. By the time we took a break for Sunday lunch I was fairly confident that I could manage the finances, and I set off back to Bristol with our new accounts ledger tucked under my arm.

Monday morning we typically met as a team, apart from the drivers, who were already making deliveries. I explained about Paul's operation and that we might not see him for a couple of months. I told everyone that I'd be managing the accounts. Sanjoy came upstairs to help me on the buying, and we rearranged the front desk team. Everyone was amazing.

Paul did come back. His operation was successful and he wisely took time to recover. I showed him the ledger Dad had created and he loved it. While Paul continued running the finances of Nova, he ditched the Simplex D and carried on using Dad's system from then on.

And ever since then I have done the financial management of every organisation I have created or worked for.

I tracked Paul and Annie down for my 50th birthday. I watched while Paul told Dad that he had used his ledger system for the rest of his career. Dad beamed.

Computerisation

Late in 1982 we recognised that using the lists (our manual stock and ordering system) was becoming unwieldy. With hindsight it was a classic example of how a business hangs onto a system that works when small but then doesn't change this when the company grows. The system was amazing, accurate and allowed us to minimise stock levels, keep a decently paced turnover of stock and importantly maximise cash in the bank, which was still a scarce resource. And this was now taking up far too much of our time, such was the size of the business.

In those days there were a few companies selling invoicing and stock software systems. This was something none of us knew about, except for Pete, who I had known from Greenpeace Bristol and who had joined us recently. So it became Pete's job to help sort us out.

It's hard to remember what life was like without personal computers, the internet, mobile and smartphones, software as a service, apps and superfast fibre broadband. A significant number of you reading this won't recognise this pre-digital era. But in the early 1980s, most of us at Nova had never seen, let alone used, a computer.

Pete had worked a short while in computing, and in particular databases, and agreed that he would spend a couple of months researching options, in between his main job elsewhere in the cooperative. He researched the right hardware and database software. Eventually he had a recommendation and a software salesman came to demonstrate the system to Paul, Pete and me. The demo looked good. It seemed to fit our needs and budget, especially as there were lease options for the hardware.

Both Paul and I were anxious that without our lists system, which had served us well so far, the business could fall apart. And we were concerned about how long it would take to implement the new database. Despite these misgivings we decided to go ahead and purchase.

Pete moved upstairs to the office and started to set up the database. It was a big task given that by then we had over a thousand product lines and different sizes that many products came in. We had grown the range of products, largely in response to customer demand (a good thing) but trying to get all this into an early 1980s database was no mean feat.

It took a long time. A very long time. What was supposed to take two months was still incomplete at six months. In the meantime, the rest of us carried on managing the business as usual, using our manual stock, ordering and invoicing system as we always had done. Although Pete was sitting near me in our small office, I mostly forgot that we were planning to computerise our beloved homegrown paper-based systems.

So it came as a shock when, nine months after starting, Pete finally and unexpectedly announced that he was ready to move from the paper-based system to the computer. I went into high anxiety. These days Paul no longer led the lists process every Thursday. I was in charge, although I had help.

We came up with a plan, which with hindsight was a masterclass in how not to launch a software implementation. We would do the weekly stocktake as usual in the morning. Pete would then input the stock numbers for each product into the computer. We would take the customer orders on paper as usual and then he would copy these into the computer. In theory we would then 'press a button' and get the purchase order for each of our suppliers in time to call the orders in first thing Friday morning, as usual.

I assumed that this process would probably take longer than usual. It did, but much longer. We typically went home around 6pm and finished the process around 10pm over dinner. But because we were using the computer we had to stay in the office. By 10pm Pete hadn't finished.

"How long will it take?" I asked.

"Maybe 30 minutes. It should be ready by then."

In those days I had not yet learned that the word 'should' is never to be trusted. Thirty minutes became an hour, then two hours and still Pete was not ready. Finally at midnight Pete announced that he was ready to produce the reports that we needed to do the orders first thing in morning. "Great, let's get on with it," I said.

Five minutes later Pete went white. "What's going on?" I asked.

"The system has crashed," he replied in a rather soft and despairing voice.

In this sort of situation you have to think of the business first. I felt a combination of anger, fear and despair. But I had to hold it together. We had to do the whole process on paper this time.

We finished at 5am on the Friday morning and I went home. I left instructions for the orders to be phoned into our London suppliers in the morning. I went to bed and had a fitful few hours of sleep.

Today the majority of social entrepreneurs have grown up in the era of digital technology, mobile phones and easy-to-use software and applications. Despite this, I still hear of time and money wasted on failed technology procurements and implementations.

Ever since the computer debacle at Nova I have made it my business to understand any technology, software and hardware that my enterprise has to design, purchase, implement or operate. Not to the level of code writing, but in all cases to use and many cases to configure to meet the needs of the business.

Learning #8: Never trust 'should'

The response was "Maybe 30 minutes. It should be ready by then." The word 'should' sneaks into conversations all the time. "This should work", "I should get back to you by…" and so on. The permutations are endless, but the unspoken meaning is "I am not sure when or whether this will happen or work". I've been wise to the word ever since.

When it is used, I will simply interrupt the conversation and ask the person to define what they mean. I'm just asking for clarity. I would rather know that there is a chance that they may not be able to fix the problem, or that a delivery may not arrive today, but will tomorrow. We can then prepare for multiple eventualities.

I never trust a 'should'.

Where the new company presided Trading remains today.

Where the new company Essential Trading remains today

Chapter 10

A big decision

I woke up the next morning tired but somehow clear. I felt calm despite how ghastly the previous night had been. I went into the office late, probably for the first time in three years. I went up to the office and found Paul. He was on his own.

"I've decided to leave Nova," I said.

To this day I cannot remember his response. I've completely blanked it out. I doubt it was great. It was complicated, as we not only ran Nova together, but we had bought a house together that we lived in. There was quite a lot of unravelling to do.

Others of my colleagues asked me to stay, but I was clear. I felt this overwhelming sense of relief. And I was tired, feeling the cumulative effect of not having had a proper break for three years. All I had done in that time was work, eat and sleep, and not much of the latter.

At the time my decision to leave just felt instinctive. It had been triggered by the previous night's computer disaster. But on reflection, I was burnt out. This was not the first time this had happened to me, and typically this was a signal that I just needed to slow down or stop for a while and regroup. I didn't recognise this at the time, but I now understand that I needed to do some personal and professional development to become more self-aware as a person and more mature as an entrepreneur and leader. Announcing my departure that morning was a first step on that journey, although I did not know that at the time.

I stayed for a month, completed some things and passed on the buying side of the business to Sanjoy. It all happened very quickly. I left without having a clue what to do next, where I would live and how I would earn a living. I just knew that I had to leave.

I was sad. I knew that Nova Wholefoods had enormous potential. We had started using our buying power to work with producer co-operatives in countries such as the Philippines. We were at the start of the growth of the fair trade movement in the UK, which we could have been part of. There was lots to do, but not for me. I was sad about that. I didn't know what was to come next, but I needed some time away from Nova. I wondered whether I would ever again have work that I enjoyed so much.

I left with nothing. I had been an integral part of building a profitable company turning over £3 million a year. But we were a workers' cooperative and these are owned and run by the people who work there. When you leave, you leave. And I did.

What Nova (and our customers) did next

I didn't really have anything to do with Nova after that. It wasn't that I left under a cloud or that I held any ill feelings. Quite the contrary; I have always felt very positive and have talked a lot about Nova for the 40 years since I left. I still remain proud of what we achieved there in the early days and still consider it my second most successful enterprise.

Nova grew and grew. In 1991 they merged with Harvest Wholefoods Cooperative, based in Bath, and moved into Nova's new warehouse, where the new company, Essential Trading, remains today. When I was writing this section of the book I went to visit and had a lovely two hours with Tim, who I had worked with at Nova and is still a member of the cooperative. Essential is a very different business than the Nova that I left, in many ways because of changes in food standards. Most products are sold pre-packaged rather than the sacks and boxes of the 1980s. The company has set up incredible supply chains with organic producers and co-operatives worldwide. They own two large warehouses next to each other on the same estate. There are multiple generations of families working together as members of the cooperative.

And what about the many customers that I remember delivering to?

One of my favourites was Warrens Wholefoods in the Pontypool Indoor Market, run by Bill Warren. In 2008 I moved near to Pontypool and went back to buying from Warrens, although Bill had left. I looked for some of the wholefoods shops set up by former miners but found very few.

Van's Good Food Shop in Llandrindod Wells is a shop that survives from the early days of wholefoods in Wales. Van was a character who had been around long before Nova and who we met on many occasions.

Suma Wholefoods, who we delivered trail mix to, have grown from strength to strength. They are the largest equal pay workers' co-op in Europe, bigger than Essential. Both companies have held onto their ethos, values and identity.

Harvest Wholefoods, while merged with Essential, still have their shop in Bath. They were one of the earliest wholefoods shops in the UK, opening in 1971.

Wild Oats Wholefoods are still going in Bristol. Set up by Mike and Lois Abrahams in 1981, they were an early Nova customer. Mike is still running the business.

We used to go to Manchester occasionally in the early days and deliver to The Eighth Day Co-op there. They were founded in 1970 and are still going strong.

Alara in Bloomsbury in London are one of the oldest wholefoods shops in London. We regularly delivered there, and then in the late 1990s I worked just around the corner, so I was a regular customer for lunch.

Many others have gone, as the supermarkets have increasingly stocked vegetarian, vegan and organic food. Personally, I would still rather get my food from a shop that has the heritage and values of the early wholefoods industry.

But the best outcome is that our mission to change people's eating habits to save the world is now mainstream, not on the alternative fringe any more. Even Waitrose published a study that states that a third of Britons have stopped or reduced eating meat. The United Nations has promoted vegan eating.

I still feel glad to have been in at the beginning of wholefoods making that impact in the UK.

I worked at the stall in Swansea Market every Saturday.

I worked at the stall in Swansea Market every Saturday

Chapter 11

I make myself redundant

At the time of leaving Nova, I didn't really know what I was doing. I left after a month of announcing my departure. It wasn't a big deal; I just left one Friday and that was that. Paul and I sorted out the house and I left on OK terms, although it would be 25 years before we met again, and I'm sure he felt let down by me at the time. We are in touch now from time to time, which is lovely.

My partner and I headed off to France in an old rusty VW camper. We went to the south of France, with vague ideas of setting up a wholefoods business there. Then we went to Ireland with the same idea. None of it worked.

After three months of mostly aimless motion, we ended up in South Wales and went to see friends at Ear to the Ground, an old Nova customer in Swansea. They had a shop, market stall and smaller wholesale business supplying shops in West Wales and asked us to join and work with them. I worked at the stall in Swansea Market every Saturday.

At six weeks, it's the shortest that I have ever worked anywhere. On week two, I had a feeling that the finances of the business were not in great shape. I asked one of the two founders if I could have a look at the accounts over the weekend. He was a bit reluctant but eventually let me have them.

Not for the last time in my life, I quickly discovered that there were some financial problems with the business. I broke down the three areas of the operation by gross and net margin. It amazes me how rarely people do this when reviewing their finances. The market stall was highly profitable, the shop was doing well and the wholesale business was losing money. Overall, the business was just about breaking even, but it struggled to pay the VAT each quarter and some months the salary bills were a challenge.

To me the answer was simple. Close down the wholesale business. I went in on the Monday and explained the situation to the founder. He wasn't happy, but I had a compelling case. There was a team meeting. I explained the situation and said that of course I would be the first to leave. This made it easier for the others to accept.

It took a few weeks, but the decision was made to close down the wholesale business. It was the right thing to do, however painful. Nova committed to deliver to the shops in West Wales. A few people were made redundant. But the shop and market stall continued to thrive.

It was the first time I had to close a business down. It was an emotional wrench for those who had worked there for some time. Inevitably some of the staff felt let down. But I was glad to have shone a light on a hidden problem. It's completely possible that the whole business – shop, market stall and wholesale – could have gone bankrupt.

For the first and last time in my career I was made redundant – by myself!

Six months on the dole

I was out of work. Given that I had only worked at Ear to the Ground for six weeks, there was no redundancy pay-out. I signed on for Unemployment Benefit, or the 'dole' as it was colloquially named in those days. Benefit payments were generally more benign than they are today. If you lived outside of a major town, all that was needed to claim was for a neighbour to sign a form every two weeks and the money was sent in the post as a cheque. There was no serious chasing up for job interviews. There was a lot less stigma.

I found a holiday cottage that was let out for six months over the winter for a very cheap rent in the village of Rhossili, at the south-western tip of the Gower Peninsula, to the south-west of Swansea. It is one of most beautiful parts of the Welsh and British coastlines. We lived a very simple existence, walking a lot. It gave me a real appreciation of the beauty and people of Wales, a country that I came back to in 2006 to live and work. More of that later.

Early learnings that have stood the test of time

Nova Wholefoods was my first social enterprise and as such I made a lot of mistakes. But I began learning the skills of business and enterprise there, and here is a recap of some of what I learned, developed and adapted ever since.

Learning #1: Intuition

Intuition is the ability to understand something instinctively, without the need for conscious reasoning. I have always had good intuition, although like many people I have had to work at understanding and trusting it.

Most of the entrepreneurs, social and otherwise, that I have known have had good access to their intuition.

Sometimes intuition comes in the form of words, but mostly it is a clarity of thought that 'just knows what to do'. I have found believing and trusting in my intuition really helpful when faced with the many decisions that have to be made on a daily basis. But that doesn't mean that every decision I made with intuition was necessarily a good decision.

The first 'career' decision I ever made started as a moment of intuition.

As I recounted in Chapter 1, I went down to the local Jobcentre to look for work. As I scanned the cards on the noticeboards my eyes blurred and I couldn't really read them. And then I had this apparently random thought: go back to Bristol and set up a wholefoods wholesale company.

If I hadn't had or acted on that intuition, my life might have been very different. Being open to intuition is something I have done ever since. Being able to spot and act on intuition is a core skill for the fast decision-maker, and in a fast-changing enterprise that's vital.

However, I learned early on that intuition, while a vital skill, on its own is not enough. In my experience, intuition and dialogue make a strong combination. My understanding of dialogue is to take part in a conversation or discussion to resolve a problem.

I have always made sure that I have a great business partner to work alongside. I was taught that early on by Paul at Nova Wholefoods, who saw in me a business partner that he could dialogue with. We met up most evenings after a day of driving lorries, and when the business grew we shared a small office. We spoke all the time – asking each other questions, talking through decisions, talking about products, customers, co-op members and much more. I have made sure that I have had great working partnerships ever since.

I can make decisions fast, mostly using my intuition, but I also know that I've been a better social entrepreneur because I have had great business partners to dialogue with.

Learning #2: Reputation is everything

At Nova Wholefoods we traded entirely on our reputation – for quality food, for always making deliveries on time and for always taking responsibility for mistakes and fixing them immediately.

It was there that I learned this really important lesson (which you can read about at 'Mondays' in Chapter 2). And I have built on this my whole career. In particular, I've always found that taking responsibility for mistakes and fixing them immediately works. Customers, staff and suppliers will forgive you if you offer an immediate apology and make a genuine attempt to rectify the problem or complaint. Frequently I have been told by customers and employees that this is one of the qualities they most value and respect about the enterprise.

Learning #3: Align values and commercial interests

Nova Wholefoods was a start-up that grew fast. We rarely had a weekly turnover that wasn't significantly larger than the previous week. We had little time to discuss strategy or articulate values. These just emerged as we went along. But it became clear quite quickly that we had values that the majority of our customers shared.

This became obvious when we supported our first former miner's family to set up a wholefood shop in their village in see Chapter 3. Miners were losing their jobs and livelihoods and it was absolutely core to the values of our workers' co-operative to find a way to help workers support themselves and their villages and towns with cheaper ways to eat.

But that was also aligned to the commercial interests of the company. We were delighted to expand our customer base into the Welsh Valleys. It was a risk, but lending stock to that one shop helped us grow our customer base, and it introduced a whole group of meat eaters to vegetarian food.

Years later when I went back to the Wales to set up Connect Assist, creating jobs was a key part of the mission of the enterprise. We talked about this to our customers and explained why it was worth them being part of this mission by contracting with us. It worked; we created more jobs and the business thrived. You can read about this in Chapter 40.

Social enterprise is about finding ways to get your values aligned to the commercial mission of the company. My early years at Nova taught me never to make the mistake of thinking that the social or environmental values of the enterprise are somehow more important than the commercial interests. They are the same.

For me, the whole point of social enterprise is to show that changing the world for the better can be done successfully by commercial enterprises. It definitely can.

Learning #4: Risk-taking

At Nova, a small business taking on the rent and responsibility for a warehouse that was far too big was a huge risk. And yet fortune favoured the brave as it was not long until the warehouse was full! The same happened for me 25 years later which you can read about at 'Raising the money' in Chapter 36.

A lot is written about risk-taking. On the one hand there is the 'buccaneer' image of an entrepreneur who takes risks with little or no thought to the future. On the other hand is the person who takes a long time to take a risky decision, going through detailed risk assessments all along the way.

I've found that successful risk-taking lies at neither of these extremes. The trick is to develop an ability to see the risks of every decision and every action all the time, so that having an overview of risk simply becomes a part of the day-to-day of leading an enterprise. Doing that I found that when bigger and more significant decisions came along I had analysed the risk already and could make a decision quickly. This was really helpful as on many occasions if didn't move fast, I would probably lose the opportunity.

Learning #5: Decision-making

Can a large group make decisions?

Workers' cooperatives are owned and managed by the members of the cooperative, who are typically employees. Rules vary between cooperatives but the general principle is that everyone gets to make decisions.

This is a worthy aim, but it does have complications. We quickly discovered this at Nova Wholefoods when we formally became a cooperative. As mentioned in Chapter 5, some people felt that this meant the cooperative needed to meet up to make every decision.

We experimented and quickly found that this did not work at all. And why should it? My view has always been that decision-making should be made by the person closest to the decision. In our case that meant that Paul should make the day-to-day financial decisions and Pete the HGV driver should make decisions about the trucks. If there was a financial implication of a vehicle decision, the two of them should make it together. Common sense to me, and an approach that I have always taken.

The question is what decisions should be made by the cooperative as a whole. In my view, that means strategic decisions such as investments and budgets. In other words, the cooperative as a whole should make only the same sorts of decisions as those made by charity trustees or company directors.

The best decisions are often made quickly

As in the quick decision-making I recalled in Chapter 1, I became a member of Nova Wholefoods after a quick conversation. It was and still is the shortest interview or pitch I have ever done, all over with both sides making their decisions in a couple of minutes.

I have spent the following 40 years wondering why people take so long to make decisions, needing second, third and more meetings to finally come to a decision that they are still unsure of. This was all over in 120 seconds and yet it's arguably the most significant career decision I have ever made. It set the course for the rest of my working life.

Tips on decision-making – a summary

-   My experience is that decisions are best made by the people closest
    to managing that decision. This is a view widely held within many
    businesses, not just social enterprises and co-operatives. And it
    makes common sense.

- Large groups can't make small decisions. It's painful, inefficient and takes a lot of time. There are times when a large group needs to come together to discuss strategy, culture and values, and that is healthy.

- I have heard it said by members of cooperatives that I have worked with over the years that they need to spend more time in meetings. I disagree. In my experience, far too much time is spent in inefficient meetings in all sorts of enterprise. Meeting time is an overhead cost and if all your staff are involved in a meeting, that's expensive.

- The trick is to find ways to streamline decision-making so that it is transparent and efficient and there is a mechanism to question decisions. It's entirely possible and has largely how I have worked.

Learning #6: Say sorry and ask for help

I learned early on that saying sorry is helpful. The truth is that every entrepreneur makes mistakes. At the start of my career I made quite a lot and even more recently I've made plenty.

Back in the 1980s it was less common to say sorry. Now it's become institutionalised, with politicians and business leaders apologising for all sorts of things, to the point where I am not sure that the public is altogether convinced.

However, I still believe in the power of a sincere apology. When Paul and I apologised to the transport tribunal for non-use of tachographs, we were genuinely sorry and realised we had broken the law. Yes, we had a good lawyer, but the tribunal chair obviously saw that we had realised our mistake and taken rapid steps to rectify this and get the company compliant with the law.

Asking for help is again something I learned early on but often in quite random situations. The day that fours tonnes of honey and broken glass ended up on a motorway slip road required me to ask for help. And amazingly, two RAC patrolmen and a policeman helped us clean up the mess.

My experience is that people enjoy helping people who ask for help. I am at a stage of life where I am delighted when people ask me for help. But I often come across people who feel uncomfortable doing so. They say things like "I didn't ask because I don't want to bother you", thinking that I'm too busy. But the old phrase is true: if you want to get something done, ask a busy person.

I'm glad that at an early stage I learned to say sorry and ask for help. Both have served me well.

Learning #7: Difficult conversations

Leadership means that you sometimes have to do the scary stuff, as I recall in 'Scary leadership challenges,' Chapter 7.

My first experience of this was walking into the cafe in Bristol following the theft of cash from our warehouse. I was shaking when I came out, but this intervention worked, and I learned for the first time that difficult conversations are part of being an entrepreneur.

I have had to have a lot of difficult conversations over the past 40 years. Some of these are covered elsewhere in the book (you can read about some of these in Chapters 18 and 29). I am often anxious before having what I think will be a difficult conversation, and yet all too often feel much better once it's over. In time, I realised that it was better to have a difficult conversation as soon as possible, to minimise my anxiety and avoid sleepless nights. And in any case they are often less difficult than I thought they would be.

I became an entrepreneur long before email and messaging were in use. Since these became an essential part of everyone's working lives, I have spent far too much time 'cleaning up' difficult conversations that some of my colleagues have attempted to have by email or messaging. And I've received emails that raise difficult issues or are critical where my first response is to seek the person out or pick up the phone. This introduces a human element into the conversation that in my experience is at the heart of understanding and reconciliation.

I have always insisted potentially difficult conversations should take place in person, ideally face to face or failing that on the phone. I understand that this can be difficult where power imbalance is at play in which case I always encourage the colleague in question to bring someone to support them, for example a trade union representative, mediator or work colleague that they trust.

My employment solicitor, who I respect very highly, once told me that "there are few problems that can't be solved by a respectful straightforward conversation". It's one of the most helpful pieces of advice I've ever received.

Learning #8: Never trust 'should'

In 'Computerisation' in Chapter 9 I remembered the first time I heard the word 'should' in a business context and learned not to trust it. Facing problems fixing a new computer system, I asked how long it would take to finish. "Maybe 30 minutes. It should be ready by then." Given how wrong that was (it took hours, overnight) and how massive the consequences, I've been wise to the word ever since.

'Should' sneaks into conversations all the time. "This should work", "I should get back to you by…" and so on. The permutations are endless, but the unspoken meaning is "I am not sure when or whether this will happen or work".

I have spent years working with employees, suppliers, managers, external advisers, technology people and others who use the word 'should' without a thought. It's never good news for them because I am on top of it immediately. It is a seemingly innocent word that I have zero tolerance for.

When it is used, I will simply interrupt the conversation and ask them to define what they mean. At first people don't understand what I am doing and are sometimes offended. But over time the people I work with begin to understand that I'm just asking for clarity. I would rather know that there is a chance that they may not be able to fix the problem, or that a delivery may not arrive today, but will tomorrow. We can then prepare for multiple eventualities.

I never trust 'should' and always challenge its use.

Part Two: Ecovillage

The first time I caught a salmon I was terrified

Chapter 12

The first Experience Week

I first went to the Findhorn Foundation in early 1984. I had read the book The Magic of Findhorn by Paul Hawken[1] over the winter, which described it as a somewhat spiritual, but not faith-based, community in the north-east of Scotland, located on a sand dune and growing wildly oversized vegetables. It was an intriguing story, albeit written in a somewhat glamorous manner.

My visit was to join the initial Findhorn Experience Week. I was part of a group of around 20 people visiting for the first time. It was intriguing and a great introduction to the Community and many of its members. Little did I know that I would be working with many of those I met for the next 12 years.

One of these was Alex. One evening he came to give a talk about the structure and organisation of the Community. I was fascinated, and once Alex, who was the finance director, had finished, I plied him with questions.

At the end of the evening, I asked if I could meet up with him later in the week. We had lunch together and continued the conversation. He was intrigued by my experience of setting up and growing a workers' cooperative. I was intrigued by every aspect of the Community he shared with me – the finances, the organisation, the charitable status and the Community's ambitions.

But what particularly got my attention was the ambition to create an eco-village (although then it was called a 'Planetary Village'). The vision for this had recently been the focus for the Foundation to raise the funds to purchase its original home, The Park, a 26-acre caravan park located on the estuary of the Findhorn River, one of the great rivers of Scotland.

Many books have been written about the Findhorn Foundation over the years, and this is not one of them. But the creation of the Ecovillage at Findhorn became the second phase of my social enterprise career, and one where I learned much of the complexity of running organisations, raising funds, creating multiple corporate structures and leading teams. It is fair to say that this is not what drew most people to live at the Findhorn Community, who typically came to find a more spiritual focus to their lives. But for me, aged 26, this was an exciting project, and having come from the world of vegetarian food and its impact on the climate and environment, I wanted to be part of it.

So, that is what I will write about next.

But just to keep my story going in somewhat of a straight line, there are few years to account for before I got to that major project. After the first Experience Week I drove back to Wales, packed up the house and three weeks later was back at Findhorn. Two months after that I was working with Alex in the accounts and finance department, managing multiple budgets and trying to make financial sense of an organisation that had hundreds of activities and budget lines and a significant debt to pay off. I worked there for two years.

Isle of Erraid

During this time, I visited the Isle of Erraid for the first time and fell in love with its rugged beauty. I made the move and lived there for nearly four years.

Erraid is a small Scottish island about a mile square, close to the south-west coast off the larger Isle of Mull in the Hebrides. The island had been developed in the 1860s, first as a building site for a lighthouse, and then as housing for the lighthouse keepers and their families.

The lighthouse and the housing were built by David and Thomas Stevenson, who were members of the Stevenson family who built most of the lighthouses around Scotland. The son of Thomas, a young Robert Louis Stevenson, visited the island during the construction, and a chapter of his famous book "Kidnapped" is partly set on Erraid.

In 1978 the Findhorn Foundation was asked to become a living custodian of Erraid, which is owned by a family from the Netherlands. At the time of writing this book, this arrangement still stands. The resident group on the island usually consists of between six and ten members, including single people, couples and families. The vision of this small community is to live as sustainably as possible.

I had multiple roles during my time on the island, including salmon fisher, tractor driver, plumber, wood chopper, builder, milker of cows (by hand, the old-fashioned way), chef, parent, vegetable grower, shepherd, boat captain and accountant, the last of which being the only thing I knew how to do when I arrived.

The time I spent on Erraid set me up for the rest of my life in a way that is hard to describe. I was a young city boy suddenly living a rural self-sufficient life. There were nights at sea that were truly dangerous. There were gales when I would be up on a roof nailing tiles on to stop the roof coming off. I delivered more than one stillborn lamb to keep the mother alive.

Until I went to live on Erraid, I was a vegetarian. As the ethos of the community was that we were self-sufficient, I felt that to be a full participant in this experience, I would need to eat the fish that I was catching on behalf of the community. The first time I caught a salmon I was terrified, yet found the courage to kill, clean and gut it. And in the process I discovered a hunter's adrenaline and elation that felt primal.

I had to learn largely physical tasks that, while I haven't used many of them subsequently, gave me a confidence that I could learn most things if I really wanted or needed to.

I surprised myself that I could do this. And it surprises others. I have spent many years at networking events and business meetings telling people about my time there when asked what I have done in my career. I've seen their surprise when they reframe who they previously thought I was. It's amazing what camouflage a business suit provides.

After nearly four years on the island, I'd had enough. It was time to get started on the next phase of my social enterprise journey – the Findhorn Ecovillage.

This was a private bungalow, constructed out of a giant whisky vat.

This was a circular house largely constraucted out of a giant whisky vat

Chapter 13

Early beginnings

The Findhorn Foundation is, as you might expect from the name, a registered charity.

For the purposes of this section of the book, I use the following terms:

1. 'The Foundation' I use to mean the Findhorn Foundation, the name of the charitable organisation, a Scottish charity, registration number SC007233.

2. 'The Community' describes the community of individuals who lived and worked at the Foundation when I was there, also known as 'members'. Over time the Community has grown beyond those who live and work at the Foundation and today has formed into a wider association, but this was not the case in the early 1980s.

3. 'The Park' was the Foundation's main property when I arrived, a 26-acre caravan park. This is on the approach to the village of Findhorn on the Moray Firth, 32 miles east of Inverness, Scotland.

4. 'The Ecovillage' is the experimental ecological building project based at The Park. Residents of the Ecovillage may or may not work for the Foundation but for the purposes of this book form part of the Community.

In the mid 1980s, the Findhorn Foundation owned a lot of property, which had been purchased over the years. The Park was largely made up of static caravans and what were called bungalows (which were really two caravans put together and turned into one dwelling). There were a few buildings that had been added over the years, mostly public buildings such as the Community Centre (a large dining room and kitchen where the majority of Community members and visitors ate twice a day) and the Universal Hall (a large meeting and performance hall with associated studios, meeting spaces, offices and a cafe).

Other than The Park, the Foundation then owned Station House, a large house split into flats in the nearby Findhorn Village, and Cullerne House, adjacent to The Park. It also owned two properties in the nearby town of Forres, one of which was a huge former spa hotel.

Two years before I arrived, there was a conference held at Findhorn entitled 'Building a Planetary Village'. The conference marked the beginning of serious attempts by the Community to demonstrate a human settlement that could be considered sustainable in environmental, social and economic terms. This was still being spoken of as the kick-off for what would become the Ecovillage, but by the mid 1980s there was little, if any, activity.

It was around the same time as this conference that the Foundation purchased The Park from the previous owners, funded by a successful fundraising appeal, which was matched with a bank loan. This was a significant moment in the Foundation's history (which had been founded in 1962) and ultimately paved the way for the beginning of the Ecovillage. The combination of the senior debt on the purchase of The Park and an overhang of financial difficulties in the 1970s meant that while the Foundation managed to break even, it could not easily generate a surplus. The balance sheet was largely made up of fixed assets comprising land and old buildings, the latter generating a high cost of maintenance.

In my previous two years working in the finance department, I had acquired a good understanding of the way the Foundation operated financially and commercially. Which meant that I understood that it would be a challenge to finance the development of a 26-acre site into an ecovillage.

The challenge was greater because in the 1980s the ethos of the Community was that many of the people who lived and worked at the Foundation lived at The Park and were provided with accommodation, typically in caravans. This had led to the perhaps reasonable expectation that the Foundation would simply be able to build housing to replace the caravans that Community members lived in.

Given the financial position of the Foundation, this was an expectation that would be extremely hard to deliver on.

The first houses

In 1986 a Community member built the first of the Ecovillage houses. It was also the first of the whisky barrel houses.

This was a circular house largely constructed out of a giant whisky vat. The Community had acquired a number of these from a nearby distillery that was keen to clear them out. This barrel house was the first and eventually the smallest. It was the Ecovillage equivalent of a studio apartment, with everything cleverly designed to fit in a small and circular space. When it was first built, you could smell the alcohol in the wood. It was an innovative exercise in recycling. By the time I came back from Erraid, two more of the barrel houses were under construction.

But we could not build the whole Ecovillage of barrel houses. They had a number of limitations, not least as a result of their size and shape. It was harder to create passive solar gain and they were small, which presented problems for insulation and lots more. Although subsequent barrel houses took on different shapes, in part to work around some of these problems, these were somewhat boutique constructions.

They also required a level of craft that, while very much in the spirit of the Community's values, were not practical for a larger, and more cost-effective, housing development.

111

The planning and thinking for the development of what became known as the Ecovillage was led by John. John was from the USA, had an engineering background and had lived and worked at the Foundation for many years. He had a gift of negotiating himself through multiple challenges and was someone who was universally perceived as a reliable and good person. I had met John a couple of times when I was first at the Foundation in the mid 1980s but we did not really know each other then.

Throughout the summer of 1989 John was putting together a scheme to deliver a cluster of houses in the north-east corner of The Park. This was an area where there were about ten caravans in a semi-circle, around a wild area of land, and surrounded by a small plantation of conifer trees on the north and east sides of the plot. Plans were being drawn up for an initial four houses to be constructed in early 1990.

About once a month, the Community came together for a meeting. This was typically a gathering of the 300 or so members to deal with issues that needed either discussion or decision. In one such meeting, just after my return from living on Erraid, John gave a presentation of what was being planned.

He ended by saying, "We need someone to come and manage the finances of this."

I went down to the front at the end of his presentation. "I'll do it," I said. It was the first time we had spoken in years and probably only the third time we had spoken at all.

"We were hoping it would be you," he said. Apparently my reputation preceded me.

I started the next week.

A number of orders for goods had been made, and there was a box of quotes, invoices and statements from suppliers.

A number of orders for goods had been made and there was a box of quotes, invoices and statements from suppliers

Chapter 14

Great project but chaotic finances

I joined John in the office the following week. He had taken over
part of a timber building about five minutes' walk from the proposed
Ecovillage building site to be the office for the project.

Most of my life I have just thrown myself into each new role. That
generally suits me as I'm an 'on the job' learner. There was no
induction, just a long list of unresolved issues. And a building project
starting in a few weeks' time.

These issues included:

- There were three individual Community members who were
  financing a house each.

- John had an assistant working part-time with him, who had said
  publicly and to the three individuals that the cost of each of the
  houses would be £20,000. When I asked to see the financial
  projections I was told that he was still working on these.

- The cost would apparently be low because a company called
  Constructive Individuals had been engaged to run a series of
  'building schools' whereby people would come and learn to do
  eco-building for a three-week programme, during which the houses
  would be '90% completed'.

- The first building school was due to start in a few weeks. Twenty
  'students' would be arriving and by then the foundations for the
  first house needed to be complete. They had not yet been started.

- There was still no building warrant from the local council,
  something that would be essential before work could begin.

115

- There was no lease or other agreement for the houses, which were being built on land owned by the Foundation, land for which it had no intention of selling the freehold.

- There was an agreement signed with Constructive Individuals to raise corporate sponsorship for various building materials in exchange for a percentage of their value. The term 'value' was ill defined.

- And for good measure, there was only one computer in the office, and I didn't have access to it.

It's fair to say that, while an enormous amount had been organised in a short period with little resource, there were a significant number of serious 'loose ends'.

I had worked in the Foundation's finance office when I first arrived in 1984. This had made me aware that much of what happened at the Community was done on trust, goodwill and a belief that things would work out positively if everyone was focused together. In my view it was an overly optimistic approach to management. Don't get me wrong, I think that this approach is really important to the success of any project. But for a project of this nature, you also need to add financial rigour, clear legal contracting, realistic cost estimates and funding that is secured.

I quickly realised that part of my job was to inject a healthy dose of realism into the situation. Necessary, but it was going to be a little uncomfortable. So now I understood my role. I had a few weeks to turn this all into a financially viable housing development operation.

A busy few weeks

It took me a couple of days to realise the extent of these problems, and I needed to move fast. At the end of day two I spelled it out to John with an analysis of what I thought needed to happen. To his significant credit he backed me up.

The next morning I informed John's assistant that he would be leaving the office and would now be responsible for getting the foundations laid for the first house. I also explained that any further expectations that he had set were not to be shared again until I had done a full financial analysis.

Getting him out of the office dealt with a number of the problems. I could take charge of the finances and I could seek to reset expectations (there was no way these houses could be built for £20,000). We needed the foundations building fast. And I needed the computer.

The next job was to do a proper costing. A number of orders for goods had been made and there was a box of quotes, invoices and statements from suppliers. I waded through these. It took a couple of days but by the end of that I had a detailed financial forecast for the project. I was grateful to Paul at Nova Wholefoods for giving me the finances to manage there as I had become much more confident with financial forecasting.

It was clear that the first house would cost closer to £50,000, not £20,000.

The next step was to visit Ian, a Community member who was funding the first house and would live in it with at least one other member. Thankfully, he was a very sensible person, warm and friendly. I met him over a cup of tea. He asked me how I was getting on in my new role and was appreciative that I had taken it on. That helped. We chatted a bit. Finally, I got down to it.

"I'm sorry but I have some bad news," I said. "I have to apologise on behalf of the Ecovillage team and the Foundation."

117

"What for?" he interrupted.

"We promised you that your house would only cost £20,000, but it's going to cost closer to £50,000."

He was silent for about 30 seconds, which felt like a long time.

"I think I had half expected this," he said. "I didn't think a house that size could really be built for that little, even at Findhorn."

I breathed a sigh of relief and took out my spreadsheet to show him the numbers.

On that occasion I had the difficult conversation and it turned out OK. It's always better to have the difficult conversations than avoid them, and in my experience, if you are honest, straightforward and, if necessary, apologetic, the conversation is most likely to go well.

For more about difficult conversations, please see Learning #7 in 'Early learnings that have stood the test of time'.

Learning #9: Learning styles

I have done almost all my learning on the job which suits me best. I have personally found it harder to learn by reading or attending training courses, while I am generally a quick learner if I do the task myself.

For many years I was somewhat judgemental of my learning style, so it was very exciting when I came across some of the research on learning styles. Everyone prefers different learning styles and everyone has a mix of learning styles. Some people may find that they have a dominant style of learning, with far less use of the other styles. Others may find that they use different styles in different circumstances.

Once I had looked into this it became clear that I am a kinaesthetic (or physical) learner. Touch is big part of this so when Steve Jobs launched the iPhone that was perfect for me. And many millions of others.

This knowledge helped me feel more comfortable in my own approach to learning. And it also helped me to understand people I was working with much better and adjust my communication to better match what I observed their learning styles to be.

At the end of the book is a link to a questionnaire where you can explore what your learning styles are.

Learning #10: Cashflow management

Particularly in the start-up phase of an enterprise, cashflow is critical and has to be carefully managed. In the start-up phase of all my enterprises, preparing a weekly cashflow report has been essential.

Early on I learned to manage cashflow well and have always made sure I know the cash position of each enterprise.

Cashflow management and awareness are key skills. When I'm coaching social entrepreneurs, I encourage them to always know what the cash position and forward cash forecast of their enterprise is, even if they are not the finance person.

Building an ecological village

Chapter 15

Building an ecological village

I had been asked by John to make sense of the money. By the end of my second week I had put together a detailed costing and financial forecast for building the first four houses of the cluster.

The first to be built was Ian's house. It was being developed as two separate apartments, one on each floor. Ian would live upstairs and another Community member downstairs. Ian had been surprisingly relaxed about his revised cost and was in the process of making the funds available.

The building school was about to start. The foundations were nearly finished. Constructive Individuals were due to arrive a week before the school started.

One of their team, Melanie, had been commissioned by John to manage a corporate sponsorship campaign aimed at building suppliers to get donations of building products such as plasterboard, electric cable, roof tiles and copper pipe.

I met Melanie as soon as she arrived. I was expecting the campaign to be in full flow; but it wasn't. She showed me letters that had been sent to the project asking for materials with which to put together a professional fundraising ask. Nothing had been done at our end.

We had to move fast. We would need some of these materials in the next two to three weeks if we were to be able to use them on the first house.

When Melanie realised that nothing had been done, she took it well, and she and I got to work. Over a long day we put together a brochure pack and letters to over 40 companies that she had researched as good prospects.

We got a designer, who worked up a brochure cover, which was a beautiful drawing of what the development would look like, complete with wind generator, solar panels and vegetable plots. Across the top it said 'Building an Ecological Village'. That was the first time we had used that name, and it stuck.

I knew this was the right name for what we were doing but was aware that 'Planetary Village' had been used by the Community since the early 1980s. But 'Ecological Village' would be more clearly understood, and at that stage we were focused on raising sponsorship from traditional building supply companies. The Community would have to put up with the change of name. If we had asked, it would have involved weeks of meetings and debate, as this was generally the consensus-making approach adopted for most decisions; but there was no time for that. It was not the last time in this project that we just got on and made decisions.

The good news was that no one even questioned the name decision. And the term has stuck, with a slight change. Today it is called the Findhorn Ecovillage and is part of a global network of ecovillages GEN which the Findhorn Ecovillage played a lead role in establishing.

Learning #11: Branding

I am a great fan of choosing a name that clearly states what you do.

Much has been written about branding over the years and I am no expert. But I've been involved in a fair bit of rebranding. My experience is that enterprise names are best when they are as close as possible to explaining what the enterprise is there to do.

The name Ecological Village, shortened to Ecovillage, has stuck and has been adopted by similar projects across the world. That's great branding.

I hope that you think I have done this choosing the name for this book.

122

It was not unusual that a plane would take off just as discussion got heated

Chapter 16

Wind power for the people

One of the earliest projects of the Ecovillage wasn't housing, it was the Wind Park. Any development, ecological or otherwise, needs to invest in infrastructure. Energy supply is a key part of this. Building the Ecovillage meant thinking about ecological infrastructure, and top of the list was energy.

In 1989 John led on this project and had identified a small patch of land that could be rented from the local farmer, with whom he had built a good relationship. The next step was to get planning permission for a wind turbine. There was, as always, a problem.

The local farmer owned land that was situated between The Park and the Kinloss Royal Air Force base. From 1945 until 2010 it was the main base for the RAF's fleet of Nimrod MR2 maritime patrol aircraft to monitor Russian ships and submarines in the Norwegian Sea.

They are undoubtedly the noisiest neighbours I have ever had, and as a Community we would have to pause debates and discussions for five minutes of 'silence' as the roar of the Nimrods on take-off made talking and listening impossible. It was not unusual that a plane would take off just as a discussion got heated, giving a welcome pause for reflection and restoration of objectivity. We lived surprisingly well with our noisy neighbours.

It was no surprise when RAF Kinloss objected to a tall wind turbine so close to the runway. John was confident that this was far enough away not to be under the flight path for take-off or landing, but we needed to get surveys done and make a strong case. This took time, but as ever John's powers of persuasion prevailed, the RAF withdrew their objection and planning permission was granted.

John had secured a second-hand Vestas 75kW turbine for £75,000. This was a very good deal. It was purchased partly by the Community, with loans made to purchase the turbine, an electrical sub-station and a very long armoured cable plus the cost of installation. John was, it turned out, extremely adept at raising funds for Community ventures from Community members, and he is still doing this today.

There was about a mile distance from the turbine to the sub-station. Almost all of the Community members came out to dig the trench for the cable – the Community at its best. A crane was hired to raise the wind turbine, and its installation was a moment of great celebration.

Today there are three Community-owned wind turbines, which have a total capacity of 750kW, suppling more than 100% of the Community's electricity needs. The Ecovillage has its own private electricity grid, with most of the generation used on site and any surplus being exported to the National Grid.

And today there are no more Nimrods flying out of RAF Kinloss.

Solar

The plan was to install solar panels on every house, principally for hot water. In the late 1980s there was not the access to photovoltaic panels there is today, so solar hot water was supplied by an evacuated tube solar collector. Today, solar panels have been installed on most of the houses in the Ecovillage.

When we started, solar collectors were being manufactured at Findhorn by Weatherwise, a company set up by a community member, which was purchased in the early 1990s by another community member, George.

Since then George has significantly grown the company, renamed AES Solar in the late 1990s. It provides solar electric and hot water,

126

plus battery storage and electric car chargers. AES has gone on to be a major UK installer of solar, with clients such as the Scottish Parliament and Balmoral Castle, Scottish home of HM The King. George has played a leading role in the UK Solar Trade Association, is a co-founder of Scottish Renewables and recently won the Queen's Award for Enterprise: Sustainable Development.

Learning #12: Community shares

Today there is a well-developed market for social investment and a number of smart investment devices, including blended grants and loans, charity bonds, community shares, crowdfunded investment and social impact bonds.

Back in the late 1980s it was innovative to set up a community share scheme. These are now a popular financial model for a range of social enterprises, including community land trusts for affordable housing, co-operatives, local renewable energy schemes and the like.

An excellent website that explains community share schemes is Community Shares. For community-based social enterprises this is a very smart way to raise finance. There is a link to their website at the end of this book.

Everyone stood in a circle by the building site holding hands

Chapter 17

Revolutionary building

The building school was booked, and the architects and the team from Constructive Individuals were on site. Our little office became very busy. Building materials started to arrive, along with invoices for payment. There were numerous demands to spend money, some on items I knew about already but inevitably many I did not. I now know this is in the nature of construction projects.

Not for the first time, or the last, in my career, cashflow was very tight. I had to draw a very fine line between being supportive and facilitative, but at the same time holding a clear line about what was and what wasn't acceptable expenditure.

And there was so much to do in a short time. At Nova Wholefoods I had discovered that I have a capacity for working hard and am a 'completer finisher'. Just as well.

We were a small office of three people and we were swamped with the demands of the architects and building school leaders, the ordering and delivery of building materials, managing the hundreds of details that entailed, and all while we were still a very new team putting project and financial management in place for the first time. It was also all without email and mobile phones, both yet to become mainstream technology.

John was consumed with the problem of getting a building warrant, the permission required from the local council to construct the building. We were one week away from the start of the building school and Moray Council's building department could not understand what we were doing, and in particular the building techniques and materials that we were intending to deploy to create an eco-building. John and the architects spent days at the council offices working through the specification of the buildings.

This approach to construction was new and alien to the building department. There were minimal pad foundations set in sand that supported timber ground beams (using local Douglas fir) and timber frame walls. These were the first houses in the UK to use cellulose fibre insulation, a key element of the 'breathing wall' system, again the first of its kind in the UK.

The breathing wall was a revolutionary means of construction, allowing for natural ventilation of the building by a controlled exchange of air and vapour, avoiding condensation and loss of heat. As we were located in the north of Scotland, heat retention was crucial. All the materials used were natural, so no plywood and no animal-based glues. Today such construction techniques and materials are widely available and understood, but in the early 1990s they were largely unheard of and, reluctantly, materials had to be imported, often from Germany, which was ahead of the UK on eco-building.

The council demanded detailed specifications of the building materials and techniques. We were told that it would take weeks for them to approve them. John told them that we did not have this time. One of his many talents was his persuasiveness, and in the end the council agreed to fast-track the decision.

It was very tense in the office as we awaited the news of John's final visit to the building department. We were days away from 20 people arriving to start the building school. So, when the phone rang, with John saying "We've got it", I cheered.

90% built in three weeks

The building school started. There were about 20 students. The ambition was to build 90% of the first house in three weeks. A big ambition.

This ambition was inspired by a United States non-profit named Habitat for Humanity. They organise people to build a house for a member of their community, largely over a weekend, so it is both a housebuilding and community building event. Their work is very inspiring.

Those three weeks were extraordinary. They combined the best of the Findhorn Community's approach to group work, including a short moment of 'attunement' at the start of the working morning and afternoon. The whole team stood in a circle by the building site holding hands and shared a moment of silence, a process of helping everyone to become 'present' to the tasks ahead. For some this was new and took a bit of getting used to, but within days the whole group felt the benefit of it.

This was followed by a discussion about the tasks for the morning, and then everyone got to work. As this was a building school, most of those attending had done little or no construction before. There was a lot of tuition by the Constructive Individuals team led by Simon and also by John.

Although I wasn't part of the building school as such, I must have made the five-minute walk from our office to the building site 20 to 30 times a day to communicate or manage one of the hundreds of daily details. At this time I was the only person in the office other than John (who was largely on site) and the architect, who was absorbed with technical drawings. I was busy with deliveries to be chased, trips to a local builders' merchants for things we had forgotten, invoices to be paid, accommodation problems from some of the students and in one case a visa issue to deal with. It was an exciting time.

Increasingly, members of the Community wanted to come and see what was going on, and in some cases to join in. This was difficult as, unlike many Community activities, a building site has significant hazards. I spent a lot of time telling the rest of the Community what was going on while trying to discourage them from joining in. I quickly got a reputation as a gatekeeper (that's the polite version), a role I seem to have had for much of my career.

On site the first of the 'cluster' of eco-houses was quickly framed, in the second week the scaffolding was raised and later that week we had a roof on. Then we hit a snag.

The insulation was a product made of recycled newspaper. We had purchased a special blower that was shipped from Germany. It was basically a large cylindrical drum about five feet tall with a three-foot diameter at the top which the insulation was emptied into. There was a pump and a large flexible tube with two water jets at the end. It was like a giant vacuum cleaner that blew rather than sucked.

The walls were timber framed with a barrier and then plasterboard on the inside, so the insulation was blown into the cavity of each wall and ceiling frame from the outside. The problem was that it was February and the wind was strong and gusty. A lot of the insulation went flying as it was blown out of the end of the hose, much of it ending up all over the builders themselves. What should have taken a day took nearly a week and delayed the schedule. All sorts of ideas to resolve this problem were debated, and in the end a makeshift tent was created out of timber and sheeting that was pushed up against each timber frame to protect the blower and the blowers from the wind. It helped a bit, but we lost time.

However, by the end of the three-week school the first house was weathertight, with walls, a roof, doors and windows, electric cables and plumbing pipes fitted and the walls and ceiling partly insulated. We had built the basics of a house.

The final attunement was a great moment of celebration, and on this occasion we encouraged the Community to come and join us. Over a hundred people joined the builders and our team as we stood in a circle around our first eco-house, first in silent contemplation and then to raise a loud cheer for the builders.

It was just one house, but it was pioneering. We had not just built our first eco-house, but we had created the first breathing wall eco-house of its kind in the UK, battling the authorities to get permission to build it. We had started building the Ecovillage.

Learning #13: Working styles and team roles

At the Ecovillage I began to learn more about how to build a successful team and came across the Belbin Team Roles. Team Role theory was developed by Dr Meredith Belbin in the 1970s. Belbin Team Roles have become the gold-standard method for identifying behavioural contributions in the workplace.

Dr Belbin defines a 'Team Role' as one of nine clusters of behavioural attributes identified by his research at Henley as being effective in order to facilitate team progress.

The nine Belbin Team Roles are: Resource Investigator, Team worker and Co-ordinator (the Social roles); Plant, Monitor Evaluator and Specialist (the Thinking roles), and Shaper, Implementer and Completer Finisher (the Action or Task roles). For more information you can see a link at the end of the book.

I have found the Belbin approach very useful.

Learning #14: Gatekeeping – protecting the enterprise

I had never thought about gatekeeping as a leadership skill, but I first discovered it at the Ecovillage. Gatekeeping has always been a key part of all my enterprises.

Gatekeeping is a form of boundary setting. It's about protecting the enterprise, its customers, its service users, its employees, its suppliers, its finances, its community and its environment. As a social entrepreneur I put the safety and wellbeing of all of these stakeholders front and centre.

I cancelled my weekend arrangements and set up in the office

Chapter 18

Stumbling over funding

In reality, the first Findhorn eco-house took some time to finish. Aiming for 90% completion in three weeks was an over-ambitious target, but we had built a weatherproof building. In any case, anyone who has ever built a house knows that the internal fitting takes much longer than you think, in part because it requires specialist skills such as electrics, plumbing, joinery and decorating. We all felt very committed to Ian, whose house this was, and his generosity, and we developed a building team who worked hard on the house so that he could move in later that summer.

Meanwhile, the next houses needed to be planned. We had another building school scheduled for April, which was only two months away.

I had spoken to Ian about the costs of the house back when I started with the Ecovillage in January. Sadly, there were two other Community members who had also been told that their houses would cost only £20,000.

The first of these was Tom. He wasn't happy about what I had to say about the cost and spent some time arguing that I had increased the costs unnecessarily.

I tried to be as patient as I could. We were members of the same Community. It didn't help that he was working for the building team that was emerging from those who had attended the first building school and were keen to stay.

After a number of insinuations, I was outright accused of manipulating the numbers, at which point I had had enough. I said that there was nothing more to be discussed.

I wrote him a letter later that day saying that unless he had deposited 25% of the funds for 'his house' by the following week, along with evidence that the rest was available, we would have no alternative but to seek another funder who would then live in the house. This was a risk as we had the next building school starting in six weeks' time.

I said nothing to the others, but close communities typically pick up what's going on, and our Community was no exception. The next day, I was approached by another Community member who said that she had plans and backers for the house.

I wanted to honour the one-week deadline I had given, and I shared in confidence that this was the position. But I saw no reason that we shouldn't discuss a Plan B. I laid out the same conditions, that we would need 25% of the estimated cost of £55,000 in a week and evidence of available funds for the balance.

Tom never came up with the deposit and so we built what became the Community's holistic health centre as well as a home. We had the second house 70% built in three weeks by the second building school. This time, the insulation was blown in from the inside, an essential redesign.

Long after I left, I went back to visit the Ecovillage in 2014. I went to look at these first houses and was delighted to have tea with Tom, the man who had failed to get the house built, and to discover that he was now living in that same house. The health centre had moved to bigger premises and he had managed to buy the house. I was very happy about that.

Sponsorship succeeds

The sponsorship campaign hadn't really started by the time of the first building school in February. We had sent our sponsorship requests and packs to over 50 companies, requesting gifts in kind of various building materials. We had prepared a rough estimate of the quantities of a range of items we would need for the four houses at the cluster we planned to build that year.

We had written to manufacturers and suppliers of plasterboard, electric cables and sockets, doors and windows, copper pipe, screws and nails, tools, tiles, hard hats and safety equipment, scaffolding and much more. I spent a lot of time calling up the people we had written to, typically to be told I needed to speak to someone else. In pre-mobile phone days, tracking people down by phone was not as easy as it is today, so this took time.

The Findhorn Community has a reputation for being alternative and from time to time it comes under criticism for its entirely benign, but nonetheless different, way of life. For this reason, I was a little pessimistic as to the response of the traditional building industry.

I was wrong. We had a really positive response. Over half of the companies we approached came back with a yes. Letters started arriving offering us much of what we had asked for, and in some cases more. In one case very much more.

A lorry driver arrived at the office one day from a well-known manufacturer of electric cable. I came out to direct him to our modest storage area and saw he had an enormous truckload of electrical cable of all sorts and sizes.

"How much of that is for us?" I asked.

"All of it," he replied.

I took a deep breath. It was probably enough cable to wire 50 homes. There wasn't enough room to store it and I had to quickly commandeer additional storage space around the Community. I spent the next two days moving it off the side of the road and into various sheds and garages. Some of it lived outside for a long time.

By the time we got to April we had taken delivery of a huge quantity of materials. This made a massive difference. We charged each housing project the materials at cost, realising a surplus to pay for the work done by Constructive Individuals and leaving the balance to cover the rising costs of our growing building operation.

Learning under pressure

After the second building school that April, the architects and Constructive Individuals left. This was the end of their contract and they had, in John's and my view, done a great job. But we were also relieved of the cost burden and agreed that we could manage ourselves.

For the most part we could. John took on the structural engineering work for which he was qualified. He also led the building schools, which he had been jointly doing already. We had Andrew, a recently qualified architect, working in the office, so he took on the design and detailed drawing, and he was soon joined by an architectural student. I took on the ordering of materials. But there was a gap that we all forgot about: quantity surveying.

The main part of this role for us was cost estimating, cost planning and cost management. I was already doing the planning and cost management, but the estimate of the amount of materials we required for each house had been done up to now by Simon from Constructive Individuals.

The problem was that both John and I forgot about this. As we got close to the date for the build of the third house, I went to John on a Friday afternoon and asked for a breakdown of the materials we needed, so I could check against our stock and place orders early the next week to arrive on time.

He looked at me and said, "I haven't done this."

"Neither have I," I replied.

We both swore.

John had a planning deadline he had to finish that weekend.
He was under pressure.

138

"I'll give it a go," I said. "Can I check with you when I have questions?"

"Of course," he replied.

I cancelled my weekend arrangements and set up in the office.

I went through all the plans, measuring every element. I was constantly on the phone to John asking questions about details such as the overhang coverage of roof tiles, the depth of the soffits and much more. I learned masses, in particular the fact that architects leave a lot for builders (and it turns out quantity surveyors) to work out by themselves. I'm convinced that this is one of the reasons that builders and architects don't always get on.

But when John and I met up on Sunday evening, we had a quantity list that he said was great, spotting a few things I had forgotten. When we got to site there were a few more things I had left off the list, which we had to go and find quickly, but I learned again one of the skills of social entrepreneurship: be prepared to quickly learn something you know nothing about.

Learning #15: Be prepared to quickly learn something you know nothing about

I am quite restless, so learning how to do new things I know nothing about, often under pressure, becomes second nature.

I realised this at the Ecovillage when I had to teach myself basic quantity surveying in a weekend. That weekend, I learned again one of the skills of social entrepreneurship. Be prepared to quickly learn something you know nothing about.

I've carried on doing this for the rest of my career, particularly as my various social enterprises have been in different fields, each presenting new questions that I have had to learn the answers to.

"Stop right there Patrick". I stopped mid flow

Chapter 19

Growing fast

By the summer of 1990, the Ecovillage was taking off. We had started the third building at Bag End (which somehow became the name of the cluster) with a third building school that summer, this time run by John.

In addition, we had started the construction of a house for Eileen, one of the founders of the Findhorn Foundation. Her son was an experienced builder and moved from the USA to lead a team of our builders on this project. The house was located right in the centre of The Park.

At this stage the houses had used a similar vernacular design befitting the original plan. John began the process of developing what became a comprehensive building code that all new buildings at the Ecovillage would be required to meet. This went far beyond UK building standards and included high levels of insulation, non-toxic organic paints and wood preservatives, boarding manufactured without the use of toxic glues or resins, roofing with natural clay tiles, water conservation features and locally sourced materials. Most important was the adoption of the breathing wall construction.

We were developing a permanent team of builders and I was scrambling around to find accommodation for them. Many of them were graduates of our building schools, which had always been the intention, but others were established builders who had heard what we were up to and wanted to come and join in.

Around this time, John moved out of the office and stood down from leading the Ecovillage. He wanted to build his own barrel house and worked freelance for us, largely as a structural engineer, which he was qualified at. He had held the torch for the development of this since at least 1982 and he is still, correctly in my view, seen as the founder of the Findhorn Ecovillage. With my help, he had taken the project to a good size and scale, and he had confidence in my leadership, something I'm very grateful for.

Leadership

John was still involved in and very much the figurehead of the Ecovillage, but I took on leading the project. There was a significant team of builders and we had about £250,000-worth of building projects on the go at various stages of completion. Alex, who then was the financial elder statesman of the Foundation, was extremely supportive, having developed the legal structure for people to invest money in the house they would live in.

I had got the finances in good shape and successfully negotiated the financial relationship with the Foundation, giving us some freedom to operate, and I had a good relationship with the finance director. With Alex's help, I had negotiated the ability for the Ecovillage development to borrow money, albeit within clear parameters.

This was a big deal and a turning point. The Findhorn Foundation and majority of the members were very debt averse. In the late 1970s it had run into financial difficulties and, although it had successfully raised most of the £250,000 to buy The Park in 1982, was still in debt and paying it off. I was well aware of this, having worked in the finance team when I first arrived in Findhorn. There was sometimes resentment about this change in borrowing policy among Community members, especially when setting annual budgets.

The day we started the third building school we had a gathering of everyone involved in the building of the Ecovillage. We all stood in a circle around the foundations of what would be our third house at Bag End, number 7. We had builders, electricians and plumbers working to

142

complete numbers 5 and 6, we had the team led by David from Eileen's house and we had the team of by now five from the Ecovillage office. We were about to start house number 4, which was to be a dwelling for three to four Foundation members, funded by a legacy donation.

As we held hands, I quickly counted how many we were – it was 70. I was a bit shocked. In just six months we had become by far the biggest of the many work teams at the Foundation (kitchens, gardens, running workshops, maintenance, etc.) and I don't think many other Community members had previously realised this. We were attracting people to come and work here because of the vision of the Ecovillage, not the original spiritual and educational work of the Foundation. This was new.

And so things changed quickly. Some of the members of the Community who had joined the Foundation's staff were resentful that builders could join our team and have an equal status. Others were understandably resentful that houses were being built with private money for the residents who could afford this.

That winter I started to attend a number of meetings to discuss this and make the case. It wasn't easy but one of the great things about being at the Findhorn Foundation was that there were plenty of opportunities to learn how to listen in a non-defensive manner. I was new to this and struggled at first, but I started to notice that the more defensive I was, the angrier other people became.

I had a number of arguments in favour of what we were doing.

1. The Ecovillage had been an ambition of the Community since 1982 and had been the vision for the successful purchase of The Park that same year.

2. We were starting to build the first house for Community members who could not afford their own house later that year, and we had plans for more.

143

3. Creating a Community building team was by far the most cost-effective means of building and over the medium to long term would mean that we could build more housing for members who could not afford to finance their own house.

4. The Community had always had a number of people with specific skills who had joined more quickly – this was just an argument about numbers rather than principle.

At the first meeting there were over 150 Community members. I said my piece as calmly as possible. Alex had coached me to just listen and let people have their say. I did. I listened for an hour to a range of opinions, complaints and eventually attacks on me, my ethics and more. It was hard not to get angry, and once or twice I tried to intervene. But there were just some people who were angry and felt that we were deliberately undermining their position as Community members.

Many people over the years have asked me what it was like to live in a community such as Findhorn. There is not a quick way to answer that question. But I do know that I learned a lot about leadership at Findhorn. I struggled to listen at length to complaints and criticisms about my leadership. It was new to me to genuinely listen to and respond to these non-defensively, while at the same time holding my position. I struggled to do this without getting into an argument. And then one day I discovered how to do this.

Look for the grain of truth

We were at a large facilitated Community meeting. I was, as usual, coming under attack in a way that I felt was unreasonable and outrageous. I was starting to respond defensively.

The facilitator said, "Stop right there, Patrick." I stopped mid flow.

"What is the grain of truth in these criticisms of you?" he asked me.

"What do you mean?" I shot back at him.

"Every criticism, however outrageous you may feel it is, has a grain of truth in it. See if you can find it and acknowledge it."

This took what felt like a long minute while I sat in silence thinking. The criticism was that I was dishonest and had deliberately lied to the Community about how many builders were required to join, and that this was changing the nature of the Community's culture.

That was quite a few criticisms at once.

I replied as honestly as I could. "You are right that I didn't know how many builders we would need. Can I explain why this has turned out differently?"

It worked. The tension in the room dropped immediately and I calmly explained why things had turned out differently than even I had expected. The majority of the people in the room were happy with that and we moved on.

As I did more of this, the criticisms died down. And I started to think more about how my behaviours and actions were contributing to some of the conflict in the Community.

This is probably the most useful leadership skill I have ever learned.

Slowly I started to win over the majority of Community members, who began to see that the Ecovillage was a welcome and necessary development and that the Community should welcome the fact that so many builders wanted to help make this a reality.

145

Restructuring

'Restructuring' is a word that is used a lot, particularly in charities. I confess to often being critical as to the value of many so-called restructures. But my first involvement in one of these was very positive.

Alex came up with a new organisational structure, which was adopted. The Community would have three main areas of activity – educational programmes (the core business of the Foundation for many years), the Ecovillage development and the trading activities (of which there were a number, including a shop, publishing business, holiday park and wind farm). Each would have a unique contribution but operate under different ground rules, for example the agreement for the Ecovillage to borrow under certain conditions.

As with everything, the new structure had to be agreed at a Community meeting. Some of the criticisms reappeared but I was in a better frame of mind around these. It took two meetings, but it was agreed.

For the Ecovillage, this was a big deal. For example, the builders could attend Community meetings. It was the start of a process of integration of the Ecovillage into the Findhorn Foundation, and it was a good thing. The 'original' Community members started spending more time with the 'new' building members, and friendships, relationships and eventually families, began to be formed. Previous positions softened.

For me, it meant that I joined the Foundation's management team. Of course, I was there to represent the Ecovillage (my day job), but I was also there to make and be accountable for decisions that affected the whole Community.

Most of all, this felt like it followed a process that was already taking place. It was a good example of where a restructure follows the emerging direction of travel. In my subsequent leadership I've always looked to restructure when it follows a direction of travel that has already effectively begun.

Public accountability

My time on the Foundation's management group was to last only three years, but it was an incredibly fertile time in my leadership development. Like any organisation there was a need for good management, and following the restructure this was reflective of the variety of work, focus and income streams of the organisation

Being a Community that had a strong focus on personal development, there was a higher than average requirement for dialogue and accountability, particularly on the part of members of the management team. This was especially required of the more entrepreneurial elements of the overall organisation, which meant the Ecovillage, and that often meant me.

I look back on this time with gratitude for what I learned, but at the time my day job was to manage the complex and largely under-resourced Ecovillage operation. We were managing to secure the building and technical skills we needed, but it was a constant challenge to find sufficient people and funds.

On top of this there was the management job. I was expected to be available to discuss decisions at fortnightly Community meetings, typically on a Monday evening and sometimes half- or full-day meetings as well. At meetings the management team would sit in a semi-circle of chairs in the large meeting hall looking up at rows of seats, also in a semi-circle, looking down on us. It could feel intimidating. At 33 years old, I was one of the youngest members of the team, and often the focus of challenge from a sizeable minority of the Community.

The approach to decision-making was one of seeking consensus. This meant that we had to comprehensively discuss a subject, which could take some time. However, if members felt that a conversation had gone on too long or was going round in circles, they could call for a show of hands on the decision or issue.

This did not, however, close the discussion. If there was a clearly identifiable minority, they would be given a chance to put their case again. After this they would be asked whether they had been sufficiently heard in order to be a 'loyal minority'; in other words, that their disagreement had been noted and heard, but they would not stand in the way of the decision progressing. Typically, they would agree, but on occasions there was a process to go through before someone would accept that they had been sufficiently heard. As a management team member I was expected to stay to the end and I can remember evenings where I got home after midnight, despite the fact that more than half the Community members had already left.

In many cases, of course, the management team would just get on and make decisions. These would be reported in the minutes, which were printed in a weekly magazine that all members received. At the next meeting, the management team had to account for their decisions and in some cases there would be pressure to overrule them.

Learning #16: Consensus leadership

I initially experienced the high level of consensus seeking and debate as a bit of a burden. However, the upside was that, once decisions were made and discussed, there would be a very high level of buy-in to these decisions, so Community goodwill would be high (such as with the digging of the wind turbine cable trench).

I began to realise that this form of governance has many benefits. I began to learn that a leadership style that welcomes dialogue as well as challenge has its value.

Learning #17: Confidence in leadership

Early in my career I was fortunate to have people show their confidence in my leadership.

This was a good thing to experience early in my career because one of the great arts of leadership is having confidence in those around you, those you are working with. As a leader, I have found it important to demonstrate that confidence by giving people projects and businesses to lead, and then staying out of the way. Of course, they have to earn that confidence, but I try not to make it too hard. Everyone is different and if the bar for showing confidence in someone was that they 'do leadership the same way as me' then I would have failed as a leader.

The grass-roofed guest lodge was on fire and the fire brigade
had been called

Chapter 20

Health and safety, opportunity and risk

The inspector calls

It was never a dull moment at the Ecovillage. I had a smaller corner office that was once John's. I was thrown out of the architect's room for 'being too noisy'. At Nova Wholefoods, I had spent most of my days on the phone, buying and selling. And here I was doing the same at the Ecovillage office. I was banished to a single office with a door (and a phone, computer and fax machine). And windows on two sides. I loved it, not then realising that in the corporate world the 'corner office' is a status symbol.

This was perfect as builders, who were often dusty or muddy, could come to one window to see me without the office getting dirty. Typically, they came to tell me they had run out of something or could not find some crucial building materials, tools or nails. By now our sponsorship meant that we had good safety clothing and equipment for all the builders – steel-capped boots, tool belts, hard hats and more.

On one occasion a man in a suit appeared. I opened the window and invited him to come into the office. He introduced himself as the council's health and safety inspector.

"I've come here to inspect safety on your building site," he said.

"Of course," I replied. "I'll walk down with you and show you the site. You'll see that we have good safety equipment for all the team."

We got to the site a few minutes later and there were all the builders wearing their bright yellow hard hats. I breathed a sigh of relief. Someone must have heard the conversation at the office and slipped out to the site to forewarn them.

The inspector said, "It's good to see that the team are all wearing their hard hats now, because when I arrived at the site earlier there wasn't a hard hat to be seen."

I groaned. I had fought a losing battle to get the team to wear the hard hats, especially when the weather was warm.

The inspector walked back to the office with me. "On this occasion I'm giving you a warning," he said. "I'll be back, and if I see anyone without a hard hat I'll close your site down." And with that he was off.

I went back to the site and called everyone together. A few hard hats were already back off. I explained what had just happened and then said that from then on if I saw anyone without a hard hat they would be instantly off the site and off the team. I told them we could not risk having the site closed down, and in any case hard hats were there to protect them. We could not risk having someone suffer a serious accident – or worse.

The next day I announced that we would appoint a safety officer for the site. I probably should have done this earlier. There had been incidents before that I had had to deal with. Like the time one of the team was so angry that he threw a hammer at one of his colleagues. On that occasion I sacked him on the spot for gross misconduct, a term that the Findhorn Community had not considered using previously. Everyone had to recognise that this was a building operation and safety was our number one priority. To be fair, everyone agreed.

Co-housing

Many people came to visit us in the Ecovillage. I would regularly get a call from a workshop facilitator saying that someone on the course wanted to talk to me about the Ecovillage. Although it could be a distraction, I welcomed this. There were so many interesting, talented, committed and sometimes wealthy people coming through each year. I was keen to see what, if any, opportunities they might open up.

On one such occasion, a woman came to visit. She was very interested in the Ecovillage and asked me to take her around. I did this a lot. We went to look at the various buildings. When we came to the Bag End cluster site I told her about our plans for a larger co-housing building for ten residents.

She listened intently and then told me that her husband had recently died. A friend had suggested that she come to Findhorn as part of her coming to terms with her bereavement. I asked her about her husband, whose name was Bev. He had apparently had a real interest in communities and the environment, but they had never been here as a couple.

She then put an unusual proposition to me.

"If I could bury his ashes under this new building, I would lend you the money to build it at a very favourable rate."

"Of course," I said, "if that is what you would like." I took a gamble as I knew I would have to take this to the management team and possibly to a Community meeting. But this was such a powerful and personal moment for her and not the moment to bang on about due process. And interest rates were very high at the time.

And so, six months later, she joined a large group of Community members as we stood around the site on a cold, windswept day. She spoke about her husband and then put an urn with Bev's ashes in the ground, in a hole dug at the centre of the areas already laid out and ready for the foundations. Then two of the building team poured concrete over the urn and the construction of numbers 9 and 10, named Bev's House, began.

The house became the first of a number of co-housing projects at the Ecovillage. These were buildings where residents had their own private and modest living/sleeping space (typically studio flats) with ensuite shower rooms and then large, shared living, dining and kitchen spaces, as well as a shared heating system. A community within the Community.

Grass roofs

As part of the management team I had influence over the Foundation's annual budget. At the time there was pressure on accommodation, both for resident members but also guests, the name given to the thousands of people who came to the Community for residential courses each year.

The majority of guests on programmes were accommodated at Cluny Hill College, a former spa hotel in the nearby town of Forres, which was purchased by the Foundation in the mid 1970s. The Park had limited guest accommodation, largely in a group of 'bungalows', a rather optimistic term for dwellings made by sticking two caravans together and creating three bedrooms plus a living space, bathroom and kitchen.

There was an urgent need to both replace this guest accommodation and create more. And right in the middle of The Park was the perfect site, a large piece of open ground called The Green, where volleyball and other games were played. It was also a popular hangout for most of the teenagers who lived at the Community, along with their friends from the area.

John had always been keen on developing single-storey buildings with grass roofs on this site, so that they largely blended in and didn't distract from this open green space at the heart of The Park. Andrew drew up plans that showed we could have a ten-bedroom, single-storey guest lodge plus a smaller workshop building at a corner of the site, while still leaving the majority of the green space for volleyball and other outdoor activities.

We posted the designs on Community noticeboards and I went to work on a financial plan for the management team. Meanwhile the designs received a lot of support. We came up with a scheme where the Foundation invested some of the surplus it had made in the previous year, and the Ecovillage borrowed the rest, with the repayments being met from additional guest income.

Meanwhile we were approached by the organisers of the Community's Youth Project. This was an organised group for Community young people that ran throughout the year, also running groups for children of guests who visited as families in the summer holidays. They were looking for a base.

We discussed funding and they said that they had been fundraising for some time to secure some form of permanent home. I discussed it at the management team meeting and got a lot of support. We came up with a plan where the Youth Project fundraised a percentage of the cost, with the Foundation contributing some from the budget for a number of years to support borrowing by the Ecovillage.

It took a while to get though planning, but as always John produced his magic with the planners. We went ahead with both buildings.

At that time we had all the construction going on in a relatively contained area. That had allowed us to add some temporary buildings for tools, safety equipment and small items of everyday use such as nails and screws.

We decided to build both buildings on The Green simultaneously and create a new site, at the same time identifying two more potential sites adjacent to The Green. We quickly found a couple resident at the

Community who wanted to build on one. We had our second multiple dwelling site.

A big opportunity

The nearest neighbours to The Park were a farming family. John made friends with them over many years, and he would regularly go around there to meet with them and update them on what we were doing. We had a clear line of sight to a large five-acre field of theirs from our office.

We heard that they were seeking planning permission to put five large houses on this field. In some ways it was to be expected that, given the Ecovillage was happening on their doorstep, they would seek to capitalise on the inevitable rise in property values.

John was despatched to see them. To cut a very long story short, they went ahead and received planning permission, but at the same time John negotiated the purchase of the land by the Ecovillage.

Suddenly we needed to raise a large sum of money. The project was about to get a lot more interesting.

The fire

By 1992 we had three building sites on The Park. The Bag End cluster was still busy, with many of the residents already moved in. We had the two grass-roofed buildings being built on The Green, with one more in the pipeline. And there were two more whisky barrel houses being built, including John's.

There was a lot to juggle: people, finances and project management. But we had more people in the office. We had two architects, we had Frances looking after the building teams and we had Lynn, who was assisting us all and managing the office.

On a day-to-day basis things were going well. The Ecovillage had generally been accepted by the Community. I was being drawn more and more into management issues across the Foundation as a whole, particularly financial management and fundraising. My memory of this time is that there were few crises. Maybe time has eroded such memories, but one has stayed with me.

I got a call at home very early one morning. The grass-roofed guest lodge was on fire and the fire brigade had been called. I pulled on some clothes and rushed down to the site. The fire had been put out but there was smoke with one wing of the timber construction looking bad. The building team had arrived and were in shock.

They were desperate to start working on it but I said no. Once the fire brigade said it was safe, I asked them to secure the building so that no one could enter. We went to the various Community meeting points and explained what had happened and asked people to stay away for now.

It was obvious what had happened. The team had been working inside finishing the woodwork with oils. The number one no-no on site was to leave an oil-soaked cloth scrunched up and lying around as they can self-ignite. We had a procedure for dealing with this, which was supposed to be followed rigorously – but hadn't been on this occasion.

The team leader was beside himself. He felt responsible and was offering to resign and pay for the damage. I got a message to his partner and asked her to come and take him home.

Once it was secure, I left a couple of the builders to keep an eye on the site and keep inquisitive Community members at bay. If they offered help, I asked the builders to tell them to go and meditate on our behalf. It was partly tongue in cheek, but of course it was exactly the right thing to do. Meditations were held (a bit like prayers) across the Community. It helped the builders to manage the situation.

I went off to call the insurers and by lunchtime we had an assessor on site. He confirmed what had happened, confirmed that we were covered, and with Andrew's and John's help I started preparing an estimate of the cost of repair. To the insurers' credit they paid in full.

It delayed the completion of the building by three months as some of the damage was structural, but thankfully it was contained in one wing of the building.

Lucky there are only 43 houses of all different sizes.

Today there are some 43 houses of all different types

Chapter 21

Field of Dreams

There was huge effort to raise the funds to purchase the field belonging to our neighbours at Findhorn, and John led on this project. He knew more than anyone how important this would be to the future integrity of the Ecovillage.

I set up a new company to acquire the land, with John as the lead director, myself and a Community member called Johnny who had a background in housing and was an enthusiastic fundraiser. The company was called Ecological Village (Findhorn) Ltd, but no longer exists as its job is long done. John named the project the Field of Dreams, in homage to the movie of the same name, and it stuck.

This was an important purchase for many reasons. A private development next to the Ecovillage on two sides but without our eco-build standards and values would have been a major long-term problem.

But this also solved a complicated problem that we had grappled with since the start of the Ecovillage. It was always going to be a slow process to develop new eco-housing for members of the Community who could not afford houses. The Foundation itself could develop housing but had neither the financial reserves nor the borrowing track record to develop at speed.

The Foundation did not want to sell off parcels of land on The Park. This was where the Community had been founded in 1962 when it was a desolate caravan park on a sand dune, and a massive fundraising effort had enabled its purchase 20 years later. Scottish law is different to that of the rest of the United Kingdom, and this is particularly so in the ownership of property. It had proven highly complex to make the legal arrangements to take private investment in housing on the

Foundation's land and it presented some risk to both the investors and the charity.

The Field of Dreams would therefore be a step change. The company was set up independently of the Foundation and would, if we purchased the land, be able to sell plots on and let people own their freehold plot and build their house, albeit subject to covenants ensuring that they adhered to the Ecovillage building code.

As with so many projects this took time, but we raised the funds to purchase the land, largely from people giving money that would convert to land purchases and some very generous donations and zero-interest loans from members, former members and visitors to the Community. That was very helpful as by and large there was no interest to pay as the loans were technically unsecured. The existing planning permission was for five houses only and we needed and wanted to put more like 40 buildings there, a mix of single dwellings, apartments and co-housing, with no guarantee that we could get this.

The Field of Dreams was a leap of faith by a large number of people, and all the better for it. The money was raised, largely down to John's powers of persuasion, and the land was purchased.

After that, there was a need to raise another £150,000 to pay for the infrastructure. This would be a high-intensity development on what was agricultural land. It needed water, sewerage, roads and access, electricity, telecoms and IT (it was the early days of the internet). And a lot of planning permissions.

By the time I left Findhorn no building had yet begun. Today there are some 43 houses of all different styles but with a common theme, that they are among the best ecological homes in the world. I have been back a few times to visit and stayed in a couple of the houses.

162

Published the first edition of his book. Simply Build Green

Published the first edition of his book, Simply Build Green

Chapter 22

Recognition and its challenges

John is one of the most creative and productive people that I've had the privilege to work with. Around the same time as the Field of Dreams purchase was kicking off, we published the first edition of his book, Simply Build Green.

John was keen to write a book that focused on the ecological and technical aspects of what we were creating at the Ecovillage. He wrote a synopsis. We had had some contact with Scottish Homes, who expressed an interest in the work we were doing. Scottish Homes were one of the largest social landlords in the UK during the 1990s. They played a major role in regenerating and improving social housing all over Scotland before disbanding in 2005.

We sent them the synopsis and asked for a grant to self-publish John's book. They agreed to a grant of £5,000 for us to produce the book and to pay John. He wrote it in what felt like record time (I've no idea how as he was so busy).

We published it in a ring binder format with recycled card, and I still have a copy of it. We created 100 copies. Subsequently a paperback edition was published, which has sold well, and if you are interested in ecological building, it is the book to read. Here is the summary.

This book provides a detailed description of the theory, practice and products used in the Ecological Village Project. The project combines standard building techniques and the basic philosophy of ecological building and its application. Some of the major issues discussed are: the use of natural materials; responsible design for energy and resource conservation; radon; the use of non-toxic material and construction methods; and renewable energy systems, including wind power and solar energy.

Simply Build Green gave credibility externally to the Ecovillage, and the fact that Scottish Homes had funded the first edition was a bit of a public relations coup. I was perhaps not surprised to receive a call from the Scottish Office in Edinburgh (this was before devolution and the establishment of the Scottish Government).

A few weeks later, two civil servants with responsibility for building regulations across Scotland came to visit. They were really interested. They wanted to visit all our building sites, and they spoke with many of the builders, asking questions about the materials that we used and why. They were particularly interested in the story of how difficult it was to get building consent from Moray Council at the beginning of the project. They were with us for hours and left saying they wanted to stay in contact.

The next thing was that John and I got an invitation to speak and exhibit at a major building exhibition in Glasgow. It cost what for us was a lot of money, but they said that they would pay for this, which they did. John could not go for some reason so I went on my own for two days, did two presentations and had a conference stand that was busy for the whole time.

After that we had lots of interest and reasonably regular visits from local authorities, housing associations and some private developers. I bought a second-hand suit that fitted well enough and I would host at least one visit a month. The Community was not known for its formal dress code and I got a lot of ridicule for wearing a suit. The way I saw it, we needed to look like we were serious about what we were doing and wearing the suit helped! Put another way, don't dress to impress others, dress to impress yourself.

We later heard that the Scottish Office civil servants who visited were at the time reviewing the building regulations and code for Scotland and they had been told that Scotland needed to have the most environmentally friendly code in the UK. They asked if they could use John's book to inform that. We said yes, they used it and the building regulations changed.

The downside of recognition

I've since learned that one of the signs of success is that you get resistance, and that success is often in the same measure as the resistance. Well, that is for sure what happened next.

As the Ecovillage gained momentum and recognition, there was resistance from within our immediate locality.

The Findhorn Foundation had sometimes had a tricky relationship with some of the residents of the local community, particularly in the village of Findhorn, less than a mile from The Park. This was understandable given that this was a 'alternative' community close to what had been a traditional fishing village. A number of Community members, notably Alex and John, had built good relationships over many years.

But the Ecovillage was growing, both in recognition and size. We were open about our development plans but the combination of the purchase of the Field of Dreams and other projects caused concern locally about expansionist development. There were other issues that were raised, unrelated to the Ecovillage, but there was no doubt that our success was attracting resistance.

Enter Sir Michael Joughin. Sir Michael was the recently retired chairman of Scottish Hydro Electric, a privatised electricity company. He had had a successful career as a farmer, as president of the National Farmers' Union of Scotland and as chairman of the North of Scotland Milk Marketing Board. He lived with his wife on the southern end of the Findhorn Village, close to The Park.

Sir Michael was a highly articulate man and an effective political operator, making him a very high-calibre critic of the Community.

He first came to my attention with letters to the local Forres Gazette. We had a history of such letters. The local paper understandably saw stories about the Findhorn Community as a circulation goldmine. But Sir Michael's letters were more coherent and made a solid case. It felt like the start of a campaign.

The next thing was that we received a letter from the recently formed Scottish Charities Office (SCO), which became the Office of the Scottish Charity Regulator. The SCO were only able to investigate a charity on receipt of a complaint or when they had reasonable grounds to suspect problems.

The letter invited representatives of the Findhorn Foundation to attend a pre-investigation meeting in Edinburgh, following a complaint. A number of questions were raised in the letter. It was clear where the complaint had come from.

The letter was addressed to the Management of the Findhorn Foundation and quickly found its way to my desk. I think a few managers had a look at it and were terrified. I read the letter, groaned and then called up Jerry, our auditor in Inverness, with whom I had a long-standing relationship.

Jerry was great and the two of us quickly prepared coherent and competent answers to the questions, heading down to Edinburgh a couple of weeks later for the meeting.

This was the first investigation that the SCO had ever undertaken. We had been told to expect a two-day meeting with officials. I was anxious but felt that it was important that the Community as a whole was not alarmed at that stage, so the fact of this investigation was kept within a very small circle.

We arrived at the meeting and were treated very cordially. We were thanked for our prompt and detailed responses. I was expecting something more confrontational. They then explained that there had been a detailed complaint and outlined the issues that had been raised. We went through each of the points, mostly dealing with supposed financial irregularities and alleged fraud. By lunchtime they said that they were satisfied that there was no case to answer on any of the matters, that the investigation was closed and that they would communicate this to the complainant.

We drove back. I should have been elated but I felt more anxious. This would neither satisfy nor stop Sir Michael.

I was right. It was quiet for a few weeks and then there was a headline in The Scotsman. It was highly critical. Then there was a deluge. The Guardian, of which I am a lifetime reader and subscriber, wrote a highly critical article. I still read the paper, but I'm not sure that I have completely forgiven them.

It started with accusations that the Community were deliberately seeking to take over the village. Then there were accusations of strange cult-like activities. Then there were accusations of widespread drug taking.

By then it became clear that I would be handling the press and I got many requests for interviews. I was selective and careful, but also felt that we could not ignore this and wanted the opportunity to put our points across calmly and rationally. In some ways this was fairly straightforward. The Community exhibited none of the attributes of cults (such as separating people from their families or institutional misogyny). And in terms of drugs, everyone had to sign a no illegal drugs agreement when they joined and failure to abide by this was an instant dismissal offence. The problem was that the journalists had no interest in hearing what we had to say – their story was much more salacious.

The training and experience that I had had dealing with complaints in a non-defensive manner was helpful. I also got some media training for myself and some others at the Foundation, which helped enormously. Just as well, as a week or so later I had a one-hour TV interview with BBC Scotland. I tried hard to avoid giving them a quote that would look bad on the news and actually was pleased. But it was hard.

Enough was enough. In The Art of War, Sun Tzu says, "If you know the enemy and know yourself, you need not fear the result of a hundred battles". It was time to change our strategy. I spoke with Alex and a couple of others and we all agreed that I should get to know Sir Michael.

I picked up the phone and dialled his home number. He answered.

"It's Patrick Nash from the Findhorn Foundation here," I said. "I think we should meet up."

"I would be delighted," he said.

We chatted in a friendly way for about five minutes. He asked me where I was from, where I had been to university and things like that. It was very cordial. He invited me to tea a few days later.

When I arrived at the house, I was welcomed by his wife, Anne. She had a lovely smile and said quietly and a little mischievously, "He has been looking forward to this". Sir Michael and I had a really good hour in his study, which had a beautiful view out over Findhorn Bay. He asked me lots of questions, probed a lot and we debated our different views in a robust but congenial manner. Frankly, I enjoyed the discussion with him more than many I had with Community members.

We agreed to meet up again and so began a regular series of tea-time meetings. Of course, I invited him to visit the Foundation and Ecovillage, but he yet wasn't ready for this.

Like any charity, the Foundation had a board of trustees and ours would convene for a three-day meeting each November. I spoke to the secretary of the trustees, and asked whether they would agree to meet Sir Michael. They did, and I made the invitation at our next tea-time meeting. He immediately accepted and we spent the hour discussing what issues he should raise and what their responses might be. It was surreal – he was asking my advice.

The big day came. As one of the management team, I was attending part of the meetings. I left the room to meet Sir Michael and we had a brief chat. He was a bit nervous. I had briefed the trustees on him and the issues that I thought he would raise and had gently suggested how they might respond.

It went well. There was again a robust but largely polite conversation. At one point it began to get a bit heated, but luckily one of the trustees intervened and calmed things down. After an hour the chair of the Trustees politely thanked Sir Michael and said that he had given the trustees some things to think about.

I accompanied Sir Michael out of the building.

"How do you think it went Patrick?" he asked.

"I think it went well," I replied. "They heard what you had to say. You know we won't always agree, but I hope we can be influential on each other."

"I hope so too," he said.

I remained in touch with Sir Michael until I left Findhorn in 1995. I last saw him in February 1996 when I had returned with a hired lorry to collect my possessions and drive them back to London. I met him by chance at the nearby petrol station where I was filling up the lorry. We had a very brief conversation.

We wished each other well and then he said, "You were a worthy opponent, Patrick."

It's one of the greatest compliments I have ever received.

I was shocked to hear that Sir Michael died just two months later. I later read that he was still "heading a campaign to have the expansion plans debated by the full Moray Council as a social issue rather than simply as a planning application and it is the only campaign he was not able to see through".[2]

Learning #18: Resistance is often a sign of success

I've learned that one of the signs of success is that you get resistance, and that resistance is typically in the same measure as the success.

When I was doing something that I felt to be important, I found it hard to not feel deflated by resistance. But any positive change has its criticism. The only way I found to face this type of resistance was to engage with it. But how could I have a positive attitude to the resistance while engaging with its protagonist? How could I have a dialogue without having an argument?

This has happened a lot in my social enterprise career. I have had resistance both externally (from customers, stakeholder organisations, communities and even government) and internally (from managers, staff and board members). My starting point is always that resistance is helpful – either as a sign of success or as good feedback to change a project for the better. But sometimes resistance is so overwhelming that I have had to seriously consider whether I am on the right path, although when that had happened and I have changed course it has ended up well.

172

Learning #19: Know your enemy and know yourself

It was a quote from Sun Tzu that inspired me to get to know the Ecovillage's greatest critic, Sir Michael Joughin. Fortunately, he felt the same way. We began a relationship that, although he did not stop being critical, definitely took the sting out of his public and media campaign against us.

I have made it a priority to try to get to know critics of all the organisations I have led ever since. This has helped me with periods of negative publicity, for example dealing with a rare demonstration against the Dalai Lama on my watch, as described in Chapter 26. And when receiving criticism from customers, staff and board members.

Of course, not all resistance has come from 'enemies'. But there is no doubt that a personal relationship always makes a big difference in any conflict. I appreciate that in these days of social media this can be harder, but where possible and realistic I always try get to know my detractors and critics.

On a water powered funicular up the side of a steep hill

Chapter 23

Financing the next stage. The Community pushes back

For some time, I had been frustrated about the slow pace of development. By the beginning of 1993, we had completed, or were in the process of building, 12 eco-houses, of which the majority were privately financed. There was nothing wrong with privately financed houses, but the majority of the Community members (including me) lived in accommodation provided and owned by the Foundation. There was some frustration that the Ecovillage was developing only for people who could afford to build their own home.

We tried a number of ways to secure funding, but the fact was that the Foundation operated on a largely break-even basis. Income from its educational programmes was around one million pounds a year, which just about covered the costs. There was little or no surplus.

The charity owned quite a few properties in the area, but these were mostly used for accommodating members and guests and running the educational programmes. I had a number of meetings with our bank where we explored borrowing against this portfolio, but given the financial profile of the charity, this wasn't a serious option. I explored other sources of finance but kept hitting dead ends.

John, Alex and I were forever being introduced to guests who had an interest in funding the Ecovillage, and to be fair there were a small number of wealthy members who were prepared to support projects from time to time, but I could not find a means to secure a sizeable source of finance to scale up the Ecovillage, and in particular housing for Community members.

I started researching how other similar organisations were financing their developments. This was easy in so far as there were not many, but hard as there was no internet or Google. I made many phone calls to track down the financial brains of various ecological and community organisations.

But, as so often in my life, inspiration was just around the corner.

Centre for Alternative Technology

One of the best things we did for the building team was an annual exchange week with the Centre for Alternative Technology (CAT), near Machynlleth in Powys, Wales.

CAT, founded in 1973, is an eco-centre dedicated to demonstrating and teaching sustainable development. It has a fabulous visitor centre with interactive displays on all aspects of an eco-life, including renewable energy, eco-building design, organic gardening and much more. It processes its own sewage in reed-beds. As it is situated on the top of an old mine, you get there on a water-powered funicular up the side of a steep hill. In 2010 they opened the Wales Institute for Sustainable Education (WISE) in a large building designed as an educational case study of sustainable architecture.

I had visited CAT in the early 1980s when I was at Nova Wholefoods, but my interest now was their latest venture – how they had created their visitor centre, built the funicular and created more housing, all funded by a share issue.

In 1991 we invited a group of CAT builders to come to the Findhorn Ecovillage and spend a week with our building team. It was a great experience for all and the following year they invited our team to visit them. I decided to go and I drove one of the Community's buses on the ten-hour journey each way.

While our builders spent time with the CAT building team, I met with Roger, who was the chief executive of their new public limited company. He was at pains to say that this was a title he was uncomfortable with. It would never have gone down at Findhorn. He generously gave me his time, explaining what they were doing and how they were doing it.

The team at CAT had done a great job of creating an off-grid ecological community, but for them this wasn't enough. They wanted to make CAT a major visitor attraction. This part of Wales attracts large numbers of visitors, drawn by the natural beauty and proximity to the coast and many beautiful beaches. It would be a perfect opportunity to attract families and other visitors and to inspire people, particularly young people, to explore a life that had a lighter effect on the planet.

The CAT team came up with the idea of creating a visitor centre that would excite and educate. They had designed a circle of buildings around a large pond, which was fed from streams up the mountain above. Each building would have interactive and illustrative exhibits on the various elements of an ecological life, including building, renewable energy, food production, travel, and sewage disposal.

Roger had worked with an excellent lawyer who I had met previously when he was doing work for worker cooperatives. They had found a way through the maze of compliance necessary to form a public company and issue shares.

CAT launched their campaign 'An Issue of Concern', and the headline appeared on leaflets and advertisements in magazines like Resurgence and The Ecologist and even The Guardian. In order to raise a million pounds, CAT had set up a public limited company and was issuing shares for sale. The alternative eco-fringe was joining mainstream capitalism. This was exciting and, if it worked, would be a breakthrough in unlocking finance to promote eco-villages, eco-building and eco-communities to mainstream investors.

Despite some visible differences, CAT and the Findhorn Ecovillage had a lot in common. We were not just building ecological villages,

177

we were running educational courses and hosting visitors. I came back brimming with information and ideas.

The Community pushes back

I spoke with John and Alex about the idea, and I spoke with others. Together we developed a proposal.

The bottom end of The Park was still a holiday park. There was a lot of unused land there for the majority of the year, with caravans and tents for a relatively short summer season. But there were big numbers of day visitors, and the attraction of the Ecovillage was rapidly increasing these.

We came up with a plan that had some similarities to that of CAT in Wales. We would use some of this land in the lower area, which had the advantage of being near the main entrance to The Park, as well as the potential to have beautiful views over the road to Findhorn Bay.

We developed a plan that included holiday lodges, homes for Community members (on a co-housing basis) and an Ecovillage visitor centre. Given that the land is on a flood plain, the buildings were designed to be raised on stilts, with water around them and walkways above the water. It looked stunning.

While this was going on, it was my job to develop a financial plan. My original thought had been to do a version of the community share offer that we had done for the Wind Park. But this was too big an ask.

The visit to CAT in Wales had been inspirational. If they could raise a million pounds, we could certainly raise the funds we needed. I made contact with the solicitor who had worked up the share offer for CAT, and he was enthusiastic too. The Foundation's management group were broadly supportive, although they had some questions.

I ploughed ahead, confident that this was the way forward. We costed the project at around £500,000, a sum that would be impossible to raise from within the Community. That drove us down the route of setting up a public limited company, in the same way that CAT in Wales had done.

Looking back, I missed some of the signals. I was open about the plans, and was asked to present these to a Community meeting. I was delighted and went armed with plan details and financial projections. I knew that there would be some push-back from a small group of people who were often critical of the Ecovillage development.

But this time there was a tidal wave of criticism. While some of this was about the project itself, what emerged was a level of resentment that the Ecovillage was steaming ahead at a pace that a significant number of Community members felt was too fast and out of their control. In my passion and enthusiasm for the Ecovillage project I had ignored some of the low-level criticism along the way, but it had not gone away and now it wasn't low level any more.

I was shocked and didn't respond well. I really could not understand how so many members wanted to hold back the development. I felt that the Ecovillage was the future of the Community but so many couldn't see it. The more I made the case, the greater the resistance was.

The meetings went on. I was still busy with the 'day job' of the Ecovillage. But the resistance was getting stronger and eventually the visitor centre project stalled.

I started to withdraw, feeling somewhat deflated by the experience. My mood was low. I felt distant from friends. I had some symptoms of depression. Was it time to leave?

We had a buddhist monk saying prayers

Chapter 24

Living Machine

I wasn't quite done with the Ecovillage yet. As it turned out, I had one project left.

One of our trustees lived in Vermont in the USA where he was involved in an interesting project piloted in the state. The Living Machine was originally designed as an ecological sewage treatment process designed to mimic the cleansing functions of wetlands.

The creators of the Living Machine were looking for a pilot project in the UK. The trustee asked whether the Ecovillage would like to build the first Living Machine in Europe. Of course we wanted to do this. John was keen, I was keen and Alex was keen. We discussed how to do it.

The basic principle, as I understood it, was that we would have to build a large greenhouse with a large septic tank on the outside of it. Because The Park had been a caravan park, it had its own sewage system that eventually went to the main sewers at one single point. We would divert this mains outlet into the septic tank, where it would settle before being pumped into the greenhouse. There would be two rows of seven large tanks in a line, which the waste would move through.

These tanks would hold a variety of plants and creatures (such as snails) that would clean the waste and turn it into water. The water chemistry would be designed in a way to ensure an active cleaning process similar to that of a wetland but requiring only 10% of the land area. If this worked, it would be a revolutionary means of cleaning sewage that could be recycled for such needs as watering gardens, flushing toilets and other activities requiring water.

181

There were a few complicating factors. Firstly, there was no money to do this and we would have to raise the cost, estimated at around £160,000. We would have probably our most complicated planning application process to date. Because of the commercial ownership of the system in the USA, there would need to be a licensing agreement, especially if we were to seek to commercialise the Living Machine technology elsewhere in the UK. There was a lot to do.

John was planning a major conference at the Foundation for October 1995 on eco-villages and this was just over a year ahead. He was keen to open the new Living Machine during the conference. So now we had a deadline.

The three of us got to it. We had worked together in pairs and as a trio for many years by then and had a well-earned reputation for getting things done. John was to take care of the planning application. Alex secured a site at the south end of The Park, just beyond the area that was still a holiday park. Alex and I set up a new company called Living Technologies Limited and I started the process of raising the funds and managing the project.

The three of us worked on this project together and it went really well. We raised most of the funds from a European Union fund with the assistance of the local economic development agency, Highlands and Islands Enterprise. We got planning permission. The licensing arrangements were in place and contracts signed. And Lyle, a former member of the Community who had worked on a Living Machine in the USA, agreed to come back to lead the construction.

By the spring of 1995 the Living Machine was in construction. A huge septic tank was created in a small hill. A large rectangular greenhouse was purchased and erected. We bought 14 large circular oil tanks of the type used by big rural houses and sawed the tops off them. These were plumbed in place and then the real chemistry began.

October came and the conference started. Lyle's team was still finishing off the planting in the tanks, but we were almost there. I had arranged a launch event and put up a small marquee next to the greenhouse. We had invited a number of local dignitaries.

I was also doing the press work for the conference so, with the addition of the opening of the Living Machine, we had a good story. Quite a few journalists responded positively to my press invitations, including John Vidal, the well-respected Guardian environmental correspondent.

On the final day of the conference some 300 people crowded into the greenhouse. It looked beautiful. The tanks were planted and awash with colour, and all you could hear was the sound of water bubbling in the aerated tanks. It was another world, quite magical.

The Living Machine was opened by Jonathan Porritt, the former director of Friends of the Earth and at that time chair of United Nations Environment and Development UK. He was brilliant. We had a Buddhist monk saying prayers, and afterwards speeches in the marquee by Hector Munro MP, the Scottish Office Minister and the Director of Highlands and Islands Enterprise. It was a moment when the 'establishment' came to the Ecovillage.

It was the last project I did at Findhorn. It was a great day but by then I knew that I was leaving so it was tinged with sadness. I would never work with Alex and John again.

The Living Machine survives and is a key element of the Ecovillage. The Scottish Environmental Protection Agency regularly conduct quality checks, and in all the years of its operation the Living Machine has never been out of compliance. The genius of the system is that it mirrors the genius of nature, in that virtually nothing goes to waste. Every organism provides food for the next step in the food chain until the cycle is complete.

Reed-bed waste-water treatment has been around for a long time, but it needs a lot of land so isn't practical in the concentration of a largely urban population. The beauty of the Living Machine is that it replicates this natural process, but in a concentrated way. I've always thought that this technology could solve many of the problems associated with sewage and waste-water treatment, but to my knowledge it has never taken off. And it seems that even now, in this time of climate emergency, somehow this issue doesn't seem to get much traction.

I often reference the Living Machine story in my talks about social enterprise. It catches people's attention. Although the Ecovillage is largely made up of housing and other buildings, in my view an eco-village isn't an eco-village unless the infrastructure is part of that. With the Living Machine we achieved that. And its work is continued today by a locally based enterprise, Biomatrix.

Let's face it, cleaning shit with plants, fish and snails is about as eco as it's possible to be.

I left Pinkerton at the end of 2003 and moved to London

I left Findhorn at the end of 1995 and moved to London

Chapter 25

Time to leave

My last year at the Findhorn Community was a difficult time, notwithstanding the excitement of the Living Machine. The visitor centre project was off the agenda due to resistance from the Community. Most of the people I was close to were carrying on with their projects.

John was as energetic as ever and I admired him for his ability to keep positive and gently move the Ecovillage along. Alex had a wide range of projects on the go. They had both left dedicated leadership roles in the Foundation, operating as self-employed agents of change and working on a number of projects. I admired how they had done this, and in what was my last year I withdrew from my leadership roles and tried my hand at self-employment too.

It didn't work and I wasn't happy. It didn't help that my personal life was chaotic at this time. I felt distant from friends. I had symptoms of depression. I had started seeing a therapist two years before, and through my therapy I began to see that it was time to leave.

I have since learned that one of the great skills of entrepreneurship is knowing when to move on. And then moving on quickly. That's harder to do when your mood is low, and mine was. The Living Machine project helped my energy and working with Alex and John on a project again helped my mood. Just enough to finally take action.

I started applying for jobs. At first I went for jobs as a charity fundraiser. As well as raising funds for the Ecovillage, I had launched the Findhorn Foundation's first public fundraising campaign in a decade, which had been very successful. I applied for jobs in Scotland but wasn't even shortlisted.

I hadn't told anyone that I was applying for jobs, but I shared this with a consultant who had helped me launch our fundraising campaigns. She immediately said, "Don't apply for fundraising jobs, apply for chief executive roles. You'll make a great CEO."

That was good for my mood. I started applying for CEO roles.

And then it happened quickly. I got my next job. I left Findhorn at the end of 1995 and moved to London.

Personal legacy

My friend Loren once said to me that he was jealous of me because my legacy would be visible for all to see long after I had left. He meant the Ecovillage, its houses, the Living Machine and more.

I replied that it was not my legacy but that of many people, and particularly John. The Ecovillage would survive, but I would be largely forgotten within weeks. And of course that is what happened. It always does.

Nonetheless, the Findhorn Ecovillage was a significant phase in my social enterprise journey. Many of the skills I have deployed since as a social entrepreneur were developed there.

Some of these are practical skills. I set up companies and learned how to raise finance. I developed successful fundraising campaigns. I worked with complex legal structures and learned how to manage procurement. I led a large team of people.

But what I most value for my learning there were the personal and interpersonal skills of leadership. I learned about communication. I learned how to stand up in front of a large room of people and listen to what they are saying, even when they are expressing different views to mine. I learned conflict resolution skills, including looking for the grain of truth in any criticisms. I learned how to stand for a position

188

while under attack, especially in the media. I discovered psychotherapy and started on a path of self-exploration that has subsequently served me well as an entrepreneur.

I went back to visit the Findhorn Community some years later and had tea with Eileen, the founder. I was well into the next phase of my journey and I was able to say to her, "There isn't a day goes by that I don't realise that I'm using a skill that I learned here at Findhorn". She liked that.

The Ecovillage's legacy

It is now generally understood that we are in a climate emergency. It is widely accepted that the human impact on planet Earth now exceeds the available capacity of natural systems to sustain it, and that western countries typically have a resource usage that 'would require three planets' to maintain if every citizen on Earth had a similar impact.

In October 2006 an independent study of the ecological footprint of the Findhorn Ecovillage was undertaken by the Sustainable Development Research Centre of the University of the Highlands and Islands (UHI) Millennium Institute in collaboration with the Stockholm Environment Institute. It concluded that the Ecovillage residents have the lowest ecological footprint of any community measured so far in the industrialised world, being half of the UK average.

Of particular significance were the results relating to food, home and energy use, and consumables and personal possessions, which were 35%, 27% and 44% of the national average respectively. Findhorn residents have an eco-footprint some 13% lower than those at the London eco-housing development, BedZED.

What I most respect about this project is that it demonstrated how it is possible to live sustainably and that eco-villages should be the norm rather than the exception. In 2022 the Intergovernmental Panel on Climate Change (IPCC) report on mitigation of climate change featured the Findhorn Ecovillage on its front cover. This is clear recognition of the work that has been done there.

It was a real privilege to have played a part in getting the Findhorn Ecovillage successfully started.

What I learned at the Ecovillage

I learned a lot of new skills while creating the Ecovillage, and here is a reminder of some of them, and how I applied them later in my career.

Learning #9: Learning styles

I have done most of my learning on the job which suits me best. Don't get me wrong, I'm all in favour of training and have spent plenty of money on training in most of the enterprises I've been part of. But I have personally found it hard to learn by reading or attending training courses, while I am generally a quick learner if I do the task myself.

I am one of those annoying people who can't remember journey directions when I am told them but will always remember directions once I have driven the journey myself (which was very useful as a lorry driver early in my career in the pre-satnav days).

For many years I was somewhat judgemental of my learning style, so it was very exciting when I came across some of the research on learning styles. Everyone prefers different learning styles and everyone has a mix of learning styles. Some people may find that they have a dominant style of learning, with far less use of the other styles. Others may find that they use different styles in different circumstances. There is no right mix. Nor are learning styles fixed across your life. You can develop ability in less dominant learning styles, as well as further develop styles that you already use well.

Once I had looked into this it became clear that I am a predominantly kinaesthetic (or physical) learner. Touch is big part of this so when Steve Jobs launched the iPhone that was perfect for me. And many millions of others. When I was at Teacher Support Network, I went to a seminar led by the former Chief Inspector of Schools who said that the secondary school curriculum in England fails the majority of young

191

people as more of them are predominantly kinaesthetic learners than any of the other learning styles.

This knowledge helped me feel more comfortable in my own approach to learning. And it also helped me to understand people I was working with much better and adjust my communication to better match what I observed their learning styles to be.

At the end of the book is a link to a questionnaire where you can explore what your learning styles are.

Learning #10: Cashflow management

I have spent the majority of my career having to watch the cashflow.

It started at Nova Wholefoods, where we had to get the lorries back from deliveries come what may by 3pm on a Tuesday so there was time to get the customers' cheques into the bank before it closed at 3.30pm and before the post-dated cheques we had issued to pay suppliers the previous Friday cleared. (See 'The business model – Tuesdays' in Chapter 2 for more.)

At the Ecovillage the building of a new house was a cashflow challenge. Building materials would arrive, along with invoices for payment. There were numerous demands to spend money, some on items I knew about already but inevitably many I did not. I had to draw a very fine line between being supportive and facilitative, but at the same time holding a clear line about what was and what wasn't acceptable expenditure. (See 'Revolutionary building' in Chapter 17.)

I realised that cashflow management would be with me from then on. And it still is. Particularly in the start-up phase of an enterprise, it is critical and has to be carefully managed.

Early on I learned to manage your cashflow well and am always up to date on knowing my cash position, today and for the next 12 months.

Cashflow management and awareness are key skills. When I'm coaching social entrepreneurs, I encourage them to always know the cash position and forward cash forecast of their enterprise are, even if they are not the finance person.

Learning #11: Branding

Much has been written about branding over the years and I am no expert. But my gut feel is to come up with a name and brand that is as close as possible to explaining what the enterprise is there to do.

My first change of name was at the Ecovillage. Early on during my time there we changed the original name. I was creating a brochure pack for the building trade to encourage companies to sponsor us with building materials and the name Planetary Village, which had been used for ten years or so, would not make sense to them. It was a classic example of a name that was clearly understood internally but was not right for anyone outside of the organisation. The name Ecological Village, shortened to Ecovillage, has stuck and has been adopted by similar projects across the world. That's good branding.

I applied this learning when I later needed to change the name of the Teachers' Benevolent Fund, a name with a hundred-year history but that sounded like it had come from the Victorian era, which it had. The new name of Teacher Support Network was much more reflective of what we were trying to achieve.

In my experience, names that clearly state the purpose of an organisation, service or product are the best.

Learning #12: Community shares

Raising funds for a social enterprise is not necessarily easy. Today there is a well-developed market for social investment and a number of smart investment devices, including blended grants and loans, charity bonds, community shares, crowd-funded investment and social impact bonds.

Back in the late 1980s there wasn't much of a market for social investment, so it was really innovative to set up a community share scheme. And this is what my colleague John pioneered for the first wind generator at the Ecovillage. It worked and a significant number of residents of the Findhorn Community purchased these shares and receive a dividend that's reflective of their original support.

I've raised a lot of money for various social enterprises since the Ecovillage but have never been part of a community share scheme again. They are gaining pace now for a range of social enterprises including community land trusts for affordable housing, co-operatives and local renewable energy schemes.

The main website that explains community share schemes is Community Shares. This is a site which is run by a range of organisations based in the UK and it states that "since 2009, almost 120,000 people have invested over £100m to support 350 community businesses throughout the UK".

For community-based social enterprises this is a very smart way to raise finance. It worked for the Ecovillage.

Learning #13: Working styles and team roles

At the Ecovillage I began to learn more about how to build a successful team and came across the Belbin Team Roles. Team Role theory was developed by Dr Meredith Belbin in the 1970s. Belbin Team Roles have become the gold-standard method for identifying behavioural contributions in the workplace.

The nine Belbin Team Roles are: Resource Investigator, Team worker and Co-ordinator (the Social roles); Plant, Monitor Evaluator and Specialist (the Thinking roles), and Shaper, Implementer and Completer Finisher (the Action or Task roles). For more information you can see a link at the end of the book.

Learning #14: Gatekeeping – protecting the enterprise

I had never thought about gatekeeping as a leadership skill, but I first discovered it at the Ecovillage.

When we started the building schools I realised that, unlike many community activities, a building site has a range of hazards. I spent a lot of time telling the rest of the Community what was going on while trying to discourage them from joining in. I quickly got a reputation as a gatekeeper (that's the polite version), a role I seemed to have for much of my career. (See 'Revolutionary building' in Chapter 17.)

Gatekeeping has always been a key part of my subsequent enterprises. This was particularly the case when dealing with confidentiality in mental health and other personal calls to the many helplines those enterprises set up or delivered for others. We developed policies and procedures and invested in technology that was a version of gatekeeping.

Gatekeeping is another name for boundary setting. It's about protecting the enterprise, its customers, its service users, its employees, its suppliers, its finances, its community and its environment. As a social entrepreneur I put the safety and wellbeing of all of these stakeholders front and centre.

During the lockdowns of the Covid-19 pandemic, I spent much time discussing with social entrepreneurs how to protect their social enterprises and charities when much of the economy was effectively shut down.

Learning #15: Be prepared to quickly learn something you know nothing about

At my first social enterprise aged 22, I knew nothing. I had to learn everything about enterprise for the first time. I found that a trick to being a successful social entrepreneur is to keep doing new things for the first time, which I did throughout my career. I am quite restless, so learning how to do new things I know nothing about, often under pressure, becomes second nature.

I realised this at the Ecovillage when I had to teach myself basic quantity surveying in a weekend (see 'Learning under pressure' in Chapter 18). With respect to any qualified quantity surveyors reading this, I would never see myself as a member of your profession; but I managed to calculate our materials requirements for a house over that weekend because I had to.

I learned again one of the skills of social entrepreneurship. Be prepared to quickly learn something you know nothing about.

I've carried on doing this for the rest of my career, particularly as my various social enterprises have been in different fields, each presenting new questions that I have had to learn the answers to.

Leadership skills

I had learned a lot in a short time at Nova Wholefoods, but it was all done on the job and at speed. Much of what we were doing was making it up as we went along. Many social entrepreneurs do likewise, especially in the start-up phase. This is a great quality to have, but I discovered at the Findhorn Community that it's not everything. For the first time in my life I received some training and began to get feedback on my leadership.

The Ecovillage was a start-up venture at the Community at that time, so of course we still did a fair bit of making it up as we went along. I have to admit that I do quite like that. But I was fortunate to learn a lot about leadership at Findhorn. Here are some of my leadership learnings from that time.

Learning #16: Consensus leadership

When I became a senior manager at the Findhorn Foundation, I initially experienced the high level of consensus seeking and debate as a bit of a burden. But the upside was that once decisions were discussed and made there would be a very high level of buy-in, so community goodwill would be strong (such as with the digging of the wind turbine cable trench).

I began to realise that this form of governance had many benefits. I began to learn that a leadership style that welcomed dialogue as well as challenge had its value. It meant that I was constantly looking for how this could improve the quality of my leadership. When I left Findhorn I had a level of leadership maturity that I'm not sure I would have achieved so quickly had I stayed at Nova Wholefoods.

I spent my 40s and 50s as a leader in social enterprises, so I'm really grateful for what I learned about leadership in my 30s.

Learning #17: Confidence in leadership

Early in my career I was fortunate to have people show their confidence in my leadership. Paul did that at Nova and Alex and John at the Ecovillage. Each time I felt a form of elation as well as the weight of responsibility. It's a good and realistic combination.

This was a good thing to experience early in my career because one of the great arts of leadership is having confidence in those around you, those you are working with. As a leader, I have found it important to demonstrate that confidence by giving people projects and businesses to lead, and then staying out of the way. Of course, they have to earn that confidence, but I don't make it too hard. Everyone is different and if the bar for showing confidence in someone was that they 'do leadership the same way as me' then I would have failed as a leader.

197

I have recruited, promoted and invested in a range of people who went on to be great leaders. None of them were fully formed as leaders when I met them. But then neither was I when people put that confidence in me. It didn't work out with everyone, but I would rather show confidence in the leadership of many potentially great people and clean up the few situations where it doesn't work out.

Learning #18: Resistance is often a sign of success – but not always

I've learned that one of the signs of success is that you get resistance. My experience is that typically the greater the success the greater the resistance.

As the Ecovillage gained momentum and recognition, there was resistance from within our immediate locality. It was the first time I had encountered resistance of a sustained nature, co-ordinated by a worthy opponent and with headlines in local and national newspapers and coverage on radio and TV news. You can read more about that in Chapter 22 at 'The downside of recognition'.

When I was doing something that I felt to be important, I found it hard to not feel deflated by resistance. But any positive change has its criticism. Again, it was a 'look for the grain of truth' moment. But this was more. This was the type of resistance that wants to stop change.

The only way I found to face this type of resistance was to engage with it. But how could I have a positive attitude to the resistance while engaging with its protagonist? How could I have a dialogue without having an argument?

What I began to realise was that the resistance was as a result of the success of the Ecovillage. And that realisation made it easier for me to engage calmly, rationally and in listening mode. It shifted the dynamic of the conversations (including the press interviews) and our message began to cut through.

This has happened a lot in my social enterprise career. I have experienced resistance both externally (from customers, stakeholder organisations, communities and even government) and internally (from managers, staff and board members). My starting point has always been that resistance is helpful – either as a sign of success or as good feedback to change a project for the better.

But sometimes resistance is so overwhelming that I have had to seriously consider whether I am on the right path. I encountered this level of resistance towards the end of my time at the Ecovillage (see 'The Community pushes back' in Chapter 23). That time I realised that the level of sustained resistance from within my own community suggested it was time for me to move on. I did and it was one of the best decisions that I ever made.

Learning #19: Know your enemy and know yourself

If you know the enemy and know yourself, you need not fear the result of a hundred battles.

The Art of War, Sun Tzu

I first came across The Art of War by Sun Tzu as the resistance to the Ecovillage was building. It was an odd book for a social entrepreneur to read, believing I was doing good in the world. But every so often a social enterprise or other well-intentioned cause will come under attack and any leader has to be ready for this.

It was reading this quote from Sun Tzu that inspired me to get to know the Ecovillage's greatest critic, Sir Michael Joughin. Fortunately, he felt the same way. We began a relationship that, although he did not stop being critical, definitely took the sting out of his public and media campaign against us.

I have made it a priority to try to get to know critics of all the organisations I have led ever since. This has helped me with periods of negative publicity, for example dealing with a rare demonstration against the Dalai Lama on my watch, as described in Chapter 26. And when receiving criticism from customers, staff and board members.

Of course, not all resistance has come from 'enemies'. But it's my experience that a personal relationship always makes a big difference in any conflict. I appreciate that in these days of social media this can be harder, but where possible and realistic I always try get to know my detractors and critics.

Part Three:
An interlude, and Teacher
Support Network

We had just taken on the hosting of His Holiness
the Dalai Lama's visit to the UK

Chapter 26

The Dalai Lama is my boss

The suggestion that I should apply for a chief executive job was great advice. On January 2nd 1996 I started work as CEO of the Tibet Relief Fund and Tibet Society. I had one member of staff and a small office up four flights of stairs (no lift) off Tottenham Court Road. I looked across the rooftops of London and could see one random tree growing out of a chimney pot. I missed Scotland.

I was CEO of a tiny organisation with a turnover of £250,000 a year that had just taken on the hosting of His Holiness the Dalai Lama's visit to the UK in June that year, less than six months away. The budget for this was £1 million and it would be make or break financially. In the absence of a CEO, the trustees had booked the Barbican in the City of London, the Manchester Free Trade Hall and Alexandra Palace in north London for five days of Buddhist teachings, public lectures, political meetings and a cultural event. It was a big production.

This is a story in itself, but not one that is particularly relevant to my social enterprise journey. The visit of His Holiness was challenging, with Buddhist monks demonstrating against him, death threats, close protection and the risk of financial ruin for the charity. But it was also a huge success, with significant profile and political support for His Holiness and the largest footfall for his UK visits to date. We even snuck him into Clarence House, without telling the government, who might have stopped it, to visit the then elderly Queen Mother, who was very keen to meet him.

Fortunately, the charity broke even on the visit, and off the back of the visit we trebled our membership and doubled our annual income.

On the final day at Alexandra Palace, His Holiness gave a public talk to over 10,000 people. Following that we had a concert featuring

Tibetan musicians, Andy Summers, formerly of The Police, Sinead O'Connor and David Gilmour from Pink Floyd. We finished off with His Holiness leading interfaith prayers with leaders from nine faiths. It was a spectacular event.

In 1997 I travelled to India and started up funding of projects in Tibetan refugee settlements in the remote area of Arunachal Pradesh in North East India. On my return we raised significant sums from the then National Lottery Fund and other funders to scale up development in the Tezu and Miao refugee settlements there.

I really enjoyed my time at the Tibet Relief Fund, but it wasn't without its challenges. The Dalai Lama commands a lot of respect but sadly there is a lot of jostling for proximity among a very small number of his supporters. The board of the charity had attracted a couple of these and I soon found myself under attack by one of them for the 'crime' of organising the successful visit in 1996. A campaign was started that was critical of me and on this occasion I wisely took this as a signal to leave. I felt that if I stayed it could get difficult.

Moving on fast

I started looking for jobs again. This time I had some urgency as I had a mortgage and was living in London. I applied for a number of jobs in vegetarian food and environmental organisations, basically causes and issues that I was passionate about and sectors I had worked in before. I had some interviews but no offers.

In desperation, I started applying for jobs in organisations that were outside of what I knew. It felt odd but needs must. One that caught my eye was a charity CEO job based near Euston. The salary was good, quite a lot more than I was currently earning. The turnover was about £5 million and there were just over 200 employees. This was all good and would represent a significant step up for me.

The problem was that the charity looked really old and dated. The main business was making grants to individuals and running residential care homes. The cause held little interest for me. I was shortlisted for interview but considered pulling out.

A friend said, "Why don't you for once consider working with people you like and earn a decent salary rather than for one of your favourite causes?"

It was a novel thought. I went to the interview and, to my surprise, the second half of my social enterprise career began.

In many ways I was sad to stop working for the Dalai Lama. He was my boss only in the sense that he was honorary president of the organisation and I arranged his 1996 UK visit. He wasn't my line manager, but we had a number of very interesting conversations.

"If you want to go with this strategy, I think you should appoint me"

Chapter 27

Reserves policy

The interview spanned a day and a half. I was asked to turn up in the morning at the offices of the Teachers' Benevolent Fund, which was in the basement of the National Union of Teachers (NUT) headquarters just off the Euston Road in London.

TBF, as it was called, was founded in 1877 by members of the National Union of Elementary Teachers (which became the NUT) to provide financial support to teachers and their families in difficult circumstances. It had attempted a half-hearted modernisation over recent years, but no serious effort had been made to change the way it was governed or operated for a very long time. Walking into their office this was really obvious.

There were three candidates. I had turned 40 a couple of weeks previously, and I was the youngest. The morning was spent getting a long lecture on the charity from three of their board members, the general message being "Don't think you can change anything here". We then had to do a 'test', which was to assess a grant application. My heart sank – is this what they want their new CEO to do?

Finally, after lunch we were introduced to the four senior managers of the charity. I hoped that this would be more interesting. Thankfully it was. The three candidates were sitting on one side of a rectangular table with the four senior managers on the other side.

I was sitting opposite Carol, their head of fundraising. I started off with a question.

"So, we have heard this morning about what we can't do. Please would you tell me what you think whoever of us gets the job should do?" It broke the ice. Everyone laughed.

209

I don't like to dominate a conversation, but this was a job interview and I had to both impress the senior managers and also let them know that I would be on their side were I to get the job. I was in competition with the other two candidates.

Carol replied first. "We have recently had some fascinating research done with teachers. It tells us that the charity is largely irrelevant. Hardly anyone that was interviewed had heard of us, they weren't interested in a retired teachers nursing home and they were somewhat disparaging of our welfare grants programme."

"So, is there anything you do that teachers want?" I asked. Again, everyone laughed.

"No," Carol replied, "but we asked them what the biggest issue facing teachers is."

"Don't tell me," I said. "Did they say stress?"

"Yes," she replied. "Do any of you know about counselling?"

I was on solid ground now. Yes, of course I did. I had been in therapy for more than five years and was part of a men's therapy group in north London. I was a trustee of a psychotherapy training charity. Luckily for me the other candidates were not strong in this area and talked about training, somewhat missing the point. I asked Carol if I could have a copy of the market research findings to take away, which she gave me.

Before we left for the evening, we were told to come back the next morning and do a presentation as part of our one-to-one interview. We were given the most recent set of audited accounts of the charity and told to present on the subject of 'What should the reserves policy of the charity be?'.

I had a trustee board meeting at Tibet Relief Fund that evening and had to go straight back to the office. I was not looking forward to it as

210

I knew it would be difficult. I asked to have the latest interview slot of the three and explained why, and fortunately everyone agreed.

Fortunately I can read a set of accounts quickly. I scanned the balance sheet. The charity had about four years' worth of reserves in investments. I called a friendly accountant, explained the situation, shared the basic numbers and asked his opinion. He said, off the record, that he reckoned after what they needed to set aside for emergencies, there should be around £3.5 million spare. He also said that the Charity Commission had recently announced that they were looking into charities that held what they called 'excessive reserves'.

This was good. I had the germ of a plan.

I gave the Tibet Relief Fund little attention at the board meeting. By the end of the evening, I had a presentation in my head. I got home around 10pm and spent the next couple of hours writing what I would present in the morning.

I didn't sleep much and in the morning went to a local printer and had acetate slides made up as well as a set of printed copies. Back before PowerPoint and projectors, we used these thin sheets of transparent cellulose acetate, onto which figures could be drawn or printed. These were then placed on an overhead projector for display to an audience.

They looked great. I headed down to the TBF office.

A ten-minute strategy

I went into the interview room. There were four trustees. They introduced themselves and then asked me to give my presentation.

The first slide was a simple spreadsheet. I talked them through my thinking that they had around £3.5 million in free reserves. 60 seconds.

I summarised what the Charity Commission had to say about excess reserves. 30 seconds.

I summarised the key messages from their research on what teachers thought of the charity and what had been said about stress at work. 90 seconds.

I had seven minutes left to pitch my strategy. I had decided to go for it. Either they wanted change or not; and if not, I didn't want the job (although I coveted the salary).

I said that I thought the charity was struggling to be relevant and that this would only get worse. I explained how a counselling-based helpline could work and that I would expect around 10,000 requests for support in the first year. I showed my rough costing for the set-up and first two years of operations. It was completely made up, but as it turned out was not a bad guess.

I explained how I would set this up, how I would involve the trustees, how I would approach the government for part funding and that I would expect the charity to underwrite the costs.

I explained that in my opinion this would be transformational for the charity and that in a couple of years it would be a significant, relevant organisation in the education sector, respected by teachers and the sector as a whole.

I looked down at my watch that I had put on the table. I had 30 seconds left. I made up my closing statement on the spot.

"If you want to go with this strategy, I think you should appoint me. If not, I suggest you appoint one of the other two candidates I met yesterday. But if you go for this strategy, I think you'll be proud of what we will have achieved together."

I sat down. There was what felt like a long silence. They looked at one another.

Then the questions came. They wanted to know all about my plan. They were intrigued. Their questions were positive and constructive.

I knew I could work with them. They then asked me the usual perfunctory interview questions and I left with them saying that they would get back to me in the next couple of days.

My phone rang that afternoon. I had the job.

Learning #20: Fortune favours the brave

My time at Findhorn had taught me a lot about leadership. One of the lessons I had learned is that sometimes you simply need to make a brave move. Of course, it is risky, but by my late 30s I had made a few such moves and most of them had worked out.

The final statement of my interview presentation for the job at the Teachers' Benevolent Fund was a risk. It was impulsive. By that stage of my career I had taken a few risks and had developed an ability to see the risks of every decision in real time as an ongoing mental process.

In this case it was 100% instinctive. My internal risk assessment said that the only person that would suffer if I was wrong would be me. Because no one else's wellbeing was at stake, I could take the risk without hesitation.

I took the accounts home on Friday evening and spread
them out on the dining table

Chapter 28

First day

I started work at the Teachers' Benevolent Fund (TBF) just after New Year 1998. I was met at the door by the finance director, who it turned out had been interim CEO for six months before my arrival, had applied for the job and had not been appointed. This was awkward. It was a shame no one had told me.

She had a month-long induction planned for me, much of which involved reading documents and visiting the charity's residential homes around the UK. Were they trying to manage me? It wouldn't work, but I did not want to upset anyone on day one.

I read through the induction plan and made a few suggestions. I wanted to start by meeting all the head office staff in one-to-one meetings and I would do this today and tomorrow. I would like to arrange to meet the key trustees (chair, vice-chair, treasurer) again in one-to-ones, and preferably next week. I would like full sets of the detailed management and audited accounts for the past five years. I managed to do this in a collaborative manner.

It's a strange feeling starting as CEO of an established organisation. Although I had done it at Tibet Relief Fund, I was the only employee when I started, so it felt more like a start-up, which is what I was used to. Nova Wholefoods was a start-up and the Ecovillage was a start-up, albeit within a larger organisation. This was different. To be honest I felt a bit of a fraud, experiencing what I now know is called imposter syndrome. I really had little idea of how to act in this situation.

Luckily, I had the plan that I had shared at interview. This would be a whole new direction for the charity, so in effect I could get back into start-up mode, except unlike before there was money available to make it happen. That was a good thought.

215

First week

I had a packed week. I met all the head office staff and on the
Wednesday visited the first of the four residential care homes run
by the charity. That was an experience. It was in Scarborough, East
Yorkshire, so was an early start to get a three hour train journey from
London .

Upon arrival I had to hear a grievance from a member of staff against
the manager of the home. I'd never done this before (another imposter
moment) but I had been well briefed by one of the senior managers.
I took the time to hear the grievance in detail and then met the home
manager to hear her position. I drafted my ruling which was that in my
opinion there were no grounds for the grievance, before handing it to
the employee and her trade union representative. I then had a tour of
the home which in my view was being very well run.

I was back in London the next day and we had the first meeting of the
Strategy and Governance Group (SG Group). This consisted of the four
trustees who had interviewed me, the four senior managers and myself.
It was a good opportunity. I went through a version of the presentation
that I had done at interview, and then we agreed to come up with a new
strategy for the charity as a matter of urgency.

The other immediate job was to review the charity's governance.

Challenging governance

Throughout my career I have met a lot of charity trustees and company
board directors, and I've been a member of about 20 boards myself. I
had never seen anything like this one at TBF.

The purpose of a charity's trustee board is to provide effective
oversight. Trustees are not employees (in the vast majority of
cases), and the history of this approach goes back centuries to a time

216

when charities were funded by wealthy philanthropists and later by organisations such as professional associations and trade unions.

The TBF had its history in the founding of what was now the National Union of Teachers (NUT). Trade unions have a particular style of governance that is often based on elections to national bodies from regional ones. This is understandable for a representational and campaigning organisation. But because of this history, TBF had a version of this as its governance structure.

We had a National Council with 40 members, and 26 of these were elected from a regional committee (13 committees sending two delegates each). These were effectively the regional committees of the NUT. In addition, the National Executive Committee of the NUT (its governing body) appointed 12 of its number to the TBF National Council, along with a further two appointees from the National Association of Teachers in Further and Higher Education (NATFHE).

If you think that is a lot of trustees (which I did), the simple explanation is that the charity was dominated by a trade union and governed like a trade union. This was the way it had been since the nineteenth century. It's just not necessarily the best way to run a charity.

Don't get me wrong, I am a strong advocate of trade unions. My view is that the demise of trade unions over the past 40 years has in large part given rise to the exploitation of employees and the worst excesses of business, particularly large globalised businesses.

The trustee members of the SG Group had been part of this governance structure for a long time and found my challenging of this difficult. But they could see that the charity had been losing its way, were ready for change and would be important allies for what lay ahead.

First weekend

It took some reminding, but the finance director somewhat reluctantly gave me the detailed management and audited accounts for the previous five years. I think it was hard for her to accept that I understood finances as I am not a qualified accountant. I'd come across this attitude before, and would again, and have learned to be understanding about it, despite the fact that it still irritates me.

I took the accounts home on Friday evening and spread them out on the dining table. I started building my own spreadsheet. By mid morning Saturday I had begun to get a picture of what was going on.

I had been told that there were challenges with the residential care part of the charity. I had also been told that these would be solved by a combination of improving occupancy and some investment. I had not yet got to the bottom of how much investment was needed, but if my visit to the home in Scarborough was anything to go by, across four properties it would be a seven-figure sum.

By mid afternoon I had a clear picture. I created a set of simple graphs and put everything away.

On Monday morning I asked the senior managers to assemble. I took them through what I had discovered. Which was that the charity was losing over £500,000 a year on a turnover of £4.5 million. Were we to continue running residential homes we would need to spend at least £1 million. That would not guarantee occupancy would rise from its level of around 55%, at least not without significant modernisation and marketing. Even then, we would effectively be running care homes as a business rather than for their original purpose of providing accommodation and care to retired teachers in their old age. And a loss-making business at that.

The final graph showed that if we carried on as we were, the charity would slide gently into insolvency.

218

I thought they would be more surprised, but to their credit the managers took this news on board. I was amazed that no one had spotted this, including the charity's auditors, although I was looking at the charity through fresh eyes, so it was easier for me to see.

I started to make some calls. The first was to the recently appointed head of homes. She had been appointed around the same time as me and was starting to work with us in a couple of weeks. I had met her once and liked her. I called her and explained the situation. I said that there would be a review process to go through but that I thought it likely that we would spend the next 12 to 18 months extracting the charity from running care homes.

"Given this situation," I said, "I would completely understand if you decided not to take the job up."

To her credit she replied, "No, I'll be doing the job. And if this is the decision, I'll work to manage that process with respect for the residents, their families and the staff."

By the end of the day, I had spoken to the chair of trustees. She and I agreed to call another meeting of the SG Group for later in the week, where I would go through it all in detail. I also spoke to the auditors, shared my findings and asked them to come for a meeting the following week with some explanations.

Learning #21: Figure out your business model early on

When I started at the Teachers' Benevolent Fund there was a business model that had been around a long time. As many of the staff and trustees had been around a long time too, no one had noticed that the business model was no longer working and that the charity was gently sliding into insolvency.

Every enterprise has a business model, whether you articulate it or not. I am a great advocate of having a clear and robust business model that you understand and review regularly. Every social enterprise is different so there is no one way to design a business model, but here are some things I have always considered in the mix:

- What service levels do your customers or service users require?

- What level of gross profit is needed to fund the growth, development and quality of these services and/or products?

- How to design this business model to ensure that there is sufficient cash at the lowest point of the month (typically when salaries are paid) or quarter (when VAT is paid)?

- How to ensure that working patterns will suit employees?

If you don't take charge of your business model, it will take charge of you and work against you. Teacher Support Network taught me that.

Learning #22: Imposter Syndrome

Imposter syndrome is a psychological occurrence in which an individual doubts their skills, talents or accomplishments and has a persistent internalised fear of being exposed as a fraud.

Starting as CEO of my first 'established organisation' was scary. I had developed confidence in many areas, but I found this hard. I felt a fraud because I had never before done a job like this. Although I suspect I looked confident on the outside, which was clearly expected of me, I could not stop this niggling feeling that I would be 'found out'.

I had never experienced this before, but I felt this on and off for the remainder of my time at Teacher Support Network. I got to understand it through psychotherapy, getting better at dealing with the episodes of imposter syndrome when they threatened to overwhelm me.

I explained what we were doing and why.

I explained what we were doing and why

Chapter 29

Strategic plan

Every charity or business needs a strategic plan. Right. The problem was that I had never produced one and didn't have a clue how to do this.

Nova Wholefoods 'just grew itself'. At least that's what it felt like at the time. We were growing so fast and almost every week we were a different business, so a strategic plan would have been a complete waste of time. The Ecovillage had architectural and building plans, and I had produced financial spreadsheets galore, but that's as far as we went.

Such 'planning' was therefore new to me. The SG Group at TBF was set up to deliver a strategy for the charity, but really they were looking to me to tell them how to do this. So I did what I always do: ask for help. I made a few phone calls and in no time at all I was on a two-day residential strategic planning workshop in the Lake District.

It was led by a consultant who had worked for a number of charities in the UK and Asia. By the lunchtime of the first day, I was convinced that he was someone our trustees would respect. I had a conversation with him and by the time I left the workshop we had come up with a plan. He and I would co-facilitate a collaborative strategic planning process that would involve significant number of trustees, staff, volunteers, donors and other stakeholders.

I explained this to the SG Group, who after a short discussion agreed with my plan. But compared with what they had imagined (me sitting in a dark room and drafting a plan for them to agree or, probably more likely, disagree with) it was a big production.

We started with a day-long version of the workshop I did in the Lake District. This was attended by members of the SG Group with some additional staff and trustees. It was excellent. Not only did it get everyone on the same page in terms of the purpose, process and language of strategic planning, but we also flushed out some disagreements and variations in understanding.

A few weeks later we hired the large meeting hall in the NUT building and had a planning day with a large group of people. We invited all the trustees on the National Council (30 of them came), all the head office staff (15), three to four staff from each of the care homes (14 came), some of our volunteers (6) and some of our individual donors (4). We were 69 people. We got the room for free, and the trustees were there for a meeting anyway, so we just paid for the travel of the volunteers, donors and care home staff. And the buffet lunch.

We had mixed people up on tables of five so that everyone was mostly working with people they didn't know. We spent the morning doing various analyses, and in the afternoon we worked on drafting high-level strategic aims. There was innovation, shared understanding, speaking truth to power and mostly a sense that we were all part of what made this charity what it is. Overall, and to my satisfaction, there was a real head of steam for change that would make the charity more relevant and much closer to teachers and schools.

Throughout the day, staff of the NUT kept popping their heads around the door. They had never seen anything like this.

Following that day I developed some more of the detail, and in little more than two months we had a strategy proposed to and agreed by the National Council. This was a first in the 123-year history of the charity. One of the trustees who was a senior member of the NUT's Executive Committee called it a 'manifesto for change' and was clapped by the other trustees. Job done.

Importantly, there were three clear commitments:

1. We would review our care home business and, if necessary, extricate the charity from these.

2. We would establish a national counselling service for schoolteachers.

3. We would make changes to our governance structure by the end of the year.

I'd been in post for just under five months and we had agreement on the most immediate things that needed to be dealt with. I was delighted. Maybe I wasn't a complete imposter.

Care homes

The first priority was the nursing and residential care home operation. By now I had been to all of the four homes on a number of occasions. On my first visits, each of the managers had pitched investments they felt were needed and we had a long and pricy list of 'urgent requirements'. The cost of these was well in excess of £1 million. I had by then been joined by Mary, our new head of homes, who had a long background in managing nursing and residential homes for older people.

Within a few weeks of taking up the CEO job, I began to understand the history of these care homes. When the charity had been established in 1877, the Teachers' Benevolent Fund (TBF) provided financial support for teachers and their families in difficult circumstances. One of the biggest structural problems was a lack of housing for women retiring from teaching and for this reason the charity had set about creating affordable housing and retirement homes.

There was a significant reason why this housing was necessary. I had previously not understood that women in teaching were subject to a legal 'marriage bar', the practice of restricting the employment of married women. So when female teachers got married they had to leave teaching. The result was that there were large numbers of single women who retired aged 60, rarely owning homes of their own and none of them having children who could look after them. The charity had stepped in and created housing and what became vibrant communities of women aged over 60. Otherwise, many of these women would have been homeless.

In the UK, the marriage bar was removed for all teachers as late as 1944, but of course there was still a generation of retired women teachers requiring homes. But by the 1980s this need no longer existed and slowly but surely the demand from retired teachers for places at the charity's care homes had dwindled. The homes were a good example of mission drift as they were no longer contributing much to the charitable purpose and were draining most of the charity's energy and resources.

There were various problems with these homes. All of them had large numbers of empty bedrooms. Many of the current residents had no connection to teaching. Investing all of this money made no sense. My assessment was that there was no longer a need for the charity to operate retirement homes at all.

We had to move fast before morale plummeted. Mary recommended that we speak to a company called Pinders to undertake a business appraisal of our four homes. We met with one of their directors, Simon. We agreed terms and he went to see all the homes. The managers were briefed. To be honest, they were smart people and could see the direction of travel, so we decided to take them into our confidence. It was the right decision as they could better manage expectations and morale among the employees.

226

Simon was back to us in six weeks. We had a detailed assessment of the viability of each of the four homes. He recommended we close one of them down, find new accommodation for the residents, seek planning permission for a brand new nursing home and sell the site with the added value that this would create. Two of them he recommended that we try to sell as going concerns, giving us an indicative valuation. The fourth was more complicated as we ran it in conjunction with two other charities and did not own the property itself. For this he recommended that we find a way of getting out of our commitments.

We took the decision to the trustees in June, and Simon came and presented. Mary and I recommended that we take his advice and that the board authorise this course of action. There was a lengthy debate. It was a bitter pill to swallow for many of the trustees who had been intimately connected to the homes. But eventually, and in many cases with a heavy heart, everyone around the table voted to agree with the way forward.

Agreement was one thing, and implementing it was quite another. There were a large number of stakeholders – the residents, the staff, the families of the residents and finally the House Committees. These committees were small groups of volunteers who helped out but who generally felt that they 'owned' that home rather than the charity itself. We guessed correctly that these groups would be the most difficult.

Again, we took the managers into our confidence, but this time we also spoke with the staff trade unions, as well as owners of a number of care homes in the vicinity of the home in north London that we planned to completely close. They were all really helpful and to their credit the news of the decision did not leak out.

Mary and I had a very difficult week when we went to each of the three affected homes to meet with, in order, the staff, the residents (with

227

the staff in the room to support them), followed in the evening by the families and then the House Committee members.

We decided to tackle the home in north London first. We knew this would be toughest as we planned to close it down. We started with the staff. Although the news had not leaked out, I think most of them expected this would happen. The home was in a terrible state, with years of under-investment. It was unlikely to pass recently announced inspection standards. It wasn't the fault of the staff that this was the case. I started by apologising on behalf of the charity, explained what we were doing, said we would work with them to find new jobs and asked for their support on behalf of the residents. It was a sad and tearful moment for many. The home manager was wonderful, as was their trade union representative, who we had invited to support the staff after we had finished.

After giving an hour or so for the staff to absorb the news, we met with the residents. We explained what was happening, that we would close the home in six months and spend that time taking them to homes in the area so they could choose where they wanted to move to. Some were sad, some were excited and inevitably some didn't really understand what was going on. Mary then spent the rest of the afternoon seeing them individually and in small groups. She was amazing.

The evening was harder. We were joined by the chair of the trustees and the treasurer. We started meeting with the families of the residents. Again, I explained what we were doing and why. Some of them were fairly angry, and early on one of them started accusing me of all sorts of bad motives. Before I could say anything, the treasurer stood up and started to defend me in a combative manner. I immediately stood up again and walked in front of him, interrupting him.

I remembered the words from a Community meeting at Findhorn: 'Look for the grain of truth, however outrageous the criticism or complaint.'

I dug deep and spoke to my accuser, a man upset that we were about to turn his mother's life upside down. "Yes, sir, this will be disruptive for your mother. And I apologise for that."

He relaxed instantly. He asked what we would do to minimise her disruption and I slowly and patiently went through what I had said earlier.

We spent the next hour with me responding similarly to a number of such criticisms. We had discussed alternative options. In one case a woman threatened to remove a legacy from her mother's will, which I encouraged her to do if that was what her mother wanted and offered to explain how to do this. At the end of the meeting, a few people came up to me and said that, although they didn't agree with the decision, they respected me. I silently thanked Findhorn for my conflict-resolution training.

The two trustees had been largely silent. The treasurer winked at me at the end and softly said, "That's not how we do it in the union."

"I know," I said. He giggled.

The final meeting was with the House Committee. This was a group of about eight older people who appeared to consider that the home was their personal fiefdom.

They were furious. I took a similar tack to the previous meeting but was a bit more robust.

Question: "Why haven't you asked our permission?"

My response: "It's not your decision to make."

229

Question: "Why are we the last meeting of the day?"

My response: "Out of respect for the people whose lives will be most affected." That was a bit provocative on my part, but it was also a fact.

Comment: "Most of the residents will die over the winter because of this. Their blood will be on your hands."

My response: This wasn't really worth replying to, so I just said that this was not our intention and that only time would tell if they were right.

This carried on for a while and eventually they ran out of steam, but not before promising to lead a robust campaign to save the home.

Save our home

I know a lot of people in the charity sector who have led incredible campaigns, but I haven't met many whose charity has been campaigned against. Fortunately for me, I already had the experience of being campaigned against by Sir Michael at Findhorn (which you can read about at 'The downside of recognition' in Chapter 22).

First, we had letters to the charity. Many of them were addressed to me and some to the trustees. Our office manager came to see me a few days after the meeting and said that we had 30 complaint letters in the post that day and asked my advice on what to do. We had a look, and they were all mostly the same, following a template that had been circulated. Together we drafted a reply, and this was used as a template to be topped and tailed.

The next day there were 50 letters. It was suggested we hire a temp to reply to these, using our template. I agreed. Someone was with us that afternoon and worked through replies. I signed all those addressed to me, often adding a handwritten note. We had over 1,000 letters in total.

In the middle of this letter campaign, I received a call from the private secretary to HRH The Queen Mother. The Queen Mother was patron of TBF, along with some 350 other charities. She had visited the home we were closing some years before, and there were signed photographs of that visit in the reception area.

Her private secretary explained that he had received 300 letters of complaint to Her Majesty in respect of the closure of a nursing home. He had an irritable tone of voice. Could I explain what was going on as Her Majesty was quite put out?

"You may remember me," I said.

"I don't think so."

"We spoke two years ago, and I arranged for Her Majesty to meet with the Dalai Lama. I was CEO of the Tibet Relief Fund at the time."

"Oh, yes, I do remember. That was very helpful of you, and Her Majesty was very pleased indeed." His tone was very different all of a sudden. "How can I help you?"

We discussed the situation, and I explained what we were doing and why. We agreed that I would send him a version of the reply we had sent to the campaign letters. I never heard anything about this again, but in August 2000 I was invited to Clarence House (along with many charity CEOs) to the Queen Mother's 100th Birthday Party.

Closing the homes

It took about two years overall for us to close the care homes. In the process, the charity reduced staff numbers from 210 when I started to 15. Our income dropped, but our expenditure dropped much more. We were no longer heading towards insolvency.

We sold the homes in Staffordshire and Scarborough. These both went as going concerns, so the residents were not affected and the staff transferred to the new owners. In both cases we retained priority nomination rights for former teachers as residents, an arrangement that worked well for all parties. In Scarborough the new owners were the home manager and our very own Mary, who had left TBF as her role was no longer required. I missed her nonetheless; she was a very good person to work with and always gave me great support and challenge.

The home that was a partnership transferred to the partner who owned the property. That took a few meetings in Birmingham, but it all worked out well in the end.

The north London home closed six months after we announced it. We spent the winter taking the residents on bus trips to a variety of homes in the area, and by the time we got to the spring of 1999 all the residents had new homes. Many of their families were appreciative of how we had managed the transition. The staff had all found new jobs and I received a very nice letter from their representative at Unison thanking me and the charity for the "professional, respectful and fair manner" in which we had managed the redundancies. The members of the House Committee were not happy but their campaign was over.

And for the first winter ever, no resident died.

We got planning permission for a new retirement home and sold the site to Sunrise Homes in 2000 for around £2 million. Mary and I were invited to the opening of the new home a couple of years later, but we got caught in a blizzard and ended up having a lovely dinner in a restaurant in north London waiting for the snow to stop, and reminiscing about our times closing down what was fundamentally not fit for purpose. I've never been back.

My first coach

The first year at TBF was very busy and I was stretched, but from the start I made it part of my job to get out and about in the charity sector. I needed the inspiration and encouragement that other CEOs were able to give me. I joined the Association of Chief Executives of Voluntary Organisations (ACEVO) and went to a number of meetings.

At one evening event in London, I arrived a bit late. I took a seat at the back and listened to this intriguing American woman talk about leadership in the charity sector. She was knowledgeable, wise and quirky. I took to her immediately and at the end of her talk went up to her and asked "Do you do coaching for CEOs?"

She did, and we agreed there and then that I would go and meet her the following week for an exploratory coaching session.

And so Lois became my coach. She was originally from Jacksonville in Florida but had been living and working for most of her adult life in London, editing Shrew, the first women's movement newsletter, and also working at the Inner London Education Authority. She had been a freelance consultant and coach for about 20 years by the time we met.

Coaching is a process that builds a leader's capability to achieve organisational goals. It is usually conducted one-on-one for a defined period and with a specific business purpose in mind. I had never had a coach before and, despite the successes I was having, I was still anxious that I would be 'found out' and needed somewhere to share what was going on for me as well as develop my leadership skills.

Lois was a brilliant coach for me. She understood my somewhat unconventional career. She supported and challenged me, and she helped me understand a lot more about myself as a leader. I received useful feedback she gave me a space to share the un-shareable. I went to see her for a whole afternoon about once every six weeks for five years.

I continued coaching for the next twenty years and have worked with three other coaches, Peter, Rosie and Jon. Coaching has been an essential part of my development as a leader and entrepreneur as well as the success of the enterprises. I honestly don't know how I would have managed without it.

Lois and I worked together facilitating two of the International Tibet Support Network conferences in Prague in 2003 and Brussels in 2006, and we stayed close friends. We were informally coaching each other most weeks as she was receiving treatment at University College Hospital in London, shortly before she sadly died of cancer in 2016.

Lois's lovely obituary in The Guardian described her well.

> *Lois used her unique 'perspective of the outsider' and her soft American accent to gently question and articulate the challenges of organisations, groups and individuals. She would then find creative ways to help them (re)discover the practical inspiration in their work and find solutions.*[3]

I often think of her and regularly have 'Lois would say this' moments.

Learning #23: Conflict resolution

Conflict is inevitable in social enterprises. Most people come to work in them because of a passion for the cause. Different interpretations of the cause and how it should be fulfilled can be a source of conflict.

During one such conflict I was asked to "look for the grain of truth, however outrageous the criticism or complaint". I stopped being defensive and took this advice. It worked. I had just tried out what is arguably the most useful leadership skill I have ever learned.

I was in the midst of a meeting with the families of the residents to explain the closure of one of our nursing homes. Some of them were angry and early on one of them started accusing me of all sorts of bad motives. I acted on this conflict-resolution advice and the atmosphere of the meeting changed instantly.

Conflict is something that is a given in any social enterprise. In all my leadership roles I have been involved in conflict from time to time. It's not possible or even desirable to agree with everyone all of the time. I have got into conflict with members of staff, directors and trustees, customers, funders, suppliers and others. Sometimes their behaviour feels unreasonable, and on occasions it's been aggressive. But there is always a grain of truth, however small, in any complaint or attack. I always try to quickly figure out what this and acknowledge it. In almost every situation this has defused the tension and allowed us to solve the conflict.

Learning #24: Be prepared to close down

I have on more than one occasion had to close down a business. It's not an easy decision but sometimes it is what has to happen. The first time was at Ear to the Ground's small wholesale company, which I write about in Chapter 11.

While in Scotland, I was involved in the decision to close a publishing company owned by a charity. The board had asked a few people to review the financial state of the company, one of whom said, "It's better to close a company when the losses are relatively small than wait and watch the losses mount".

That was great advice. So, when it came to closing the retirement home business, I applied the same logic.

Learning #25: Mission drift

The business model of social enterprises and charities is perhaps more complex than in other sectors. The social mission is as important as the commercial business. But they should both be relevant. If not, the organisation runs the risk of 'mission drift'.

It is no good fulfilling a social mission but draining the resources of the enterprise, and therefore its ability to fulfil that mission. Equally, it's no good simply making money but no longer fulfilling the social mission. The job of a social entrepreneur is to keep these two in balance, working together.

The TBF homes provide a good example of mission drift because they were no longer contributing much to the charitable purpose, but they were draining much of the charity's energy and resources.

Learning #26: Coaching

Coaching is a process that builds a leader's capability to achieve organisational goals. It is usually conducted one-on-one for a defined period and with a specific business purpose in mind. I had never had a coach before and, despite the successes I was having, I was still anxious that I would be 'found out' and needed somewhere to share what was going on for me as well as develop my leadership skills.

My coaches have supported and challenged me and helped me understand a lot more about myself as a leader. It has been a space to share the un-shareable. I have typically had half a day coaching session about once every six to eight weeks.

Coaching has been an essential part of my development as a leader and entrepreneur as well as the success of the enterprises. I honestly don't know how I would have managed without coaching.

Carol and I went to the House of Lords to meet Lord Fulton.

Carol and I went to the House of Lords to meet Lord Puttnam

Chapter 30

Do we need counselling?

By autumn 1998, we had done a lot at TBF. We had a new strategy.
We were in the midst of exiting our care home business. We were
changing how we delivered our welfare grants programme, speeding
up the process and cutting out some of the older and somewhat dubious
approaches that the charity had hitherto taken.

I was spending quite a lot of my time meeting key people and
organisations in the education sector, but it was hard to be taken
seriously. TBF was seen as an old-fashioned welfare organisation,
effectively the NUT's retirement charity. As much as I talked about
the mental health challenges associated with the particular nature of
teaching, I struggled to get people to listen to what we were setting up.
We would have to find a way to cut through.

It didn't help that, despite the new strategy, many of the National
Council members were resistant to change, so that slowed things down.
Good governance is there to support the development of a charity, but
as I discovered from talking with other charity CEOs, the opposite was
sometimes the case. I was spending a disproportionate amount of time
speaking to my 40 trustees. It didn't help that some of them had an
outdated notion that I was a kind of glorified secretary for them. Katy
our office manager had been putting pressure on me to get a personal
assistant (PA), which after a long call from a trustee asking what train
she should take to a meeting, I gave into. I never thought PAs were
very 'start-up', and this was the first and last time that I have ever had
a PA. But it did help.

The SG Group had worked hard on the strategy, for which I was very
grateful. But then they had to deal with modernising the trustee board.
Having 40 trustees was too many. I did some research and the average

239

number for a charity of our size was between five and seven. I shared this with the group, who didn't look happy. This was going to be a 'turkeys voting for Christmas' situation.

We came up with a plan, which was basically this:

1. The National Council would remain but meet quarterly not monthly. It was to be constituted in the same way. They would not be trustees but would act in an advisory capacity.

2. They would cease making welfare grant decisions (which they had always made) but would be responsible for advising on grant-making policy.

3. Twelve trustees would be appointed by and from within the National Council. They would also meet quarterly.

4. The charity would be reincorporated as a company limited by guarantee with charitable status, giving the trustees the limited liability protection that they currently did not have.

5. While we were at it, we expanded the charity's objects in terms of geography and supporting trainee teachers.

The December meeting was a couple of weeks before Christmas. I had banned alcohol at board meetings soon after I joined, as it was clearly disruptive to sensible discussions. On this occasion I arranged for drinks to be served, along with mince pies and cake, but only at the end of the meeting. The decision to fundamentally change the governance structure of the charity was the last item in the agenda, so a timely debate would be necessary if they wanted a drink before it was time to catch their trains home. It was a high-risk strategy, but the vast majority agreed to the changes. There was, as I expected, some push-back, but it was half-hearted.

I was learning political intelligence from the best – trade union members. I would need this as my greatest political challenge in this job would come in the following few months.

Counselling service

I was impatient to get on with setting up the counselling service for teachers. All this strategy, governance and restructuring was all very well, but it was not the core work of the charity.

Looking back at this time, I think I started to understand some things that have served me well since. One of these was that, as a charity CEO, it's important to focus on the work and its impact, rather than all the logistics of getting there. Too much time can easily be spent on strategy, restructuring and governance. It is important, but it does not on its own get the work done.

Secondly, I began to realise that I am a fundamentally impatient person, but that despite having been criticised for this most of my life, especially at Findhorn, impatience is a useful quality for a social entrepreneur. It served me well at Nova Wholefoods (even if it was tough for others around me) and it was serving me well at TBF (and I hope I was being less difficult to work with).

I felt that the best time to launch the counselling service would be at the beginning of the school year, which meant September 1999. We had less than a year to get this off the ground.

Carol, the head of fundraising and marketing, was returning from maternity leave in November and was the most entrepreneurial member of the senior management team. While she was away there was a very competent fundraiser who had stood in for her, so we agreed to keep her on to create capacity for Carol to help with setting up the counselling service.

In the summer I had made a number of enquires of people who ran helplines, looking for someone who could advise us. Eventually I came across Linda. She was an independent consultant working in the employee assistance programme (EAP) industry made up of companies that provide counselling and other support to employees.

Linda came and met us at the office. We had a good discussion about what we wanted to do. We wanted a predominantly counselling service, but we wanted the ability to support any issues that teachers would come to us with. We were open to how this would be delivered, but we were reluctant to set up our own in-house counselling service, especially in London. We also wanted some involvement from our trustees in the process of setting this up.

We cooked up a plan. Linda would organise for us to visit four to five of the main EAP companies in the UK. She would pick the ones that she felt were most suitable for our requirements. Once that was done we would issue a simple tender document and ask for price quotations.

During that winter, two of the trustees plus Carol, Linda and I went to visit four EAP companies. It was a very useful learning process for us all. We knew what we wanted but we had absolutely no idea how to implement it. Outsourcing was clearly the best way to do it. We had early trains on frosty mornings to Leicestershire, Oxfordshire, Milton Keynes and Essex. We spent a few hours at each and by the end of the exercise there were three of the four that I felt we could trust our service with. They were really keen to work with us and could see that we had potential and were serious. Linda was excellent and made sure that each company answered all of our questions, plus the questions that we didn't know we had, but she did.

And Linda introduced me to two words that became a major part of my life for the next 20 years, 'tender' and 'outsourcing'. Completing a tender is a formal process where businesses are invited to bid for contracts from public or private sector organisations, which need specific skills for a project, or goods and services on an ongoing basis. And outsourcing is the process of obtaining goods or a service by contract from a third party supplier

We made it clear that we hoped to launch in September 1999 and that we expected some 12,000 calls in the first school year. This was 2.6% of the schoolteacher population in England and Wales, which I think these companies thought was a tall order for a brand new service. We also wanted a pilot programme in May for a couple of months, just to prove concept and iron out operational issues before the main launch. We wanted some of the counselling staff to have been schoolteachers. We did not want any face-to-face counselling, which all of the companies suggested we have. We said telephone only, with the possibility of adding email in a year or so (which some of them expressed discomfort about).

At the start of January, Linda issued the tender documents to the three companies we were interested in working with. Impatient as ever, I could not wait to see what came back.

In the end we went with the Leicestershire company, called First Assist. They made the most compelling offer in terms of counselling and engagement with teachers, and their price met our budget. It was a good decision. It was February. We were on track.

Doing the politics

Early in my time at TBF, I got to know Steve Sinnott, who at the time was deputy general secretary of the NUT. I liked Steve immediately and decided to tell him about my ambitions for a counselling service for teachers. He understood what I was talking about, but he cautioned me to stay close to the NUT on this. His very useful advice was that if the TBF strayed too far from the NUT, my ambition would be harder to realise.

243

Steve arranged for me to meet with the general secretary, Doug McAvoy. Doug was a legend in the trade union movement and a formidable political operator. I was anxious before meeting him. It was a one-to-one. After the pleasantries, we had a discussion about the counselling service plan. His position was that the NUT provided counselling already, so we ended up debating mental ill health and how best to solve it. We did not agree, but I have a feeling that he enjoyed the debate. We agreed to stay in touch as the project developed. It wasn't a no, but neither was it a yes.

The relationship between the NUT and the TBF was the most important relationship we had. As described earlier, our National Council was 95% made up of NUT members, of which 30% were members of their Executive Committee. Local and regional associations of the NUT made donations totalling some £120,000 a year. And the NUT mailed all their members annually asking them to make a regular donation (which for historical reasons was called a subscription) and these brought in some £200,000 a year. It was vital that the NUT supported the counselling service along with the other changes that I was making.

The NUT were supportive of our move to close the care homes, which can't have been easy for them. I'm sure that they had a similar number of complaint letters as we had, and I know that some of their associations had not donated that year because of it. It was important that I didn't push my luck and Doug very cleverly signalled this to me. I got the message.

Steve Sinnott became general secretary of the NUT in 2004. He died very suddenly in 2008[4]. Doug McAvoy retired as General Secretary of the NUT in 2004 and died in May 2019[5]. They both were great supporters of Teacher Support Network and I have a lot to thank them both for.

The Minister's impossible challenge

I was determined to get government funding for the counselling service. The service itself was going to cost about £500,000 a year to deliver and would require significant marketing and publicity to succeed. We had come up with an overall budget of £1 million a year including marketing, staff and overhead costs.

This was more than TBF could afford. As part of the strategy development, we came up with a three-year financial forecast. As always, I was heavily involved in this, and Carol and I came up with a plan that would support a stronger fundraising campaign based on delivering the counselling service and making the charity something that was attractive to schoolteachers in a way that it currently was not.

We worked out that the charity could afford about half of the cost of the counselling service from our operating costs. Of course, we had reserves to fall back on, but having just stemmed the losses from the care homes (which wouldn't kick in until the year 2000), I didn't want to set up another large annual deficit.

But it wasn't just about the money. I wanted the government to endorse the service. That would be a big step and everyone would take notice – the unions, the education authorities, headteachers, the press and importantly teachers themselves. We needed something like this to get us off the ground.

Around this time, I made an approach to Lord David Puttnam, the Oscar-winning film producer. He had recently become a Life Peer and was focusing on education projects. He was a friend and colleague of Estelle Morris MP, who was Minister for School Standards at the Department for Education and Employment (DfEE).

I just had a feeling that Lord Puttnam would be interested in what we were doing. He was involved in education politics from the House of

Lords and he had written about mental health. I found out the phone number and called his office. His assistant answered, we spoke for about 15 minutes and to my great surprise a meeting was arranged on the spot.

Carol and I went to the House of Lords to meet Lord Puttnam. He was really lovely and very generous with his time. We spoke for about an hour. He wanted to know all about what we were creating. Finally, we broached the subject of funding. He was completely relaxed and asked us to send him a one-page summary and offered to speak with Estelle Morris. And then he took us on a tour of the hidden rooms of the House of Lords.

David, as he asked me to call him, was as good as his word and a couple of weeks later I got a call inviting Carol and I to meet Charles Clarke MP at the DfEE. At the time, he was parliamentary under-secretary at the DfEE, and went on to be appointed Secretary of State for Education and then Home Secretary.

He was big in the Labour Party, having been chief of staff for former Labour leader Neil Kinnock and playing a key part in the modernisation of the Party. We were briefed by David to keep our pitch short and listen carefully to what he said.

We did what we were told. We had worked on a summary that covered who we were, what we planned to do and why we wanted £500,000 a year from the department. All in five minutes.

He listened intently and then said, "We will fund you if all six teaching trade unions agree to support what you are doing. Apologies, I have to go now." And with that he left the room.

I was elated. This was a YES. But with a sting in the tail. To this day, I still think that the minister may have assumed that, given the competition between some of the teaching unions, and the fact that we were so closely connected to the NUT, we didn't have a chance of achieving this, and so his promise was easily made. In the excitement of being back in start-up mode again, or just plain naiveté, I thought we can do this.

Advisory group

David Puttnam called. "How did it go?"

We met again, this time in his favourite Italian cafe in Westminster. We discussed tactics. He agreed it was a tough challenge, but achievable. He suggested that we put together an advisory group that included all the unions, as well as other key education sector organisations. We came up with a list on the back of a napkin.

I expressed my concern that hitherto I had struggled to get taken seriously. Then he had a genius suggestion.

"You'll need a public affairs professional."

He suggested Neil Stewart. With Charles Clarke, Neil had worked as a member of Neil Kinnock's staff when he was Leader of the Opposition. They were friends.

We quickly arranged a meeting with Neil at his office. He ran a successful public affairs and conference business. We discussed the challenge from the Minister, and he quickly came up with a plan.

1. Draw up a list of organisations we want in the advisory group.

2. Find a chair who is suitably independent but knows everyone.

3. Secure meetings with the general secretaries and leaders of these organisations.

4. Get written commitments of support from all these unions and other organisations.

5. Go back to the minister and secure financial commitment.

By then it was the end of February and we needed to get the commitment before the end of June or we would miss our September launch. Four months. It was going to be tight.

Change the name

Neil said the Teachers' Benevolent Fund name was a problem. I agreed but had felt this would be a change too far. He convinced me that I had to get this done as soon as possible. It was simply too old-fashioned.

Neil set up about 15 meetings with leaders in all the target organisations. It was a whirlwind. He and I went to meet them all in a four-week period, trying to get it all done before the Easter break when the three largest teaching unions held their annual conferences. Sometimes we had three of these meetings in the same day.

But the response was generally positive. There were lots of questions, which we got better at answering.

Question: "Our organisation already supports teachers with stress, so why do we need this?"

Our response: "Does your organisation employ counsellors?" To which their answer was always no.

Question: "Will we have to pay for this?"

Our response: "No."

Question "Will you be poaching our members to join the NUT?"

Our response: "This has nothing to do with membership. We won't be asking callers which union they are a member of, as that's not relevant to the counselling process and in any case is confidential information."

Question: "If the DfEE fund this, how will you stay independent?"

Our response: "This is a great question. However, as the counselling process is confidential, we will not disclose anything of what we learn to the DfEE or indeed anyone else. This is where our independence is rooted.

Question: "Isn't the job of TBF to look after retired teachers and the union to look after working teachers?"

Our response: "It's the job of TBF to support teachers with the problems of the time. Once that was welfare grants, now it is mental health. There is no one else doing this for teachers in a systematic way."

And my personal favourite:

Question: "Do we need counselling?"

Our response: "If you mean teachers, yes. We have research that suggests that stress is a big issue among teachers and many would welcome this support. If you mean you personally, I can't comment on that."

That always got a laugh.

Neil gave me a great political education and as a result my confidence rose daily. I was enjoying this.

We did change the name. Following conversations with some of the trustees, we went to their next meeting with a 'compromise' proposal and the name became TBF: Teacher Support Network. It would work for a while.

249

We find a chair

Neil and I met with David Puttnam again. We were making good progress, but we needed a chair. We met at the House of Lords and he brought along Josie Farrington (Baroness Farrington of Ribbleton). She had a background in education and local government and had recently become a government Whip.

Josie listened intently to our plans for the counselling service. She asked lots of questions. At the end she said, "I would love to do this, but it's a conflict with my government position."

Neil asked, "So who would you recommend?"

"Nicky Harrison," she said.

Both David and Neil were thrilled. "That's a brilliant idea," said Neil.

"I'll call her," added Josie.

I had never heard of Nicky Harrison, but I was about to meet someone who would be a big part of my life for the next nine years.

Neil and I met Nicky in a cafe in Highgate, north London, near where she lived. She was quite brusque, with a wicked sense of humour. She had chaired the Council for Local Education Authorities and was currently chair of both the National Foundation for Educational Research and the College of North East London. Most important to our venture was that Nicky had for many years been a member of the Burnham Committee that negotiated teachers' pay. She knew all the teaching unions and their general secretaries well.

After about an hour and numerous coffees, Nicky agreed to become chair of our advisory group. She made a list of demands, including expenses. I agreed, and it was all done.

Within a month, we had the trade unions all keen to be part of the advisory group. It had taken a while to get a meeting with the NUT to discuss this, but eventually we met with Doug McAvoy and his senior team. Nicky led the way into his office, flinging her arms around Doug. They were old friends, and the NUT came on board.

Along with the NUT, the rest of the teaching unions joined the advisory group: NASUWT[6], ATL[7], NAHT[8], SHA[9] and PAT[10]. We also had a number of other organisations represented including the Teacher Training Agency (TTA)[11], the schools inspectorate OFSTED[12], and the Local Government Association[13].

Government backing

In early June of 1999 we were back at the office of Charles Clarke at the DfEE. This time Neil and Nicky were with Carol and me. Neil and Charles were old friends and colleagues. Nicky knew Charles from the Labour Party. If he was surprised that we had pulled off his challenge to get all the trade unions around the table, he hid it well. He already had a file with letters of endorsement. There wasn't much more to be said. He agreed the funding of £500,000 a year for three years from September. After the meeting was over I sat with the civil servants and sorted out the details.

I went back to the office. I was a bit stunned. We had made it. In a few short months we had got the National Council, the NUT, the other trade unions, the employers, much of the education establishment and now the government to agree that a counselling service was the right thing to do. The Teacher Support Network (as I was now calling us in conversation) was fast becoming an important education sector player.

We had been impatient and tenacious, but also deployed considerable political intelligence, seeking help where we needed it. In some ways I was completely out of my depth, and without David Puttnam, Neil Stewart and Nicky Harrison we would never have persuaded so many of the leading players in the education sector to come on board.

Learning #27: Political intelligence

In their book *Leadership PQ: How Political Intelligence Sets Successful Leaders Apart*, Gerry Reffo and Valerie Wark define political intelligence as "the leadership capacity to interact strategically in a world where government, business and wider society share power to shape the future in a global economy".

By the time I arrived at TBF I was ready to operate in a more overtly political environment, negotiating with trade unions, government and the wider public sphere. This was absolutely necessary to achieve our aims. And I needed help which I got by asking.

Many social enterprises and wider third sector organisations operate in a political environment, or at the very least have politics that are central to their purpose and values. The ability to operate politically is an essential social entrepreneurship skill.

Learning # 28: Social entrepreneurs can be impatient for growth

I've met a lot of entrepreneurs in social enterprises, charities and small to medium businesses and many of them are impatient. Maybe the job requires impatience, or maybe it just suits impatient people.

Either way, I found that my impatience for growth helped growth to occur. Whether that is growth in impact, number of people we helped, problems solved, turnover and more. I am convinced that this was a positive use of my impatience.

Early in my career I was impatient and demanding of others but lacked people skills. This was often counterproductive. By the time I got to Teacher Support Network my impatience was tempered – but it was still needed. It's entirely possible that if I hadn't been so impatient to establish the counselling service, it may never have been launched.

We named the service Teacherline

We named the service Teacherline

Chapter 31

We launch Teacherline

That summer of 1999 was a frenetic and busy time. We completed a pilot service in Camden in May and June and had some great data and testimonials that supported our case. We set a launch date in the first week of September, just as teachers would start going back to work after the long holiday.

Up to then, it had felt like a project being run by Carol and me. Now the whole team swung into action and there was an excitement that most of the staff said they had never experienced before. It helped that we had recently moved into a larger office space upstairs, still in the NUT building. The charity was renewing.

We named the service Teacherline, borrowing from the success of Childline[14]. We hired a press officer – the first ever for the charity. We put in place an elaborate launch day with events in five cities as we were keen to have this reported across the UK, not just in London. We sent posters and leaflets out to most schools across England and Wales. We had a short video made by my sister Polly, a film producer.

On the morning of September 8th, I was at the BBC TV Centre at White City, west London, at 6am. I was on the BBC TV news followed by two hours sitting in a studio doing mostly local BBC radio live interviews, plus a short slot on Radio 4's Today programme. Carol was doing the same in the studio next door. Between us we did over 30 live radio interviews that morning.

I then went on the Nicky Campbell radio show for an hour at 9am. This was the hardest as it had a reputation as a combative phone-in show. Sure enough, 15 minutes in the producers managed to get a teacher and a nurse arguing about which had the most stressful job. I managed to come over as a calm voice of reason, only because I had been briefed on how to avoid getting into a row on live radio, which of course was the purpose of the show.

I then headed over to the Trades Union Congress building where the London launch event was being held. The service was formally launched by Estelle Morris MP, Minster of State for School Standards (and later Secretary of State for Education and Skills).

She was joined by Nicky Harrison, Doug McAvoy, Anthea Millet (CEO of the Teacher Training Agency), Tom (the leader of the counselling service and a former deputy headteacher) and me. Following a few short words from each of us, there was a press conference and photo call. I then thanked the minister and the others who had spoken, did three more radio interviews and a live TV interview and headed back to the office.

Marion, my new PA, had organised a celebration lunch and there was a huge cheer when Carol, Nicky and I arrived. All the staff were there, as well as a number of the trustees, Steve Sinnott and others from the NUT. It was a lovely moment.

The press interest went on all afternoon, and I finally did my 35th live radio interview on the Radio 4 PM programme before going home.

And most importantly, we took nearly 500 calls on the helpline that day.

Trainee teachers

The following week I went to the call centre in Leicestershire. I was keen to listen to some of the calls, as well as meet the team. I was surprised to be told on arrival that I could not listen to calls. I didn't make a big deal of it then, particularly as I was primarily there to arrange the launch of our latest venture.

One of our greatest supporters was Anthea Millet, the CEO of the Teacher Training Agency. Carol and I had met her early on and she had taken us seriously.

256

As well as joining the advisory group, Anthea was keen to get a Teacherline for trainee teachers, who she felt were particularly at mental health risk when working on their first classroom placements.

So, in early November, we were back in the radio and TV studios launching Teacherline for trainee teachers. It was run by the same team in Leicestershire. Again, we had a blaze of publicity and the calls started coming.

By the end of 1999 we had taken 4,500 calls and were collecting anonymised data on the impact of the service. This meant that we were learning a lot about workplace-related stress among teachers. It was time to start cementing our position as experts in the field, although I knew that this would be a longer-term project.

Learning #29: Media training

Earlier in this story I describe myself as an on the job learner. This has largely been the case in my career but there are a few notable exceptions. The most notable of these is media training.

Towards the end of my time at the Ecovillage there was a sustained attack on the integrity and legality of the organisation accompanied by a deluge of requests for media interviews, many of these combative. I quickly got some media training for myself and some others at the Foundation, which helped enormously.

In the run up to the launch of Teacherline I got more training, this time for Carol and me. We were put though our paces by a former TV interviewer. I learned to sit on my hands as I have a habit of using my hands when I'm talking, which is a bad look on TV. Again it was incredibly helpful.

Media training is a good example of a skill that needs updating all the time.

I met with 80 teachers and school staff in a village hall

Chapter 32

Just around the corner

Most of what I have done in my social enterprise journey is spot ideas that are 'just around the corner'. In most cases these are neither original ideas nor do they stare you in the face. They are somewhere in between. Maybe there is a hint of them in a conversation. Or they may be an extension of something that is already happening, just doing it slightly differently. They exist in a type of mental and intuitive peripheral vision.

The Norfolk Well Being Programme was one of these.

In autumn 1998, I discovered an organisation called the Centre for Stress Management run by Professor Steven Palmer. I went to meet him and explained what we were planning to do at Teacher Support Network. He was very interested and we discussed my plans.

He told me about a project he had worked on. Norfolk County Council had recently undertaken a survey of levels of stress across different professional groups among the council's employees. One of the groups that had come out with the highest levels of workplace stress was headteachers, with teaching staff only slightly better. The council were keen to do something about this.

I went to Norwich to visit the council's safety officer, who had commissioned the survey. We had a great talk and he was very open about their findings. He said that there was pressure to do something about reducing workplace stress in Norfolk schools, and after half an hour he took me off to meet the head of education personnel. He and I started talking and we were soon on the same wavelength. He took me to lunch at a local pub and a couple of hours later we had a plan.

I went back to the station to get the train to London and called Carol. I explained how we had come up with a plan to develop a school wellbeing programme. We were looking at a two-year programme across as many of their 550 schools as possible. We would ensure that there was a research study. We had done a 'back of the envelope' costing and it came in at about £100,000 over two years. The head of education personnel was confident that if we shared the costs 50:50 the council would grant our charity the exclusive right to deliver and exploit the Well Being Programme outside of Norfolk.

"Do you think the trustees will back us paying 50% of the cost?' I asked her.

"Let's go for it!" Carol replied.

This was the start of something big. And, as so often happens, it was 'just around the corner'.

Norfolk Well Being Programme

The trustees agreed to the part funding, a contract was drawn up and, after a first failed attempt, we appointed Ray to run the project. He had been a teacher and schools adviser in Norfolk, was well known and well liked by schools in the county and had a significant understanding of the issues we wanted to address.

Ray began work at the start of 1999, so was building the project as I was in the thick of getting Teacherline off the ground. I therefore couldn't give the Norfolk programme as much attention as I wanted to, but I think Ray liked that. He had a lot of autonomy in creating the programme and I was happy about that. I have always preferred working with people who like to be left to make things happen, because I understand it. I don't like breathing down people's necks, and I don't like anyone doing that to me. I would go to Norwich every few months and we'd spend a few hours together, which was always a pleasure.

In the second year I met with 80 teachers and school staff in a village hall somewhere in the middle of rural Norfolk. It was a day of feeding back on how the Well Being Programme had worked in their schools. It was inspirational and I wished that all the staff and trustees of Teacher Support Network had been there to see it. I found a great article about the project in the Times Educational Supplement that I think describes it well.[15]

From early 2000, we started getting enquiries about the project from other local authorities. They were contacting Ray for advice and with requests to visit. Ray was always good at communicating with me about this, albeit sometimes after the fact. The funding for the Norfolk programme would be over at the end of the year, and this was the moment for us to take it beyond Norfolk, as per our original agreement.

I started discussing this with Ray in the early summer. He was interested but understandably non-committal. I wasn't offering anything concrete at that stage, but he was interested in doing more. We kept up the dialogue. In the meantime, he told me about an interesting meeting he had had with Northamptonshire Council, who were doing something similar with their schools. This was led by Steve, who had also been an adviser in Northamptonshire Education Authority and was a trained counsellor providing support to teachers and school staff as part of their own wellbeing programme.

Learning #30: Ideas are often just around the corner

My experience is that the best ideas are already close by. Frequently, looking at something in an inquisitive way helps me to see the previously unseen. Sometimes successful innovations are completely original, although for me more often they're not.

In my experience, the best innovations I have been involved in making happen came from ideas that were 'just around the corner'.

These are typically neither original ideas nor did they stare me in the face. They were somewhere in between. They are ideas that are close by but not quite yet visible.

Often the idea is hinted at in a conversation. Or it may be an extension of what is already happening, just doing it slightly differently. These ideas exist in a sort of mental, emotional or intuitive peripheral vision. Sometimes it's a feeling that just won't go away.

I keep looking around the corner.

press conference

I presented it at the conference

Chapter 33

High profile

By spring 2000 we'd had around 8,000 calls to Teacherline. There was good data coming through that was starting to give us a picture of the state of wellbeing among teachers. The Norfolk Well Being Programme was starting to deliver positive results. We had launched a benefits, debt and money advice service from the office, run by a former Citizens Advice manager who had a teaching background.

In under a year we had gone from supporting around 700 teachers a year to over 10,000. We had a public profile. We were beginning to be taken seriously by much of the education sector. We had brought the trade unions together to support Teacherline and got the government on board.

There were some internal noises about slowing down and consolidating. I largely ignored these as I think consolidation is overrated. My view is that we had only just started and if we slowed down the pace, we would be unable to capitalise on our success. At the time there we some 450,000 teachers in England and Wales and supporting just over 2% of them was a drop in the ocean. When one of our trustees expressed a view that maybe we had solved teacher stress and could relax, I didn't know whether to laugh or cry.

I spoke with Neil again and we decided to hold a conference of our own after Easter. I had attended three teaching union conferences that Easter, run by ATL, NUT and NASUWT, and was a guest of the union at each of them. At NASUWT I got a short speaking slot in the main conference hall, and we ran a meeting at the NUT which was standing room only.

In advance of our own conference, we commissioned some research that took anonymised findings from our helpline data and tested some of the assumptions about teachers in surveys and focus groups. The results were really helpful and suggested that the 2% being helped by Teacherline were the tip of the iceberg of a much bigger problem of mental ill health among teachers.

We held the conference in May. David Puttnam agreed to speak, we had a panel with Doug McAvoy, the general secretary of the NUT, and Nigel de Gruchy of the NASUWT. We had workshops on mental health in schools, the role of counselling and the Well Being Programme in Norfolk. After the usual morning of radio and TV appearances to talk about the research, I presented it at the conference. It was a great success, largely down to Neil's team.

Following this event, I started getting invited to speak at other conferences and meetings. I made it a rule never to turn down a speaking event, however small. This served Teacher Support Network well and helped get the message out. The more we were in the media, the more teachers called Teacherline and the more they benefited from counselling. It helped that Neil's company's main business was organising conferences and he put me up as a speaker for everything and anything that was even vaguely relevant. We really owed a lot to him.

It was at one of these conferences that I eventually met Steve from Northamptonshire Council. I had heard of him from Ray in Norfolk, who rated him highly as someone who was doing similar work to us. I had been speaking about teacher wellbeing and a man about my age started asking questions. We had what felt like a full-length conversation between the two of us in front of the whole conference. He didn't give his name, but I guessed.

During the break I went to find him.

"You're Steve from Northamptonshire?"

"Yes," he said.

"Would you like to come and work with us and get Well Being Programmes into every school in the UK?"

It was the fastest job offer that I have ever made.

"Can I go home and think about?" he replied.

"Yes, but don't think for too long."

He called me the next day and started work that September.

Worklife Support start-up

Steve's role was to take the Well Being Programme beyond Norfolk. Carol agreed that if we were to capitalise on the success of the Norfolk programme, we had to have someone credible. I had made sure that the two of them met over the summer and she agreed Steve was the person to do this. We wanted to keep Ray on board and ideally have him come and join us to set up programmes, but we agreed he wasn't right to lead on this.

Steve and Ray met in Steve's first week and agreed that this all made sense and that Ray would decide on his next steps once the funding for the Norfolk programme ceased at the end of the year.

Steve went on the road and started meeting local authority education officers and headteachers. We'd had enough enquiries to keep him going for a while. In the meantime, I had a bigger problem to solve.

I met with the charity's solicitor. Stephen Lloyd was the top charity lawyer in the UK and played a huge part in making social enterprise the force it is today. He helped many people and organisations get off the ground and to create the legal and commercial structures that allowed them to thrive. He did this for me for six organisations, charitable and commercial, that I set up, and I have a lot to thank him for to this day.

On this particular occasion we sat in his office and tossed around ideas. We were a charity but this would be a trading activity. It could be seen as primary-purpose trading, but the objectives of the charity were restricted to teachers, and schools had a lot of other staff. The community interest company structure, which Stephen was later responsible for establishing, was not yet created. Social investment, although there was a market for it, was not as available as it is today. In the end we decided to go for a traditional share company with the charity owning the shares.

Stephen was my solicitor from 1998 until his retirement in 2014. He very sadly and unexpectedly died later that year[16].

So Worklife Support was born. I toyed with the idea of calling it Well Being, but we could not register the company name. We set the company up and started trading. In the early days it was a wholly owned subsidiary of Teacher Support Network, so I led on the new company as part of my job as CEO.

Like any new company it took a while to get customers. I therefore had to start raising money. The charity agreed that, if necessary, we could dilute their shareholding if this raised suitable finance. Stephen talked about this with the trustees, an important discussion that laid the groundwork for our eventual investment offer.

In the end we traded for a couple of years before we raised the funds we needed. We scraped by with investments and loans from a few individuals, and Steve and I put a lot of effort into sales.

One of the challenges charities can face is moving from a fundraising mindset to a sales mindset. Actually, I don't think it's that different, but I am forever meeting people (including fundraisers) who say that they 'don't like to do sales work' or feel intimidated by it.

But selling products and services is about building great relationships with people. I discovered that when setting up Worklife Support. Our customers and potential customers were teachers, headteachers and local authority managers. In other words, interesting and socially motivated people who were dedicating their lives to the education of young people. These were people who I generally shared values with. I wanted to find out about them, why they did what they did, what their challenges were and most importantly what made them passionate about what they did. What was 'sales work' felt like an opportunity to have really interesting conversations rather than simply selling something.

But of course there is another aspect of selling. Winning. I got to know the director of education for the London Borough of Greenwich, who Nicky had worked with many years previously. He was fascinated by what we were doing and, after a number of meetings, purchased an employee counselling service for all his staff. It was Worklife Support's first significant contract. I was so excited when we won it; it was the closest I have felt to catching a salmon, a form of primal exhilaration.

We need to raise investment

I have set up a number of companies that started as subsidiaries of charities. At the time it was fairly standard in the charity sector. But since my days at the Ecovillage, where we had to raise finance for every venture, I felt that charities should not be financing their subsidiary companies if they were at the start-up phase because of the high level of risk.

So I started creating created a business plan and investor pack for Worklife Support. I started visiting all the social investors that I could find over the course of 2001, but to no avail. Finally, we got a break. Someone got us an introduction to the Great Eastern Investment

Forum, which was an investment pitch event that happened a few times a year in Cambridge. Being Cambridge, the companies seeking investment were typically tech and biotech start-up companies.

In order to get onto this, I had to go to Cambridge and be assessed as suitable. I was there on the morning after 9/11, and of course everyone's attention was on this shocking event. I was met by the organiser of the Forum, who had brought along someone called David, who ran a venture capital fund in Cambridge.

I liked David immediately, little knowing that he would be another person who would be significant in my career. He was older than me, very well spoken and well dressed. I had been told to prepare an eight-minute pitch, covering the business, its services, the market, the financials, what investment we required and on what terms. I went through the presentation. David gave me detailed feedback, which we discussed, and then I did it again. It was much, much better. I could see that.

David was smiling and said, "We don't typically invite service businesses to the Forum," and then looking at the organiser said, "but I think we should make an exception here."

A few weeks later I was back in Cambridge for an 8am start. There were ten companies who had eight minutes each to present. Following that there were small breakout rooms and the 150 investors attending could choose to visit up to three of the companies for a longer discussion. The Forum had a high success rate for investment.

I met the organiser, who said, "You're a bit of an unusual company for us, so I hope you don't mind that we've given you the smallest breakout room."

No kidding. It could barely fit ten people including me.

I was nervous doing the big pitch, but David had prepared me well. I was the only presenter who wasn't a tech company. Most of the 150 guests were tech investors. But they had all been to school once. I must have touched something as a I got a cheer when I finished.

The three breakout sessions were completely rammed. It was standing room only with people spilling out the door. I was still speaking with potential investors out in the street over an hour after the event was finished.

I was elated. We sought £500,000 of investment for a relatively small percentage of the shares, with the charity owning the vast majority, and I was confident we would get this in no time at all.

I could not have been more wrong. It was another 10 months before we raised the investment.

Email counselling service, which was immediately successful

Chapter 34

Overreaching

Digital transformation

Teacher Support Network developed a new strategy towards the end of 2001, with a major focus on developing as 'thought leaders' in the area of the wellbeing and mental health of teachers. The profile of the charity was growing rapidly, and I was keen to use this platform to help many more teachers

It is hard to remember, but in 2001 digital technology was basic compared with what we are used to now. I had a mobile phone which was quite large and I could only use it to make calls and send texts. I had a laptop and used email a fair amount. That was about it. I remember I had been reading about what was coming next in technology in the Economist and went into the office the next day and announced, "From now on, I want us to have a digital version of every service we provide".

That became a main strategic objective of our new plan. And we got on with it straight away. I looked around for people who were talking and writing about digital technology in charities and quickly came across Howard, the founder of Fundraising UK. He came and spoke to some of our staff and trustees, and we spent a morning exploring possibilities such as email counselling, online advice and guidance and benefits checkers. He put me in touch with Jason of Think Digital, who we worked with for years as we developed our digital offerings.

Today this process is called digital transformation, and transformation it certainly was. By the end of 2001 we had a rudimentary online advice service on the Teacherline website and were running an email counselling service.

I tracked down the person who had recently set up an email service for Samaritans, the charity that works to ensure that fewer people die by suicide. To my knowledge, this was the first email service helping people in challenging circumstances. Samaritans were so generous with their time and expertise, and after a bit of a tussle with our counselling team, we launched our own email counselling service, which was immediately successful, particularly at reaching teachers who felt uncomfortable picking up the phone to speak to a counsellor.

By the end of 2011 we had helped 15,000 teachers on the phone, and a further 10,000 online. This was working.

Too much start-up

On reflection, I set up too many organisations at that time. We set up three charities to mirror what Teacher Support Network was doing in Wales, Scotland and Northern Ireland, largely driven by the recent devolutions that had established what are now the Senedd, Scottish Parliament and Northern Ireland Assembly. I even started up a non-profit in the USA, initially following a request from the two main teaching unions there, who had seen what we had done in the UK. All these were subsidiaries of Teacher Support Network.

But they weren't as easy to run, and I was working in areas where I did not understand the culture, politics and funding environment so well. I enjoyed the USA project, particularly because I met John, who became a great business partner.

I think it added to a sense among the trustees and some of the staff that I was more focused on starting the new rather than taking care of the core charity. Steve and I were working hard to get Worklife Support off the ground. It took a lot of my energy and took me away from the day-to-day of Teacher Support Network. I think that I hadn't learned to delegate properly, so a few things fell through the cracks. We had a former member of staff who took us to an employment tribunal, and although we won easily, it added to a sense that all was not well.

I shared how I was feeling with Lois, my coach. She recommended that I share how I was feeling with the management team. So I did. I told them that my mood was low. I told them that I had heard some negative comments about me and how that made me feel. I shared that I wasn't sleeping well. I felt vulnerable doing this. They were lovely and I received a lot of support. It helped.

Higher profile

One the things I enjoyed about my job was profile building. These days it's one of the most important jobs that a CEO does. I have always experienced myself as being shy, typically feeling anxious entering a networking event. But I liked public speaking, I liked media interviews and, once I'd got over my anxiety, I quite enjoyed a networking event.

Up to then we had been pushing hard at getting opportunities for speaking at conferences and events. But something was changing. We were getting more requests for me to speak. Some of these were at school staff events, some were trade union events, some were national policy conferences, and then one day there was an approach to speak at an international conference in Geneva.

Someone had heard of our work and I was invited to speak about what we were doing for teacher wellbeing. The conference was hosted by the Club of Geneva, an organisation taking an international lead on workplace health. The main sponsor was Motorola.

I was invited for the whole three days of the conference, and I accepted. I'd never been to Geneva. I'd never spoken at such a large conference. My speech was on the second day. On the first night, this energetic British woman came up and introduced herself as Rusty, who was chairing my session the next day.

"Was that a random allocation to you?" I asked. "Did you pick the short straw?"

She laughed. "No, I picked your session. I'm one of the sponsors and I think what you are doing looks a bit different."

Rusty's comment took me by surprise. On the one hand it was a casual comment; on the other hand it was significant. Rusty knew the employee assistance industry well, largely as a result of her experience at Motorola. She quickly understood what we had been doing at Teacher Support Network.

Put simply, we were aiming to provide a service that was a lot more holistic than just a mental health support programme. We had started to recognise that if a teacher came to us experiencing anxiety or depression, the likelihood would be that there were a number of underlying causes. These could include housing, finances, family problems, problems at work, bullying and harassment, medical conditions and much more. If we were to help teachers, we had to provide support for all of these problems, rather than just offer counselling as a response.

We had started to do this. We had a successful money advice service and we worked on bullying and harassment. But we had a lot further to go and wanted to provide a service that could offer a response to almost anything that teachers and their families needed help with.

That evening we talked about this and I shared my frustrations. At that point we were still outsourcing our service to employee assistance programme (EAP) companies and it was a struggle to get them to embrace this holistic approach. Rusty was the first person I had met in this industry who really understood this.

We talked late into the evening. The next day a packed room heard me talk about what we were doing for teachers and in schools. Rusty gave

276

a brilliant summation at the end and invited questions. There were a lot, and it was a really exciting conversation.

Rusty and I spent pretty much all of the rest of the conference talking. We stayed in touch afterwards. This was a really significant meeting. I had just met the woman who I would create my next and most successful venture with.

Worklife Support takes off

Worklife Support was going well. By late 2002 we had a number of Well Being Programmes up and running. Steve was doing a great job of getting local authorities engaged, and off the back of Greenwich Council we now provided a number of employee counselling services. We were running Governorline, an advice service for school governors that I had negotiated and which was funded by the government.

I was technically leading Worklife Support, but most of the work was being done by Steve, assisted by Ray, who had joined us when the Norfolk funding ended. Every month or so Steve and I would get together for all or part of the day, often at his home out of London. These were really creative sessions and kept the enterprise growing and developing during the time when there was very little money. My relationship with Steve was at its most creative then and I enjoyed working with him a lot.

It was a stretch for the company to pay the salaries. We would never manage any further growth without working capital. We needed additional people both to sell more services and deliver the programmes.

Some months after the Great Eastern Investment Forum in Cambridge I got a call from David, who had interviewed me. He asked how we had gone with the investment. I told him how we had lots of interest but that it had slowly dried up.

"Do you think the charity's ownership was an issue?" he said.

"Yes, it was. The potential investors got cold feet when we talked about that," I replied, "but we could hardly avoid talking about it."

Most of the potential investors just could not understand a charity 'owning' a company. I've come across this a lot. There seems to a mindset among some wealthy people that charities should be run by volunteers and entirely funded by donations. The reality could not be more different. Most charities that earn over £1 million a year have very mixed income streams, including commercial income, government contracts and sponsorship, alongside donations and grants.

David said, "Why don't you come and visit me? Bring your numbers."

So a couple of weeks later I travelled up to see David. He lived in a beautiful old mill house in a village outside Cambridge. I told him in detail about all the investors that I had met and what feedback they had given. They had liked the business but were put off by the charity/company relationship.

We went through the numbers in detail, and he asked questions about every row on the spreadsheet. The investment requirement was still £500,000. Then he gave one of the best pieces of business advice that I have ever received.

"Find a way of doing everything you need to do for half the money, and I guarantee you'll get the investment. Come back in a couple of weeks when you've done that."

This was a challenge. Trying to achieve the same levels of income growth but with half the money. I played around and got it down to about £300,000. I went back to see him.

David quizzed me on the numbers again, and after a couple of hours we only needed £250,000 investment and had some additional headroom on costs.

"Now," he said, "have you heard of the Small Firms Loan Guarantee Scheme?"

The scheme allowed companies to take out a bank loan that is guaranteed by the government rather than the individual directors. The funding was provided by all the major banks.[17]

I was on the phone to our bank manager the next morning and arranged a meeting.

I have made it my business to cultivate good relationships with the banks and their managers that I have banked with over my whole career. In 21 years of banking with our bank I had only had two managers – each called Gary. I have been able to call them up any time and across a number of companies and charities have borrowed nearly £8 million in total. I regularly advise entrepreneurs to borrow from banks early in their career to get a good credit history.

It took a while but in the end we received a loan of £250,000, fully guaranteed and with a one-year repayment holiday. This changed everything.

For Worklife Support to thrive it needed a full-time managing director. It needed someone who understood the education world but was suitably commercial. I discussed it with Steve and he didn't think it was him. I spoke with the Teacher Support Network management team and it was inconclusive. I wasn't sure that I wanted to go out to recruitment. And I was very clear that it should not be me as that would require a new CEO for Teacher Support Network, plus the old CEO being around as managing director of Worklife Support wouldn't work well. I tossed this all around in my head for a couple of days but didn't come to a satisfactory conclusion.

I find it difficult to wait for a solution to an intractable problem to emerge. Fortunately, on this occasion I only had to wait 48 hours.

Two days after the management meeting, Carol came into my office and announced that she would like to take on the Worklife Support role.

I was genuinely surprised and hope that I didn't show it. Carol had not been the most supportive of setting up Worklife Support, questioning whether it would be a distraction (she wasn't wrong there). I said that it would be good for her to speak with David as I was considering asking him to chair the board of directors.

David agreed that this was the right thing to do. We closed the funding from the bank, Carol became managing director, David joined the board of directors as chair and Steve became operations director for Teacher Support Network. It all happened in under a week. When the right solution appears, things have a way of falling into place quickly.

Worklife Support thrived under Carol's leadership. She created some difference between the company and the charity, which felt uncomfortable at times, but it was the right thing to do. In 2013 the company launched the London Well Being Programme, alongside the London Challenge, a school improvement programme launched by the government the same year.

Within a few years, the company was turning over £2 million a year, making a profit and comfortably repaying its loan. Some 10% of schools in England and Wales were involved in some form of Well Being Programme. In 2007 research from Birkbeck College stated that "staff wellbeing is key to school success".[18]

Profit with purpose.

Learning #31: Opening up to colleagues

A lot is said about the loneliness of leaders. I had shared how I was feeling with Lois, my coach. She recommended that I share how I was feeling with the management team. So I did. I told them that I was feeling depressed. I told them that I had heard some negative comments about me and how that made me feel. I shared that I wasn't sleeping well. I felt vulnerable doing this. They were lovely and I got lot of support. It helped.

I think even at that stage of my career I felt that as CEO I had to keep my emotions largely to myself. But that was a mistake. It's important to be able to open up to work colleagues, albeit that it's important to choose wisely which colleagues.

Learning #32: Raising investment

Raising investment for Worklife Support was the first time I had attempted this for a business start-up. I had been struggling to raise finance for some time when I received some help from a corporate finance adviser who reviewed my financial plan and gave me one of the best pieces of advice I've ever received.

"Find a way of doing everything you need to do for half the money, and I guarantee you'll get the investment"

He was right. I re-worked the numbers, sought funding for half the money and soon secured the investment required. I have subsequently shared this piece of advice with many social entrepreneurs.

It is easy to underestimate the work and time involved in raising finance for a social enterprise. And it is a job that has to be prioritised above all else, in order to meet the multiple demands of investors, financiers and banks.

Having said this, I always encourage social entrepreneurs to borrow from banks and other lending institutions as early as possible in your career. The sooner you borrow, the stronger your credit record and reputation will be. My experience is that as I borrowed more it got easier.

I'm sure we can do it better ourselves

Chapter 35

Contact centre

In 1999 we had launched Teacherline with First Assist, who were a great company in many ways, with a strong clinical focus. That was what we really needed at the time as the service was focused on counselling.

But the development of a digital element of the Teacher Support Network service had changed things. We supported teachers with a lot more than just mental health or stress at work. We were providing advice on benefits, debt and money issues, we were helping teachers deal with bullying and harassment, and much more. We had an online advice library of information and gave advice on a very wide range of issues related to teacher wellbeing. As a result we were providing a lot more advice and support – to 93,000 teachers in 2003 – all free at the point of use. This was a long way from the 700 a year we had supported when I joined the charity in 1998.

We had worked hard with First Assist to try to get their telephone and email service better integrated with our digital platform and the other services we provided. Sadly, I think their clinical strength was a weakness when it came to those discussions. We liked them, but they just could not agree to the level of integration we were looking for. So, we started looking for another supplier.

In 2003 we moved the service to another employee assistance company. They promised that we would have a fully integrated service, with telephone advisers sending digital advice as a response to a call, smooth transfers into money advice and other specialist areas, and adoption of new technologies such as web chat that were emerging. They also demonstrated an impressive database that we would be able to access for research, press enquiries and reports, all of which were vital for us to develop our thought leadership.

After a year I was disappointed that very little of what we had been promised had been delivered. I met with the directors of the company to express this disappointment and they promised to implement all that we had agreed. This never materialised.

During this time, I was speaking to John in the USA a lot. We had been working together on the Teacher Support initiative there. John was an expert on workplace health solutions in the USA, Europe and worldwide and had been very helpful in the start-up phase of Worklife Support. He had a keen understanding of the direction of travel of this industry and his sense was that our approach to digital integration was ahead of the rest of the industry in the UK. He encouraged me to go to the International Employee Assistance Professionals Association (EAPA) conference in the States and arranged for me to meet a lot of industry experts. I met the founder of Beating the Blues, the UK's first online cognitive behavioural therapy platform. I met the founder of Hummingbird Coaching, pioneers in digital behavioural coaching. I was inspired.

After I got back from the USA I was having a drink with some of my management team when I remembered the conversation with Rusty where I had shared my frustrations with the EAP industry and my hopes of creating a holistic service. "I'm sick of the UK EAP companies. I'm sure we can do it better ourselves" just popped out.

There it was again – an idea just around the corner.

What I learned at Teacher Support Network

Learning #20: Fortune favours the brave

My time at Findhorn had taught me a lot about leadership. One of the lessons I had learned is that sometimes you simply need to make a brave move. Of course, it is risky, but by my late 30s I had made a few such moves and most of them had worked out.

The final statement of my interview presentation for the job at the Teachers' Benevolent Fund was a risk, which you can about read in 'A ten minute strategy' in Chapter 27. It was impulsive. By that stage of my career I had taken a few risks and had developed an ability to see the risks of every decision in real time as an ongoing mental process.

In this case it was 100% instinctive. My internal risk assessment said that the only person that would suffer if I was wrong would be me. Because no one else's wellbeing was at stake, I could take the risk without hesitation.

Learning #21: Figure out your business model early on

Every enterprise needs a business model. The trick is to figure it out early on. In the early days of Nova Wholefoods (see Chapter 2), ours was built around a combination of customer requirements and cashflow. It was a great framework, and as the business grew and our supply chain changed, we still had a model that balanced being able to get a customer order to them within three days while keeping the stock at an optimal level and the cash flowing.

My next job at Ear to the Ground (all six weeks of it) was spent undoing a company, and you can read about that in Chapter 11. At the core of its problem was that there was no business model with this sort of structure that served customers and the company.

Years later when I went to Teacher Support Network there was a business model that had been around a long time. As many of the staff and trustees had been around a long time too, no one had noticed that the business model was no longer working and that the charity was gently sliding into insolvency. You can read about this in Chapter 28.

I am a great advocate of having a clear and robust business model that you understand and review regularly. Every social enterprise is different so there is no one way to design a business model, but here are some things I have always considered in the mix:

- What service levels do your customers require? Your business model must above all else be designed to deliver on these.

- What level of gross profit is needed to fund the growth, development and quality of these services and/or products? This may well be a greater percentage of turnover at start-up (to fund investments and repay loans) than later on.

- How to design this business model to ensure that there is sufficient cash at the lowest point of the month (typically when salaries are paid) or quarter (when VAT is paid)?

- How to ensure that working patterns will suit employees? I didn't think about this in the early days of establishing Nova Wholefoods, assuming that new cooperative members would work as hard Paul and me. It's a mistake I haven't made again.

If you don't take charge of your business model, it will take charge of you and may work against you. Teacher Support Network taught me that.

Learning #22: Imposter syndrome

Starting as CEO of my first 'established organisation' was scary. Up to then I had either worked starting up an enterprise (Nova), scaling a project from scratch (Ecovillage) or recreating a tiny organisation (Tibet Relief). This was different and there were lots of people who thought I should act and behave in a way that was alien to me.

I felt a fraud because I had never done a job like this. Although I suspect I looked confident on the outside, which was clearly expected of me, I could not stop this niggling feeling that I would be 'found out'.

At the time, I was five years into psychotherapy, so quickly learned the name for this condition. Imposter syndrome is a psychological occurrence in which an individual doubts their skills, talents or accomplishments and has a persistent internalised fear of being exposed as a fraud. Yes, that was me. Although outwardly competent, someone experiencing this phenomenon does not believe they deserve their success or luck. Yes, that was me too.

I had never experienced this before, but I felt an imposter on and off for the remainder of my time at Teacher Support Network. I got to understand it better through my therapy and got better at dealing with the episodes of imposter syndrome when they threatened to overwhelm me, but it wasn't until I was starting up another enterprise from scratch that it genuinely left me.

Learning #23: Conflict resolution

Conflict is inevitable in social enterprises. Most people work in them because of a passion for the cause. Different interpretations of the cause and how it should be fulfilled can be a source of conflict.

While the Ecovillage had a start-up mindset, moving fast, making change and taking risks, we operated within a larger organisation. This was inevitably a source of conflict. The more successful we became, the more complaints we heard. After a while these began to bubble up into full-blown conflicts, and I was often in the centre of these.

As a senior manager, it was obligatory for me to attend Community meetings, and these seemed to come along all too frequently. At first my attitude was somewhat combative. I was too defensive, seeing it as my role to defend the Ecovillage against the rest of the Community. This was not at all helpful as it just exacerbated every area of conflict.

Then at one memorable meeting I was asked to "look for the grain of truth, however outrageous the criticism or complaint". I stopped being defensive and took this advice. It worked. I had just tried out what is arguably the most useful leadership skill I have ever learned. You can read more this at 'Look for the grain of truth' in Chapter 19.

I have used this approach many times over the subsequent years. One of the most useful moments was some years later at Teacher Support Network.

I was in the midst of a meeting to close one of our nursing homes, meeting with the families of the residents. Some of them were angry and early on one of them started accusing me of all sorts of bad motives. Before I could say anything one of the trustees stood up and started to defend me in a classic combative manner. This was about to go horribly wrong.

I remembered the words of that Community meeting at Findhorn to look for the grain of truth.

I dug deep and spoke to a man upset that we were about to turn his mother's life upside down, who had just said something hurtful.

I replied "Yes, sir, this will be disruptive for your mother. And I apologise for that."

He relaxed instantly. He asked what we would do to minimise her disruption and I slowly and patiently went through what I had said earlier. You can read about this in Care homes in Chapter 29.

Conflict is something that is a given in any social enterprise. In all my leadership roles I have been involved in conflict from time to time. It's not possible or even desirable to agree with everyone all of the time. I have got into conflict with members of staff, directors and trustees, customers, funders, suppliers and others. Sometimes their behaviour feels unreasonable, and on occasions it's been aggressive. But there is always a grain of truth, however small, in any complaint or attack. I always try to quickly figure out what this and acknowledge it. In almost every situation this has defused the tension and allowed us to solve the conflict.

Learning #24: Be prepared to close down

On a few occasions I had to close down a business. It's not an easy decision but sometimes it is what has to happen.

The first time was at Ear to the Ground's small wholesale company, which I wrote about in Chapter 11. It was the right decision, but that didn't make it easy for anyone involved. I was the first to put myself forward for redundancy, so it made it a bit easier, but for others it was harder. But the decision saved the rest of the business.

A few years later I was involved in the decision to close a publishing company owned by a charity. The board had asked a few people to review the financial state of the company, one of whom said, "It's better to close a company when the losses are relatively small than wait and watch the losses mount."

That was great advice.

In 1998, and new at Teacher Support Network, I remembered those words when I had to close the charity's much-loved nursing homes. This was harder as it involved residents and their families, 200 employees and a number of long-term supporters of these homes.

But I remembered the advice. I had worked out that we were losing around £500,000 a year running these homes. Every day we delayed would just increase the losses, eating away at financial reserves that the charity had built up over decades. You can read more about this in Chapter 29.

Social enterprises and charities can't trade at a loss for long, and once losses occur more than a few months in a row, you have to start asking the question as to whether the project, the department or indeed the entire enterprise is better closed down. It is always better for everyone involved to have a planned closure than a sudden bankruptcy.

Learning #25: Mission drift

The business model of social enterprises and charities is perhaps more complex than in other sectors. The social mission is as important as the commercial business. But they should both be relevant. If not, the organisation runs the risk of 'mission drift'.

It is no good fulfilling a social mission but draining the resources of the enterprise, and therefore its ability to fulfil this mission. Equally, it's no good simply making money but no longer fulfilling the social mission. The job of a social entrepreneur is to keep these two in balance, working together.

The Teacher Support Network homes provide a good example of mission drift as, although they were no longer contributing much to the charitable purpose, they were draining much of the charity's energy and resources. You can read more about this at 'Strategic plan' in Chapter 29.

Learning #26: Coaching

I found my first coach shortly after I became CEO at Teacher Support Network.

Coaching is a process that builds a leader's capability to achieve organisational goals. It is usually conducted one-on-one for a defined period and with a specific business purpose in mind. I had never had a coach before and, despite the successes I was having, I was still anxious that I would be 'found out' and needed somewhere to share what was going on for me as well as develop my leadership skills.

My first coach understood my somewhat unconventional career. She supported and challenged me, and she helped me understand a lot more about myself as a leader. I received feedback, challenge, support and a space to share the un-shareable.

Coaching has been an essential part of my development as a leader and entrepreneur as well as the success of the enterprises. I went to see coaches for twenty years and honestly don't know how I would have managed without them.

Learning #27: Political intelligence

There is a lot written about the different qualities of intelligence required by entrepreneurs. In their book Leadership PQ: How Political Intelligence Sets Successful Leaders Apart, Gerry Reffo and Valerie Wark define political intelligence as "the leadership capacity to interact strategically in a world where government, business and wider society share power to shape the future in a global economy".

I had first operated in a political environment while at university, in the green politics of that time within the anti-nuclear power movement and the Campaign for Nuclear Disarmament (you read more about this in the Introduction to the book).

I came across the term political intelligence in the 1980s. Although Nova Wholefoods did not appear to operate in a political environment, it was a fundamentally political enterprise. Our mission was to change the world through what people ate, knowing that this would have a positive impact on equality, cost of living, land use, health and climate. And workers' co-operatives are highly political, forging a different economics that is fair and equitable.

At Findhorn I had a crash course in leadership and that required political intelligence. Whether that was negotiating in consensus meetings or dealing with external criticism and attacks, I was developing my political intelligence. By the time I went to Teacher Support Network I was ready to operate in a more overtly political environment, negotiating with trade unions, government and the wider public sphere. This was absolutely necessary to achieve our aims.

Many social enterprises and wider third sector organisations operate in a political environment, or at the very least have politics that are central to their purpose and values. The ability to operate politically is an essential social entrepreneurship skill.

Learning #28: Social entrepreneurs can be impatient for growth

I have always been impatient. Ask my family to choose a few words to describe me and 'impatient' will almost certainly come up.

I've met a lot of entrepreneurs in social enterprises, charities and small to medium businesses, and many of them are impatient. Maybe the job requires impatience, or maybe it just suits impatient people.

Either way, I found that my impatience for growth helped growth to occur. Whether that is growth in impact, number of people we helped, problems solved, turnover and more. I am convinced that this was a positive use of my impatience.

Sometimes impatience is unhelpful. At Nova Wholefoods I was horribly impatient and expected our newly hired staff to work as hard and be as adaptable as me. Without anyone to coach my leadership style, I was impatient and decisive but lacking in relationship skills and sometimes basic compassion. My mindset was typically that I could do most people's jobs better than they could – a classic entrepreneur failure, for which my only excuse was that I was young and naïve (read more about this at 'Hiring people' in Chapter 4).

By the time I got to Teacher Support Network my impatience was tempered – but it was really needed. It's entirely possible that if I hadn't been so impatient to establish the counselling service, it may never have been launched.

I still have to watch out for the downside of this impatience. It has served me well but can get in the way.

Learning #29: Media training

In Learning #9 in Chapter 14 I describe myself as an 'on the job' learner. This has largely been the case in my career but there are a few notable exceptions. The most notable of these is media training.

Towards the end of my time at the Ecovillage there was a sustained attack on the integrity and legality of the organisation accompanied by a deluge of requests for media interviews, many of these combative. I quickly got some media training for myself and some others at the Foundation, which helped enormously. Just as well, as a week or so later I had a one-hour TV interview with BBC Scotland. I tried hard to avoid giving them a quote that would look bad on the news and was pleased that I didn't fall into that trap. But it was hard. I had never been so grateful for training before. You can read about this at 'The downside of recognition' in Chapter 22.

In the run up to the launch of Teacherline I got more training, this time for both Carol and me. We were put though our paces by a former TV interviewer. I learned to sit on my hands as I have a habit of using my hands when I'm talking, which is a bad look on TV.

Again it was incredibly helpful. On the day of the launch I had an hour on a combative radio phone-in show and managed to come over as a calm voice of reason, only because I had been briefed on how to avoid getting into a row on live radio.

Media training is a good example of a skill that needs updating all the time.

Learning #30: Ideas are often just around the corner

Social entrepreneurs are innovators. Being innovative means doing things differently or doing things that have never been done before. There is a lot written about inspiration, enterprise and innovation. But how does innovation occur?

My experience is that the best ideas are already close by. Frequently, looking at something in an inquisitive way helps me to see the previously unseen. Sometimes successful innovations are completely original, although for me more often they're not.

In my experience, the best innovations I have been involved in making happen came from ideas that were 'just around the corner'. These are typically neither original ideas nor did they stare me in the face. They were somewhere in between. They are ideas that are close by but not quite yet visible.

Often the idea is hinted at in a conversation. Or it may be an extension of what is already happening, just doing it differently. These ideas exist in a sort of mental, emotional or intuitive peripheral vision. Sometimes it's a feeling that just won't go away.

Teacherline and the Well Being Programme were the most successful services that Teacher Support Network launched. Both of these were hinted at in a snippet of a conversation (at 'Reserves policy' in Chapter 27 and 'Just around the corner' in Chapter 32). All I did was listen to that and then act. Often the role of the innovator is less having the idea than listening for it and making it happen. It was Thomas Edison the great inventor who said, "Genius is one per cent inspiration, ninety-nine per cent perspiration." He was right.

I keep looking around the corner.

Learning #31: Opening up to colleagues

A lot is said about the loneliness of leaders. I think this was particularly the case for me at Teacher Support Network as I was in a more traditional working environment. I did not have a business partner all the way through in the same way as I had with Paul at Nova, John at the Ecovillage and Rusty at Connect Assist.

In the middle of my time at teacher Support Network I went through a period when my mood was low. I shared how I was feeling with Lois, my coach. She recommended that I share how I was feeling with the management team. So I did. I told them that my mood was low. I told them that I had heard some negative comments about me and how that made me feel. I shared that I wasn't sleeping well. I felt vulnerable doing this. They were lovely and I received a lot of support. It helped.

I think even at that stage of my career I felt that as CEO I had to keep my emotions largely to myself. But that was a mistake. It was important to be able to open up to work colleagues, albeit that it's important to choose wisely which colleagues.

Learning #32: Raising investment

Raising investment for Worklife Support was the first time I had attempted this for a business start-up. I had been struggling to raise finance for some time until I received some help from a corporate finance adviser who reviewed my financial plan and gave me one of the best pieces of advice I've ever received.

"Find a way of doing everything you need to do for half the money, and I guarantee you'll get the investment"

He was right. I re-worked the numbers, sought funding for half the money and soon secured the investment required. I have subsequently shared this piece of advice with many social entrepreneurs.

As I recalled in Chapter 34, it took in all 10 months to raise the money to invest in and scale up the company. And it took up a lot of my time. Every potential investor had lots of questions and answering these involved spreadsheets and slide decks, as well as multiple meetings. It was a job in itself, and I was largely doing this on my own.

I was wise to this when I was raising funds to start up my next enterprise, Connect Assist (see Chapter 36, 'Raising the money'). But even so, that was complex and took the best part of a year.

It is easy to underestimate the work and time involved in raising finance for a social enterprise. And it is a job that has to be prioritised above all else, in order to meet the multiple demands of investors, financiers and banks.

Having said this, I would always encourage social entrepreneurs to borrow from banks and other lending institutions as early as possible in your career. The sooner you borrow, the stronger your credit record and reputation will be. My experience is that as I borrowed more it got easier. The first time I borrowed from NatWest Bank it was £100,000. Because I always repaid as agreed, I have borrowed many millions of pounds from them across 20 years for a variety of ventures.

Part Four: Charity helplines and job creation

"Is that one available" I asked

Chapter 36

Side project

From the moment of that drink with some of my management team onwards, I had two jobs – my day job (Teacher Support Network) and my side project (the new contact centre). It's extraordinary where the energy comes from, but I had a new purpose and threw myself into it. We would create a contact centre that would deliver what we wanted for Teacher Support Network, with full integration of all services, phone and digital.

Teacher Support Network was in good shape. My CEO day job was as full on as always, but Carol was doing great with Worklife Support, and Steve was looking after our services and operations. I was still spending a lot of time on speaking and media work but with amazing support from Vic as Director of Communications. The team was doing well.

Although I didn't have much time, I felt that I had more headspace. I could start to think about this new venture. As always in these situations, I built a spreadsheet. Over the next few years there were hundreds of versions of this.

I was backwards and forwards with John, who played a leading role in developing the thinking for the new venture. Although she was busy with Worklife Support, Carol was, as always, a brilliant sounding board. I spoke with David, who always had an ability to seek out what no one else had spotted. I was also talking with Stephen, our solicitor, who had a particular ability to come up with innovative legal and corporate solutions.

The benefit of having a lot of minds on a challenge is something that I have learned over the years. For me, the best innovations and enterprises are ones that have involved a lot of dialogue in both their conception and implementation.

However, despite all these brilliant minds, I kept feeling that there was something or someone missing. I could not quite put my finger on it. And then a strange thing happened.

One morning Steve came into my office. He sat down and told me that he had decided to leave. I knew that he had been training as a psychotherapist, which I fully supported, and that he wanted to pursue this as his career. So he had a side project too. Of course I was upset as working with Steve on the start-up of Worklife Support had been really creative.

And then I realised what was missing.

We needed to recruit someone to run the operations instead of Steve. I immediately thought of Rusty, who I had met in Geneva. We had stayed in touch so I knew that she had left Motorola. I messaged her and asked if she would be interested. She said yes.

This was brilliant. Although we had met only a few times since the conference, I knew instinctively that she was someone I could have a brilliant time creating an enterprise with. We had to follow due process on recruitment, so we put the job pack out and I sent Rusty a copy. We got back quite a few applications, including one from her.

On the day of the interviews we had four candidates shortlisted, including Rusty. But she didn't show up. What was going on? I had my PA keep trying to call her but there was no reply. Five days later I got a message that she had had a very nasty skiing accident and was in a Swiss hospital with her leg in plaster. She said to go ahead and appoint someone else.

I often wonder how the next year might have turned out if she had got the job.

Starting up

I was starting up another enterprise. Always my favourite position to be in, but this time I didn't really have the bandwidth to do it myself, and in any case I'm much better starting up with a business partner. The person we appointed to 'Rusty's job' was not the right person for this.

I made a move that was a mistake, although of course I didn't know that at the time. Never get someone to set up a business for you, only with you.

There had been quite a lot of preliminary work done on setting up the contact centre. I had a deadline to produce an outline business plan. There were four things that I had focused on.

First was vision. The vision for a holistic service would be front and centre in this new enterprise. We wanted to be in a position to help people with a wide range of challenges across all parts of their lives. Mental health, housing, finances, family problems, problems at work, bullying and harassment, disabilities and medical conditions to name just a few. While mental health would be a key part of the services we provided, it would be just one part.

Second was scale. I had worked up a number of scenarios for the new contact centre. These ranged from setting up a small in-house operation at one end of the spectrum to setting up a contact centre that would provide an outsourced helpline and digital services for many charities at the other.

The numbers suggested that the overheads of a small in-house operation would be very high and that the charity would lose the cost-benefits that it was getting from outsourcing, which we had done from the start. In other words, it would cost a lot more money, around 30% more.

303

The third area of focus was location. I wanted to create an enterprise that had as much benefit for its employees and their community as it would for charities and the people that they served and supported. If this was successful, we would need to employ a lot of people, so it made sense to look at an area of the UK that had high unemployment and lack of opportunity. We explored the West Midlands, the North West of England and the North East.

But we chose South Wales. This was one of the best business decisions of my life, although it was some time before I realised why. We chose it partly because it is two hours by train from London (where many of the UK's charities are based) and partly because it had a long history of high unemployment.

The fourth focus was technology. This would be vital to the success of the enterprise. With John's help, I came up with a very simple outline specification of what we thought we needed and asked Jason to research what would be the best options for us.

Teacher Support Network's helpline contract with PPC was up for renewal in early 2006. This was only a year away and ideally we would have to be up and running before then. That was a big ask, but I felt that if we missed the moment, we would lose the momentum.

I did what I thought was right and asked one of my senior team to take the lead on establishing the company. He lived in South Wales, so it made sense. We backfilled some of his job, and to his credit he threw himself into it.

His main areas of focus were to find premises, recruit to the key positions and work with Jason to make the technology decisions. I would focus on raising the money.

Raising the money

It wasn't that long since I had raised the investment for Worklife Support. That had taken a long time, and we didn't have that much time.

By then I was on about version 50 of the spreadsheet, which showed that we required around £1.3 million of investment to set up the company. I asked David if I could spend some time with him going through the numbers, and sure enough by the end of our session the sum we required was down at £870,000. That was still a lot of money to find for a start-up that hadn't started yet.

I began with the bank and went back to Gary, the manager. This time he was open to an unsecured loan. I had prepared a business plan and he promised to come back to me quickly.

In the meantime, there was a new business park being built at Nantgarw, near Pontypridd and Caerphilly and just north of the M4 motorway above Cardiff. The location looked good and so did the building. It also had the advantage of being in an area that was potentially eligible for some funding from the Welsh Development Agency (WDA).

I went to Cardiff to meet the WDA. They laid out a long list of reasons why we should locate the new business in South Wales and we discussed financing options. I then went to look at the premises. It was a new business park with a number of the buildings still under construction. I was shown the proposed building, which was around 6,000 square feet. There was one the same size across the road that was also being built, which had a car park against a woodland of beautiful trees.

"Is that one available?" I asked.

It was. And that is the one we went for. We took on the rent and responsibility for a building that realistically we only needed about one third of. We barely had the funds to pay the deposit. We would have to find tenants wanting to sub-let part of the building. Not for the first time, I took a risk on renting a building that was way too large.

It all comes together

It was the summer of 2005. I managed to take a holiday, although I'm not sure how as I was really busy. But it all started to come together.

Jason's team came up with a long list of possible technology platform providers. We required a telephony solution that would integrate with a customer relationship management system (CRM) that had digital channels and a knowledge base as standard (or 'out of the box' as it was named). They shortlisted to five and over that summer we met them all and had extensive demonstrations of the software. We decided to go with a platform none of us had heard of before called RightNow. This was also a good decision, again better than we could have imagined.

The trustees agreed that we should establish a contact centre that would provide an outsourced helpline and digital services for charities, not just Teacher Support Network's services. They agreed a three-year contract at a 10% cost reduction on what was being paid to the existing provider. We had everything in place – the building and technology platform, finance in principle agreed with NatWest Bank and WDA, a leasing company to pay for office fit-out and the technology and a fair amount of individual investment.

The problem is that each of the three external funders would not agree until the other two had. I met with them all, and I tried everything I could. We had deadlines to sign the lease on the building, to sign the RightNow contract and a start date of February 1st 2006 to begin

306

delivering the new Teacher Support Network service. It was stressful. It felt like it could all slip away.

I had a final call with Meurig, one the senior managers at WDA. I explained the situation in detail. I ended by saying, "If WDA doesn't jump first, the business will not launch, and that would be a massive loss to South Wales."

It was a risk, but sometimes laying it on the line is the only option.

"Leave it to me," he said.

"I need to know by Friday this week." It was Tuesday.

On the Thursday and Friday we had a two-day senior management and trustee meeting for Teacher Support Network. We had decided to have it in Cardiff. We were in the bar of the hotel on Thursday around 6pm when my phone rang.

"Check your email," said Meurig. "You've got your money."

Learning #33: Side projects

Many people start up their enterprise while doing another full-time job. It is typically a needs-must situation and gets called a 'side project'. Twitter and Instagram both started as side projects.

If I was in government, I would create some form of tax relief or grant incentive to support company employees to pursue side projects. I'm convinced this would unlock a lot of energy, creativity and enterprise.

Learning #34: Never ask someone to set up a business for you, only with you

I had assumed that Rusty would come to work with me at Teacher Support Network, and when she couldn't, I made a huge error. I felt

307

under pressure and panicked, making a decision that I soon realised was wrong. I had someone working for me rather than with me to set up the new venture. When it didn't go well, I felt that he was the wrong person. But it was me who made the mistake of appointing him to do this, and that was the greater error.

Rusty would take the challenging calls at any hour of the night

Chapter 37

First call

Following the visit to Wales to check out the premises for the contact centre, the next few weeks were frantic. I had to get the financials all in place, contracted and the money into a bank account. I got the lease agreed and signed. My manager became managing director (I'll call him MD) and he was really busy getting the building fitted out. He recruited for the main management roles and started recruiting for the ten staff we would need to deliver the Teacher Support Network service. We also needed tenants to sublet at least half of the building in order to make the numbers work.

MD worked with the local head of a government agency who was running a new project to support mental health at work in Wales and which rented space upstairs in the building. It had funding from the Welsh European Funding Office. I did not pay enough attention to this project – which again was an error. I was much more focused on the transfer of the Teacher Support Network service to the new company, which we named Link to Life. The name changed to Connect Assist in 2010.

In the first week of January 2006, I went to meet the new team. The building looked great, with almost all the work complete. MD had recruited some excellent people: Dee, who had worked for Teacher Support Cymru, and Sharon, who had come from Lloyds Bank, stayed with the business until long after I had left. But the people who had been recruited for the two main operational management roles were in my view not right. I spoke with MD about this, but he was convinced all would be OK.

I was conflicted between my intuition that all was not well and wanting to support MD and the team he had assembled. It has always been my view that it's best to support managers to do their job. In any case, I had assumed that MD would lead the company and that, once it was set up, I would step back into a non-executive role. He assumed that too.

There was an intensive month of training for the new staff, and on January 31st, six hours ahead of plan, the service was transferred from Teacher Support Network's existing provider and Link to Life took its first call.

Rusty

My intuition was correct. In the spring, John, who was by now a director of Link to Life, came over to Wales. We arranged for him to spend a week at the contact centre, and at the weekend MD, John and I had an off-site meeting. John confirmed my suspicions that MD wasn't up to the job and at the meeting we discussed this openly with MD who agreed to focus on sales. I negotiated an arrangement whereby I would be CEO of Link to Life two days a week and CEO of Teacher Support Network three days a week, with my salary and costs being paid in proportion.

Things moved fast after that. In September MD announced to me that he was leaving for a new job. I called John and told him. Then I remembered what should have happened two years before. I picked up the phone to Rusty. We hadn't spoken for a while, and I had no idea what she was doing workwise.

"Do you remember that company you were going to help me set up in Wales? How would you like to come and work here?"

I explained what had happened with MD. I reckoned that she could stay in London and like me could go to Wales part of the week, though I'm not sure I was altogether certain this would work for either her or the business.

312

"I've just accepted a job at Ernst and Young," she said.

That was a setback. I was silent for a minute.

"Could I persuade you to change your mind?"

She paused. "I'll think about it."

She did. We went backwards and forwards for some weeks. In the end, Rusty agreed to visit the contact centre. And then she joined the company. By then it was October, MD was still there and inevitably it was hard for both of them. About six weeks in she took me to one side and said,

"I don't think you have a viable business here."

That was a bit of a shock and we discussed what she meant. She meant that the operation needed a significant overhaul. Her plan was to move in to the business full-time to sort out the operation. She did not think she could sell to other customers before that was done, and it would take some time. This was the first of 11 years of tricky conversations. We haven't always agreed, but Rusty has the best instincts of anyone I have ever worked with. On that occasion I quickly agreed.

Rusty has an extraordinary ability with people, and she quickly gained the trust of our new employees. This was harder with the managers who had been hired at the start. Dee and Sharon got on well with Rusty, but the other two did not. One of them left soon after and months later sought to take the company to an employment tribunal but withdrew the case the day before it was due to be heard.

It would have been a very difficult time for Rusty. I was her CEO and her main customer, and that wasn't an easy dynamic for either of us, but particularly for her. I would arrive every one or two weeks. We would have dinner and she would tell me what was going on.

313

She was creating the building blocks of our subsequent success, creating a team that could deliver the quality of work required to help people in challenging circumstances. Rusty would take the most challenging calls at any hour of the day or night. It meant that callers received an extraordinarily professional service. This was one of the ways that she won over the majority of the staff.

Difficult two years

The mental health at work project was a muddle and we typically didn't get paid for months. The cashflow was really tight. At one point, we were called to a meeting about the project. The lead partner announced that we would not be paid what we were due. This was outrageous as they had been responsible for the mess that the project was in, cutting Link to Life out of the management. They owed us a six-figure sum and we faced bankruptcy if all or most of it was not paid.

I had spent much of my time for the company trying to find new customers or projects. We did all sorts of things that we hoped would bring in income. We did a piece of wellbeing work for a City bank, using the RightNow technology platform to deliver a 360-degree assessment programme. We started taking calls for a small coaching company. We had long discussions with a coaching company in the USA to be part of their supply chain. Rusty got some work with Beating the Blues, whose founder I had met in the USA, supporting clients using their online cognitive behavioural therapy product. There were other things we tried. They all helped us bring in some money, but we had really not found the direction for the company.

It was hard but it wasn't all bad news. We had kept a good relationship with the WDA, which had by then been absorbed into the Welsh Government. We were talking to them one day and they mentioned SMARTCymru. This was a grant programme that supported Welsh

314

businesses to develop, implement and commercialise new products, processes and services. I spoke to my old colleague Jason, who had helped me with the digital transformation of Teacher Support Network, and we came up with a scheme to create a social network based on coaching, going by the rather quaint name of 2isbetter. This was the early days of social networking and SMARTCymru liked the idea.

The idea never got off the ground, but a lot of good came out of it. We hired a young technical genius to run the project and he quickly got a handle on all of the company's technology. He was a director of the company when I left. We began to build a team of software developers, which laid the foundations for the company's technology business. And it was one of the few initiatives that kept us financially afloat in those difficult days.

Meanwhile, Teacher Support Network was using the contact centre as a showcase, which had always been part of the plan. I brought as many people as I could muster from the education and charity sectors to see what we were doing. Rusty, Dee, Sharon and the team always put on a brilliant visit. One of these was from officials from the two trade unions of staff in higher and further education, NATFHE and the Association of University Teachers (AUT), who were in the early stage of merger talks.

I was trying to persuade AUT, who had a wealthy welfare fund for members, to merge this with Teacher Support Network to create a new charity. They liked what they saw so much that this is what happened, creating a new helpline and in the process transferring their assets of over £1 million to Teacher Support Network.

A year later the new University and College Union (UCU) commissioned Link to Life to create a new database using the RightNow platform. This was the first time that we sold the RightNow platform to an organisation on its own and not as part of a helpline.

It was a turning point for the company. We had found a new service configuring databases, which would later turn out to be a major part for the company's work.

The main issue was that we were a business that was dependent on one contract (over 80% of our annual income). If we could not resolve that, the company would be over before it had got off the ground.

The situation was not sustainable. It wasn't OK or really fair for Rusty to be responsible for the operation and do all the business development, with a little help from me. But the business could not afford both of us. We had to do something.

I had always stayed in touch with the benevolent funds. These were charities like Teacher Support Network that gave financial support to particular groups of people, often those who worked or had worked in a specific industry or professional group. They had a membership organisation called the Association of Charitable Organisations. At a meeting with their director, I was sharing what we were doing at Link to Life.

"Have you met Turn2us?" she asked.

I had not even heard of them.

She made an introduction and a few weeks later I met their CEO. Turn2us were a new initiative of the Elizabeth Finn Care charity. They were in the early stages of setting up a website and helpline that would provide benefit checks and access to grants to people in financial hardship.

Jolanta was very interested in what we were doing and told me that they would shortly be issuing a tender for a consultant to help them design their helpline. Would I be interested in applying? Of course I said yes.

By the time I was off the phone she had bought two more glasses

Chapter 38

Turn2us

Rusty and I made a proposal for the consultancy work. It was the helpline that we were really interested in, but this was the only way that we could get their attention. We had to grapple with the potential conflict of interest. Would we be in a position to recommend outsourcing their helpline when we were a helpline outsourcer? We decided to be up front about this, giving Turn2us the opportunity to decide whether they saw this as a conflict. Rusty and I drafted the proposal but decided to bring in another consultant who we knew well to add independence, and she and I went to the pitch.

The pitch went well. One of the panel members was a consultant who had helped with the initial strategy for Turn2us. He was fascinated that we used the RightNow digital platform. After the pitch was over, he sought us out and we spoke a lot about it. He was very keen on this software, which was a big plus for us.

We didn't win the consultancy work, but we were on their radar. A few months later, they called us to say that the tender process was beginning. The tender was for an initial pilot programme, and they planned to scale up if the pilot was a success. They hoped that we would be submitting a tender response.

Of course we were.

Rusty and I worked hard drafting what we thought was a strong response to their requirements. I had previously written grant applications, business plans and impact reports, but this was my first tender.

The helpline would support people in difficult financial circumstances by taking callers through a review of whether they were receiving the correct state benefits, using benefit checker software developed by Turn2us. Huge numbers of people were not receiving the benefits they were entitled to. The helpline also planned to help callers find sources of funding from over 3,000 grant-making charities.

We had a fair bit of knowledge from our money advice work. My background as the founder of Teacherline was very helpful. But Link to Life was a new, small business and there were more established companies that would almost certainly be a safer bet for Turn2us. We had to make a virtue of our size and youth, so we spoke to our ability to be a collaborative partner, allowing us to be flexible in a way that a pilot helpline would require. As our second-largest customer, they would get attention that would be unlikely if they were a smaller customer among many others. Finally, we wrote about our values focusing on creating jobs in the Welsh Valleys and why that was important.

We had never costed a tender of this nature before and we called up everyone we knew who could help us. We had to find a price that would be competitive up against much larger companies, while at the same time making us money.

We submitted the tender documents and were called for a presentation and interview. We had the last interview slot of the day at their offices in Kensington. The advantage of this slot is that it means you can have a peek in the visitors' book at reception and spot your competitors. We recognised two of them.

There was a lot at stake for us that afternoon. It was a curious feeling pitching for a large contract knowing that the future of our company depended on it. I was nervous and hoped that this didn't show. Rusty did an amazing job of convincing them that we were a safe pair of hands. We seemed to get a positive response and answered a lot of questions. When we came out after an hour, we felt pleased about our performance and very nervous about the outcome.

It was late afternoon and we hadn't had lunch. We went to a pub across the road and had a bite to eat and a glass of wine each. We were uncharacteristically silent, but we both knew this would be make or break for the business.

My phone rang. It was Jolanta. "We would like you to be our helpline provider and partner."

I looked across at Rusty with a huge smile while I continued speaking with Jolanta. By the time I was off the phone, Rusty had bought two more glasses.

Manic Depression Fellowship

The Manic Depression Fellowship, now named Bipolar UK, is a charity focused on direct service provision to meet the needs of individuals affected by bipolar disorder. Rusty had made contact with them and they were keen to have us run a 24/7 helpline for them. She hosted a visit to our contact centre by their trustees, where her background and expertise in mental health and social work went down very well.

We launched the second week of May 2008 with a relatively small helpline. We were expecting approximately 100 calls a month based on their current size. What they failed to tell us was that they had been consulting with the BBC Eastenders team on a bipolar story around the characters Stacey and her mother Jean.

The story aired on the Friday that week. The charity's new helpline number was posted at the end of the episode. We took an entire year's worth of our target helpline call volumes over that weekend. Rusty, Sharon and the team were amazing.

Going full-time

It was getting harder for me to do two jobs. The trustees of Teacher Support Network were happy with this, and in any case my salary was being paid by both organisations, but I was feeling dragged in two directions. I spoke with Rusty about leaving Teacher Support Network and moving to Link to Life full-time.

This wasn't an easy conversation. She had effectively led the business through its first two years and had turned it into a business capable of winning Turn2us and other customers. She had turned the staff she had inherited into a high-performing team. She had put strong clinical governance and processes into place. She was well liked by our customers.

I wasn't sure how my working full-time would be for her. A great business partnership takes time to develop and, because of the odd situation of me having two jobs, I hadn't given this as much attention as I should have done.

But we both agreed that the Turn2us win was a turning point and that it was time for me to come on board full-time. I would focus on sales and finances, with her focusing on operations, account management and people. We would run the business together.

I joined Link to Life full-time at the end of April. I met with the managers on my first day and made it clear that my job would be to focus 100% on growing the business and getting us on a sustainable footing. We were committed to creating jobs and growth opportunities in the Valleys and that is what I would focus on. That would mean that I would expect to be on the road doing sales and business development most of the time.

"If you see me in the office more than a day or two a week, please come and ask me why I'm not doing my job," I said to them all.

There were no weeks in the next nine years when they needed to ask.

We were on track to turn over £1.3 million that year and were growing for the first time in two years. But we were highly dependent on one contract, with it representing 80% of that turnover. Although the Turn2us pilot was going well, there was little indication as to how much or how fast this would grow, if at all. We were not as financially stable as any of us would have liked.

Learning #35: Consulting as a means to win work

Early on at Link to Life (Connect Assist) we used consulting as a means of winning what turned out to be a significant customer, Turn2us. While we did not win the consulting work, the charity discovered who we were.

We quickly found that in order to win a sale of a service to most charities, we needed to spend time with them listening to what their challenges were, dialoguing with them about solutions and ultimately co-designing the new service with them.

It was a good approach, and it became a key part of the process of winning a number of our larger customers.

Learning #36: Be up front with customers

When we pitched for the Turn2us consulting work we had to be up front about a potential conflict of interest. How could we recommend outsourcing their helpline when we were a helpline outsourcer? We decided to give Turn2us the opportunity to decide for themselves whether they saw it as a conflict.

We continued this approach after that. My experience is that customers appreciate straightforward discussion rather than a traditional sales pitch that might fudge difficult issues such as conflicts of interest.

Learning #37: Understand the finances

For all the enterprises that I have set up, and for most of the other organisations I have run, I have been the financial manager alongside the day job. We grew Connect Assist with me as finance director as well as CEO, and it served us well.

I am not suggesting that every social entrepreneur should be their own finance director. But I do recommend developing a good understanding of the enterprise's finances. Understanding the profit and loss, balance sheet, cashflow and sales pipeline on a monthly basis is vital. I have always needed a strong understanding of these to make good financial decisions, in order to react appropriately to challenging situations and to convince banks, investors, customers and other external stakeholders that I have a grip on the finances.

I always recommend to social entrepreneurs that I meet that they can answer financial questions immediately with a current knowledge of their financial position. In my experience this gives people confidence like little else.

Connect Assist Rebrand

Chapter 39

Sales

By mid 2009 we were nearly 30 people working at Link to Life, new jobs we had created in three and a half years. This felt like a big achievement. But it was still a hard slog to grow the business.

The Turn2us pilot was looking successful, and we were in discussions with them about scaling up this service. This took up a lot of Rusty's time as well as managing the ongoing relationship with Teacher Support Network. I typically spent Monday in the office catching up with Rusty and the team there. I would then get the train to London and spend three days visiting charities, attending networking events and doing everything possible to create opportunities for us to find new work.

Rusty and I spoke a few times most days, typically on the phone. We weren't great fans of meetings. While meetings are of course at times necessary, I have found that there is an inverse relationship between the amount of time spent in meetings and the level of real communication. Short, regular spoken communication works best for me (and preferably not email), and it turned out for her too.

Around this time Rusty called to say that she had found someone that I should talk to. He had applied for a contact centre team leader job but she felt that he would make a great salesperson. She asked him in again and this time the three of us met. I agreed with her and we hired Adam.

Adam had a background in telephone sales and within a few weeks he was calling around 50 charities a week to arrange meetings for me. He was targeted to get three meetings a week for me, but regularly got five. It was a busy time as typically these charities required multiple meetings and proposals before a decision was made. I had been a charity chief executive for ten years, so had a degree of understanding of this, but it did mean that it was taking on average nine months between a first meeting and signing a contract.

Sales were challenging. We were sometimes trying to persuade a charity to set up a helpline for the first time. Or we were trying to persuade them to outsource their existing helpline, which was being delivered by their own employees in-house. More often than not there was shock or even outrage at this suggestion. Selling our helpline offering was harder than I thought it would be.

A rebrand works well

We had to up our game. We needed a number of smaller customers to balance out the two large ones we had. We needed to get a more coherent message to the market.

Rusty had been introduced to Paul, a local marketing specialist, who came to meet us. He brought a very different perspective and asked us many questions about who we were and what we did that I struggled to come up with coherent answers to.

Paul helped us come up with a new name, Connect Assist, that we were really happy with. But more importantly, he helped us look at how we were communicating what we could do for charities and other customers. We described these in three simple products:

- Multi-channel helplines.

- Digital service delivery.

- Online organisational feedback.

These contained a bit too much jargon for my liking, but they worked. It suggested that we had an offering that was beyond the traditional telephone helpline. We were by now using digital communication including web chat, text messages and online information, advice and

328

guidance. We could collect feedback about organisations and their clients online and present it in an engaging manner.

It began to work. We created a demonstration website that I could take to meetings. I was able to show charities how they could use their website and helpline in an integrated manner to give their clients more choice to get support and advice more quickly, and importantly **help more people for less cost.**

This last factor was really important. The impact of the 2008 financial crisis was severe and many organisations, especially charities, were having to manage with less income, at a time when demand for services was high. This accelerated in 2010 with the coalition government and the adoption of austerity as a deliberate policy.

We had a solution. We could either deliver a fully digital helpline at around 30% less cost than most charities could do it themselves, or if they didn't want to outsource to us, we could help them gain some of these efficiencies by developing the digital elements of their own helpline.

From early 2010 we started using this approach and found that there was a lot more interest. Adam was finding it easier to get meetings and I was doing a lot more of them. Many more charities wanted to come and visit us at Connect Assist and see for themselves how we operated. Rusty was busy hosting visits, which she did an extraordinary job of, sometimes hosting two or even occasionally three organisations on the same day.

When people came to visit us, it was a game changer. After a coffee, Welsh cake, introduction and signing of a non-disclosure agreement, Rusty would take them into the contact centre where they could put on a set of headphones and hear both sides of a helpline call. It was transformational. They would come back into our meeting room after 30 minutes of this and be so impressed that they would start telling us what they wanted us to do for them.

329

We had found an approach to converting interest into opportunities and then into customer relationships. We offered partnership, which meant that we would work closely with each charity to create and deliver the uniqueness of their service. This might mean who we employed on their helpline service, what hours it was open, how their website changed to deliver their service and much more.

Innovation

Innovation is a word that's used a lot in enterprise. There are a few different definitions but as far as I can see it boils down to this: Innovation is the implementation of something new. At the heart of Connect Assist's offer was our approach to innovation. Our starting point was to understand how we could help our clients do something new. That made our job not just easier but far more interesting.

During my first year full-time in the business, I began to find my voice and approach. It emerged, meeting by meeting. In my early meetings I started by talking about myself, what I had done at Teacher Support Network and how we were applying this at Connect Assist. This wasn't bad, in so far as I had a strong and positive reputation. It's often what got me through the door.

Adam, Rusty and I worked on the messaging in advance of getting meetings. On the phone, Adam would cover the ground in terms of what Connect Assist was about and seek to arrange a meeting with me.

I would then start the meeting by finding out as much as possible about what each charity's challenges were. Were they finding it harder to raise funds? Were they struggling to meet growing demands for their services? Did they need to cut costs? Were they unhappy with their digital presence? Were their service users demanding different services?

330

I found that charity CEOs and directors really wanted to talk about these and other questions. Sometimes 45-minute meetings stretched to a couple of hours. They wanted these discussions, and Rusty and I were able to give them that time. Sometimes we started co-designing some new approach, process, service or digital component during these meetings. We were innovating, typically piecing together a new solution using some existing components of the charity, some of what we could provide and discussing how to make these work to solve challenges.

Sometimes we just helped them talk through a problem or challenge that we would be unlikely to directly help them with, but we provided a sounding board. Either way it was great.

I was enjoying myself. I had worked as a charity CEO in London for over ten years, but I had spent more quality time with charity leaders in those six months than I had in all those years. I began to learn a lot and gain significant insights. And more and more charities came to visit the contact centre.

They were not only charities. There was one piece of innovation that stands out from this time, from a part of the National Health Service.

NHS Plus

NHS Plus was established in 2009 to deliver the Health for Work Adviceline in England for employers of small and medium-sized businesses. It was an occupational health advice service, with a focus on mental ill health and musculoskeletal problems. The Adviceline covered all aspects of health that employers needed to understand, including employment and health and safety legislation. It was funded by the Department for Work and Pensions (DWP)[19] with a fairly substantial budget, and the service was subcontracted to NHS Direct,[20] a nursing helpline.

Following the 2010 general election there was significant downward pressure on all government budgets and the Health for Work Adviceline was no exception. They came to visit Connect Assist to discuss how they would meet their new budget target to cut the costs of their operations to 25% of what they were now while at the same time creating a dramatic increase in the number of business owners contacting the service. It seemed like an impossible task.

This was just the sort of challenge that we liked and we were getting confident at designing and delivering to meet these. We spent an afternoon with their team at our contact centre and by the end we had a plan. There was a very tight time pressure to deliver this, including securing agreement from the DWP, so a good proposal had to be created, which we drafted for them.

From our perspective the solution was straightforward. We would build a new Health for Work website that had a solid library (or knowledge base) of information and guidance, and then add in email and web chat alongside the telephone service.

We located the front end of the service (phone, email and web chat) in our contact centre, with complex advice cases being transferred in real time to a small group of occupational health nurses.

Best of all, we got this new service live in two months as there was a budget deadline. The total cost including the contact centre, nurses, website, content and database was under 25% of their previous budget.

NHS Plus were delighted as we had saved the Adviceline. The Department for Work and Pensions were delighted as they saved on cost. Unfortunately, the nurses weren't happy, feeling that their professional position was being undermined by having Connect Assist's advisers taking all the initial calls. However, after a few months they were delighted as they were only taking cases that they were uniquely qualified to advise on.

In early 2010 Adam secured me a meeting with the Royal British Legion. I went to their office on Borough High Street in London and had a very stimulating two hours. They asked me to come back to present to members of their senior team. Of course I said yes.

That was the start of a three-year pre-sales engagement with the Royal British Legion. The best was yet to come.

By the middle of 2011 we had created 41 jobs

Chapter 40

Values at the heart of the enterprise

In the midst of the hard work and constant demand of running a business, it was sometimes possible to forget why we were doing it. However, every new job created was a reminder. By the middle of 2011 we had created 41 jobs, which we were very excited about. This is why we had set up in the Welsh Valleys, and it was working.

And we weren't just creating jobs. We were creating growth opportunities for the people who came to work at Connect Assist. Rusty was the driving force, seeking opportunities for professional development and promotion of our people. One of our initial staff team, Sharon, had become contact centre manager. Steve, who initially joined for the social media project, was running technology, both for the contact centre and for our rapidly growing digital service and CRM system business.

But it didn't stop there. I have never met anyone who has such an understanding of and dedication to diversity as Rusty. She would hire advisers who lived with disabilities, life-limiting health conditions or other barriers to employment. She wanted to give everyone possible the chance to work with us, particularly those that other employers might be wary of employing.

That year we undertook a survey of our workforce. Some 45% had joined us after a period of long-term unemployment and 30% had a life-limiting health condition or disability. One of our longest-serving team members joined us after a very long period of unemployment as a result of a serious kidney condition. He was in and out of hospital for a long time, but we always kept his job open. He became one of our top performers.

Rusty was a legend in the local job centre. She hired a call adviser with Tourette's syndrome, which surprised many, but he eventually became a team leader. At one stage we employed a woman with quadriplegia, who was not only an outstanding call adviser but was training as a counsellor, and once qualified she left us to pursue that career.

Rusty made it her business to learn about the life story of all our staff members. She discovered that a significant number of their families were financially dependent on the one salary that they were earning from us. Rusty therefore created a 'friends and family' recruitment incentive and, as soon as we could create the jobs, we had a number of families with two or three people working with us, often across more than one generation.

For us, as well as every other business, managing cashflow was absolutely vital. But the cash situation of a business is all too often a well-kept secret, known only by directors and the bank manager. We took a different approach. We were up front about our cashflow and approach to managing our finances with employees and customers, making it clear that this meant that no employee or customer would ever face a sudden financial shock (as subsequently happened with our closest competitor). Our employees really valued this as so many of them had faced multiple redundancies in former jobs, to the extent that they typically asked questions about cashflow in staff meetings. Customers valued our being open about this, evidenced by the fact that invoices were almost always paid on time.

When customers or potential customers visited the contact centre and listened in on calls, they regularly commented on the empathy of our call advisers. They were of course very well trained and supported by Rusty and Sharon, but their empathy was typically a key part of their personality before they came to work for us.

Empathy was one of the core values of Connect Assist and we applied it across the entirety of the business. Despite the additional work and administration involved, we also adopted an environmental standard, displaying the ethic of least negative impact on the environment and our locality.

This approach built staff confidence. Rusty took her turn taking calls in the contact centre, which also won staff confidence. We did all business travel by train. One of the particular successes was a democratisation such that no one person in the hierarchy was so important that they couldn't travel on a second-class train. These decisions matter.

In 2001 Save the Children reported that in Rhondda Cynon Taf, where we were located, 17% of children lived in extreme poverty. And in 2019 research conducted by the End Child Poverty Network found that Wales was the only UK nation to see a rise in child poverty over the previous year, with the worst electoral ward being in Rhondda Cynon Taf (at 47%). We had located in one of the poorest areas in the whole of Europe. One result of this was that most of our advisers had life experience of much of what they were presented with by callers to the helplines.

It took us time, but we began to talk about this. We started any presentation or proposal talking about the reasons for locating in the Welsh Valleys. We talked about the qualities of our people, their lived experiences and empathy. We gave charities and other potential customers a picture of what they would be part of by working with Connect Assist.

It was a compelling narrative, and it was a key part of our growth. I had worked my whole career in social enterprises with social and environmental values, but there had always been something missing. I never really understood what it was until then. Connect Assist was values-driven through and through, in what we did, how we did it and the difference it made to everyone involved – our staff, our charity customers, their clients and service users, and the community that we were based in.

Learning #38: Empathy is a leadership superpower

Empathy is incredibly important in leadership. It means that in every circumstance I learned to really listen to what people are saying, sense what they are feeling and try at all times to have a clear understanding of their lived reality, what they are experiencing in that moment or in their lives as a whole.

Empathy is the ability to understand another person's thoughts and feelings in a situation from their point of view, rather than your own. It is not the same as sympathy, where we may be moved by someone's thoughts and feelings while nonetheless maintaining emotional distance. At the end of the book is a link to a nice article on empathy if you want to read more.

Empathy with staff and work colleagues is important as it builds trust. As a social entrepreneur, the team looked to me for leadership and reassurance, but most of all understanding and empathy. If I could offer that most of the time, it helped build a team that people wanted to be part of.

The same applies across all parts of the business. Empathy was a core behaviour of Connect Assist across the business and what we looked for when recruiting. Customers, employees, suppliers, colleagues and even departing customers commented on the empathy that they felt from the business as a whole. It was a core part of our success.

We could put the VQ-80 in our customer's list.

We could put NCVO on our customer list

Chapter 41

Enterprise growth

National Council for Voluntary Organisations

Around this time Connect Assist won a small but significant piece of work.

The National Council for Voluntary Organisations (NCVO) champions the not-for-profit sector. They have a diverse community of over 14,000 member organisations employing over a third of the voluntary sector workforce in England.

For some years they had operated a helpdesk service that took calls and emails from members asking questions on a range of issues, including funding, employment, governance and more. It was outsourced to a larger company. The contract came up for re-tender. It would be a new departure for Connect Assist, as it was much more of an information service rather than support for challenging circumstances, but we went for it as we were keen to build a relationship with NCVO.

It was a big day for us when we won the tender, following a detailed proposal and presentation to NCVO at their London office. We implemented the service and soon were advising charity managers and trustees. And we could put NCVO on our customer list.

But it didn't end there. Some months after we had started delivering the NCVO member helpdesk, I met up with their director of membership and enterprise. This led to Connect Assist becoming a trusted supplier of NCVO, and that endorsement was extremely valuable.

NCVO were keen to help us promote our work. They had seen what we were achieving for their member helpdesk, so I started delivering a series of workshops on making charitable services digital.

They were a great success and got us in front of about 20–30 charities for a couple of hours every six weeks or so. It was a great way to promote Connect Assist as well as learn a lot about the challenges faced by charities. NCVO's CEO Stuart would typically come and introduce each workshop.

Tender writing

We were beginning to regularly submit responses to tender proposals. Prior to the Turn2us contract, I had never submitted a tender response but this activity was to become a big part of my life for the next seven years.

Tendering refers to the process whereby governments, companies and charities invite supplier organisations to submit bids for projects within a finite deadline. A tender proposal typically takes a few weeks to complete and mostly involves providing a detailed response to a large number of questions asking how we would fulfil the requirements of the service, including operations, quality and cost, as well as our qualifications and experience as a company.

When you are a small and less experienced company this is difficult. There are a number of barriers, not least a horrible little test called 'financial standing'. This is designed for the purchasing organisation to avoid becoming a large customer for a small supplier, and it was a problem we had to overcome. Rusty and I decided that the best way to overcome this problem was to partner with larger organisations and we started looking for potential partners, otherwise we would not stand a chance.

I have found over the years that often when I make a decision, an opportunity to test whether that is a good decision comes quickly.

Happy Tender Christmas

I could write a whole book about the procurement industry. There are of course many advantages for government and other organisations in terms of seeking best value. But there are a number of apparent habits of procurement managers that as a supplier are problematic, especially for small businesses.

The worst habit is the Christmas and summer holiday deadlines. I can understand that, from the perspective of a procurement manager, getting a tender document and specification produced is a big job, and so for them the Christmas or summer holidays are a hard deadline. But in this case the deadline is set with no thought for the supplier, who might also have family or holiday plans.

My first experience of this was in December 2011. In the same week we were notified of two large government contracts, both of which we felt, with the right partner, we had a chance of winning.

The deadline for submission was in early January. I had a family Christmas followed by my first holiday in a long time, as did Rusty. I called up the procurement manager for each of the contracts and tried to negotiate extensions of their deadlines. Neither of them would budge.

Adam, Rusty and I looked at it. Our largest contract was up for re-tender the next year, so we really needed to win another large contract in case we lost that. We made calls to our largest two customers, who agreed to partner with us.

We then timetabled the tender writing. There was nothing for it but to devote much of our Christmas holidays to this.

All three of us wrote elements of the two tenders and once we were back in January we compared them and spent the next week and a half finalising the responses. We negotiated the partnership agreements.

We submitted both tenders, were shortlisted and went to the final presentations.

In the end we won the contract for the Money Advice Service (MAS) contact centre, in partnership with Turn2us. It was a big step up for both our organisations. Interestingly, MAS told us that as well as a very competent tender response, they were very attracted to our values and the fact that they too would be creating jobs in the Welsh Valleys.

The digital business takes off

We had been using the RightNow digital CRM system since we started in 2006 and had become a UK implementation partner. RightNow held a conference each year and a few of us went. It was an opportunity to learn more about the software and where it was heading. We were always excited to know what new functionality would be available in the next year and how this would be of value to our charity customers.

By the end of 2011 we had 11 organisations using the RightNow software and had become one of the more active members of the implementation partner network. We had started to build a reputation as a successful configurer and developer of RightNow.

We were at the annual RightNow conference in late October 2011 with our developer and sales teams plus a number of our customers who used the software. We were completely surprised when they announced that RightNow was being sold to Oracle, one of the largest software companies in the world.

I was momentarily concerned that we could lose a business that we were gently building up. But I didn't need to worry as by the end of the conference we had a number of RightNow's larger customers approach us to develop and support the RightNow applications in their organisations.

By the end of 2012 we had added a further ten customers for whom we were developing, implementing and supporting RightNow. These included a number of charities including Beatbullying, Chartered Accountants Benevolent Association (CABA) and Licensed Trade Charity but also private and public sector organisations including Sussex Police, Travelport and Sitel. This work accounted for nearly 15% of our turnover and was growing fast. It was also delivering a higher percentage gross profit margin.

We closed the year of 2012 with turnover of over £2.5 million and 76 jobs. This was quite an achievement, as we lost our first customer to another provider that year, but such was the growth of the business that we did not lose any jobs as a result.

Learning #39: Find a higher-margin product or service

Most social entrepreneurs are looking to grow and scale their enterprise. The challenge is how to do this. Growth requires investment and investment requires profitability.

Very early in my career I discovered the value of the high-margin product. At Nova Wholefoods, trail mix was our highest gross margin product. We could mark up the ingredients at a higher price than selling them individually. I'm convinced that without this additional profit we would have struggled to finance the growth of the business.

Ever since then I have looked for the high-margin product or service to support business growth, and when I have found it, up have gone the profits and the cash balances. At Connect Assist we found a higher-margin service in our digital services development.

The procurement process forces enterprises to push down the gross margin percentage, particularly when you are a small or medium enterprise competing against larger companies. There is a real need to find a service or product that delivers a higher profit margin as a counterbalance. This approach always worked for me.

Learning #40: Stay on top of digital and IT projects

Today the majority of social entrepreneurs have grown up in the era of digital technology, mobile phones and easy-to-use software and applications. Despite this, I still hear of time and money wasted on failed technology procurements and implementations.

I did not grow up in that era so had to learn the hard way, when my first computerised business process failed (which you can read about in Chapter 9). Ever since then I have made it my business to understand any technology, software and hardware that my enterprise has to design, purchase, implement or operate. Not to the level of code writing, but in all cases to use, and many cases to be able to configure to meet the needs of the business.

I am not mistrustful of technology and digital experts, but I insist that they explain themselves in normal, jargon-free language. I want to be able to use the systems to a reasonable level.

I have generally found that technology experts come to respect me because I make an effort to speak their language and understand what they are telling me. I make the effort to learn how to use the systems that they have implemented. Digital empathy.

It was therefore a big day when I got this feedback from a digital consultant who had helped us implement a customer relationship management (CRM) system:

> *In a world of talkers, Patrick is a doer. He is extremely innovative, pioneering and loves technology. How many CEOs do you know who hands-on manage and use their CRM? That's Patrick.*

Setting up in the valley was probably the best business decision of my career.

Setting up in the Valleys was probably the best business
decision of my career

Chapter 42

Welsh Valleys again

I wrote in Chapter 39 that choosing South Wales as our business location for Connect Assist was one of the best business decisions of my life, but it was some time before I realised why.

At the time, the decision was made because the Welsh Valleys had a long history of high unemployment, in particular since the closure of the coal mines in the early 1980s, which I had become very aware of when working with mining families at Nova (in Chapter 3). There were other reasons too, including easy access to London, where most charities, our customers, were based.

We made much of why we had located there to create jobs in an area that needed them. We also made a lot of the fact that we created growth opportunities for the people we employed. All of our managers and team leaders were people who had joined in entry-level jobs, and they got promoted because they were incredibly talented, as well as hard working. One of the problems of high unemployment is that this talent rarely gets an opportunity to thrive. It was beginning to be clear that this was perhaps one of our greatest achievements.

When I say 'our' achievements, in reality the bulk of the credit for this must go to Rusty. Yes, I had created the context for this, but it was Rusty who spotted talent that our people in many cases didn't know they had, and then nurtured it. Today the company is almost entirely led and managed by these people.

However, perhaps the main reason why locating there was such a great decision is empathy. In Chapter 40 I referenced the role of empathy as a core value of Connect Assist. The core of our work was supporting people in sometimes extremely challenging circumstances, and that required a high degree of empathy on the part of the adviser on the phone. We didn't use scripts, as most contact centres do. We expected, trained and coached our advisers to empathise with the callers, gain their trust and gently but with purpose lead them to a place where they could receive support, guidance and the beginning of a way out of the challenges they faced.

We found that this quality of empathy was in the heart of many of the people of the Welsh Valleys. And that's why setting up in the Valleys was probably the best business decision of my career.

Blended team

By the spring of 2012 we were running 20 helplines from the contact centre. We had three teams working there. Turn2us had a dedicated team, Money Advice Service had a dedicated team and the remainder of the helplines were managed by what we called a blended team.

Each team had its areas of expertise and particular qualities, but the blended team required a particular set of skills. They had to be able to swap between different customer helplines from one call to another. Our computer voice system would deliver a call or email to an adviser who was available. Their computer screen would identify which phone line the call was coming from and show the relevant CRM screen so that they could start answering that call and collect appropriate data while they were speaking. There would be days when they could answer calls from ten to 15 different organisations. These helplines fell into two types of service, which we called transactional and transformational.

Transactional services were those where we were largely providing information and a degree of advice, but where it was unlikely that our advisers would be called upon to offer emotional support to an individual. These included services such as the NCVO member helpdesk and a number of employment-related services.

Transformational services were those where the caller would be likely to present with a set of challenging circumstances for which they needed support. At that stage in our journey these were largely the helpline of an industry benevolent or welfare charity, which included the food industry, the accountancy profession, and the licensed premises and hospitality trades. We ran an extraordinary service called Txtm8, a text message service for young people who had questions about their health, in particular sexual health advice. We ran a service commissioned by Save the Children called Eat, Sleep, Learn, Play!, which provided essential household items such as cookers, children's beds, books and toys to the UK's poorest children.

Often our blended team call\advisers would be a first source of support before perhaps transferring the caller on to speaking with one of our counsellors, getting them access to grants or benefits or some other intervention. Sometimes this meant linking up with the support staff of the charity whose helpline they had called. Either way, this was a set of helplines where there was a lot of challenge and complexity that the advisers needed to manage.

On top of this there would be regular high-risk situations. At the start of each call, the caller was read a short statement about confidentiality, so that they knew that in almost all cases we would not divulge any details from the call. At the same time we made it clear when we would be forced to break confidentiality if the adviser felt that there was a risk of harm to the caller themselves or to anyone else as a result of their circumstances.

These circumstances could include risk of suicide, self-harm and disclosure of current or historical abuse. The blended team had to be ready for such calls, even if days went by before they received one. It takes a special kind of person to do this, and in many ways I think the greatest achievement of Connect Assist is that Rusty recruited, taught, trained and coached exceptional people who could handle the extreme nature of such calls while at the same time dealing with the complexity of working in the blended team.

351

The Royal British Legion has extremely high brand awareness
and that is because of the Poppy Appeal

Chapter 43

The year of the Legion

Money Advice Service challenges

Implementing the Money Advice Service (MAS) contract was a significant challenge throughout 2012. Initially there was an expectation that there would be a volume of calls, emails and web chats for a team of over 50 people and we had been scaling up to meet this demand. We were part way through the scaling-up process in the autumn when we were suddenly informed by MAS that these volumes would not be achieved. We had to make a number of our new staff redundant, which was not something we were happy about. Then MAS demanded that we hire more staff, despite the fact that they did not contractually have to pay us for these.

This was our first experience of delivering a major public sector contract, and under pressure we had signed a highly complicated and frankly one-sided contract. It was a very steep learning curve for us and a very tough time for everyone. Rusty and I had to balance the demands from the customer, the needs of our staff and the financial risk. There were some very difficult conversations and sleepless nights.

It took another year before we could stabilise the impact this had on us. For that year we were losing a lot of money on this contract, which was very challenging for the business, but eventually we managed to renegotiate the fees. Great credit should go to the contact centre team who worked on this and really did a brilliant job of rising to the many challenges presented by this service. Today, some of Connect Assist's most talented staff started with us on this contract.

The longest opportunity

Meanwhile, I was still spending the majority of my time visiting new charities and other potential customers. By mid 2012 we had 32 customers that we were providing services to and in addition we would typically be pursuing around 50 potential opportunities at any one time.

I had designed a sales pipeline methodology that worked well in terms of predicting the financial performance of the company. Its basic principles were as follows:

- If we had a successful initial meeting with a customer that led to a visit, activity or second meeting, we would estimate the size of the contract and assign 10% income and direct costs (people and technology) to the financial forecast for the year.

- If we were asked to produce a proposal or quotation, or were shortlisted as part of a tender process, that figure would rise to 33%.

- Once the customer had agreed that they wanted to go ahead and sign a contract with us (verbally or in writing) the figure would rise to 70%. You would be surprised how many organisations said they wanted to sign a contract with us and then not do so.

- Only when a contract was signed would it go in at 100%.

We reviewed all the sales opportunities at a monthly sales meeting. Opportunities would move up and sometimes back down the various levels of the sales pipeline, depending on where we were in discussions or negotiations. Typically, a sales opportunity would disappear after six to nine of months of low activity. Other entrepreneurs I have met have commented that they think this approach is pessimistic – but it worked so well that we always met our sales and profit targets each year.

There was, however, one opportunity that stayed in the pipeline for three years. There were occasional discussions about whether I should stop spending time on this, but we always agreed that I should persevere.

It was the right decision. It turned into the most high-profile, most exciting and largest ever contract of mine and Rusty's time at Connect Assist.

Back in early 2010, Adam had secured me a meeting with the Royal British Legion. I spent the best part of two hours talking to one of their managers, a former army officer, and his colleague.

A few months later I went back to do a presentation for a number of the Royal British Legion operations team, including their director of operations. She discussed their latest strategy, Pathway for Growth, which was focused on putting the beneficiaries of the Legion at the heart of the charity. The talk was of having a contact centre as the first port of call.

Months went by. I kept in contact and eventually was back in their office in early 2011. This led to a visit to Connect Assist by some of their managers, and in July that year I was asked to propose a contact centre and digital service pilot to run from November 2011 for six months.

We were excited by this, and I sent in the proposals at a modest cost of £60,000. The feedback was positive, and I was asked to prepare contracts. Then it all went quiet again. I had been dealing with a particular manager but after a couple of months of getting nowhere I was told that he had left the charity.

This was not the first or last time this had happened to me. The London charity sector had notoriously high staff turnover. I started again and this time eventually had a phone conversation with the operations director. She told me that they were likely to put the contact centre and digital platform out to tender soon and would be using a consultant named Ian to manage this process.

I made contact with Ian and in early 2012 was back at the Legion's head office for a meeting with him and Carol, the new assistant director of operations. This time they gave me a couple of hours and I went through what we could do. It was a good conversation and they told me then what the tender timeline would be.

The tender was, as is often the case, a two-stage process. The first stage was a PQQ (pre-qualification questionnaire). Typically, these are just to sort out which of a wide range of suppliers could qualify to deliver the services being tendered. In this case, the Legion's PQQ was much more detailed, although I think that was to our advantage.

I duly submitted the PQQ and about three weeks after the submission date I was told by Ian that we had passed to the next stage but there would be a delay while they rethought some elements of their specification. I reiterated that we were keen to submit a full tender and he was very encouraging.

As before, the months dragged on. I would call Ian once a month and he repeated his position. I didn't know whether I sounded keen or desperate. I was on holiday in August when I got a call from our office saying that the full ITT (invitation to tender) document had arrived.

I had a look through, emailed off a set of questions for us to submit, cleared most of my diary for the month when I returned from holiday and went back to the beach.

When I returned, Rusty and I went through the document again in detail and then I headed off home to write the tender with minimum disturbance. By the time I had finished I had written a huge document of 202 pages and entitled 'Big Enough to Deliver, Small Enough to Care'. We knew that we would be by far the smallest company bidding for this work, so we needed to make a compelling case.

The tender document demonstrated everything that we could deliver. I made a strong case for Connect Assist as the best partner for the Royal British Legion, due to our heritage and experience in the charity sector, the fact that we helped people in challenging circumstances and so on. I littered the document with quotes from satisfied customers, the best being from the then chief executive of NCVO:

The team at Connect Assist impressed us with their understanding of our organisation. This coupled with their innovative solutions and ability to harness the latest technology made them an obvious choice when we decided to review our service requirements.

On the day the ITT was due to be submitted, I went to a printer who printed three copies of the document, two for the Legion and one for us. I got these bound and personally delivered them to the Royal British Legion's office.

And then it went quiet again. After a couple of weeks I called up Ian. He was very apologetic and said that we would get an email in a week. Two weeks later the email came saying that they had shortlisted from four companies down to two and that we were one of the two.

I was a combination of ecstatic that we were down to the last two and furious that they had not just made a decision. Rusty calmed me down by reminding me that we were still in the running.

A couple of weeks later a team from the Legion came to visit us at Connect Assist. We had established a well-oiled machine for prospective customer visits. We cleaned the building to within an inch of its life. We had fresh coffee and Welsh cakes ready for their arrival. Ian, Carol and two other members of the Legion team came and we gave them plenty of time in the contact centre, listening to calls, seeing how we managed email and web chat, understanding the digital platform and getting an insight into how we collected, managed and stored client data.

You could see that they liked what they saw. When they returned to meet Rusty and me in our boardroom, it was all smiles and lots of talking. Finally, we asked them what would happen next and they said that we would need to present to the operations director and her team at head office in London. They gave us the date.

It was a massive problem. Rusty would be half way through an overseas holiday. I was due to be in Berlin the following day for a wedding and had booked travel. But in true Connect Assist style we came up with a solution. Rusty had previously worked with a local company to produce a few short videos to showcase the company and the work we do, and on this occasion they excelled themselves. In the video she introduced the company and then there was a filmed example call from a veteran (played by one of our call advisers who was a veteran) speaking with one of our call advisers. We even had Rusty's mum playing a veterans' widow. It was brilliant.

On the day of the presentation, I was in London with Sharon, our contact centre manager, Steve, our technology director, and Lucy, our trainer, whose husband was in the Royal Air Force. We showed the video and then did a short presentation focusing on what we knew their key areas of questioning would be. We made a big deal of 'Big Enough to Deliver, Small Enough to Care' and focused heavily on the values and purpose of our business, including some statistics I had found on high levels of veteran unemployment in the Welsh Valleys. I honestly don't think we could have done better. I went straight from the presentation to Berlin.

Two weeks later Ian called me on a Friday morning. I was sitting in my car at Newport station about to drive to the office.

"You have won the tender," he said. "The Legion want you to run the contact centre and digital platform." I fought back tears. I had carried the tension of this for nearly three years.

We spoke for about ten minutes about the next steps, but all I wanted to do was call Rusty. He rang off and I called her straight away. I am not sure how I got the words out, I was so emotional, but she knew.

I drove to the office. We held a meeting of all the staff and everyone was really thrilled. It was one of the best days ever in the history of the business. It would potentially be the largest contract we had ever won, and it was the highest-profile charity we had worked for. And with the Welsh Valleys being one of the strongest military recruitment areas in the UK, our team felt a strong affinity for this work.

Building the Legion's service

It was always busy at Connect Assist. The truth is that every successful enterprise is busy. If you aren't busy then you probably aren't as successful as you could be.

Implementing the new Royal British Legion service was a big project and kept a lot of us very busy indeed. It was a team effort between Connect Assist and the Legion. The key elements of the implementation included specifying and creating the CRM and digital channels, creating a knowledge bank of information, recruiting a contact centre team, with at least half being armed forces veterans or their families, training that team and setting up the infrastructure.

A key part of the new service was ensuring that all of the Legion's regional offices were linked up to the contact centre. The plan was for the contact centre to be the single point of entry for all services, but with a good proportion of enquiries seamlessly passed on to the relevant regional office. There were 16 of these. The Legion was also setting up a high street pop-in centre in each of these regions, where members of the armed forces community (serving, veterans and families) could call in and seek help and, if needed, arrange a meeting with a local adviser.

359

So, this was not just a new service for Connect Assist; it was a new way of working for the Legion and its staff and volunteers. It was a big change and, like any organisational or operational change, needed to be carefully negotiated and implemented.

A couple of weeks after we had won the tender, Rusty and I attended a large meeting at the Oval cricket ground in London. We met most of the managers and staff from all the regional offices, as well as a number of the head office welfare staff. We presented what the contact centre would be about and how it would work. We showed the video we had made for the tender presentation and they completely got it. It was a huge success, and I believe that for some years it was used as a training video at the Legion. Rusty and Sharon also hosted a number of visits of regional office staff to the contact centre in the first year, which was really helpful in building a strong relationship between the contact centre and the rest of the Legion.

We had the Legion's team of advisers in place and in training by the beginning of April 2013. We started with a team of eight advisers plus the team leader. Over half of them were armed forces veterans. We took the first call at the beginning of May. It was the plan to start slowly, but soon it was clear that the volume of enquiries was significantly higher than the Legion had predicted, and by the end of June the team had doubled to 16.

There are about six weeks of each year when the Royal British Legion has extremely high brand awareness, and that is because of the Poppy Appeal. It was not the job of the contact centre to manage the logistics of the appeal, but it was inevitable that there would be a lot more of the armed forces community seeking help then because of the high brand awareness of the Appeal. My days at Teacher Support Network had taught me that it was awareness that drove helpline demand rather than the scale of need.

In May we took just over 3,200 enquiries and this had grown to over 8,200 in September. The increase of the team to 16 was ahead of the Legion's predicted staffing requirement, so it did not increase. In October we took over 15,500 calls and in November it was 13,500. Although this reduced in December, it was still around 9,000 calls with an additional 1,200 emails and webchats, and in January it bounced back up again.

We needed a larger team and in January Sue and Carol agreed to reorganise their budgets. By March 2014 we had 23 advisers on the Legion's contact centre team.

The Royal British Legion service has grown from strength to strength. Today the core contact centre team comprises the same number but increases by six people for the period of the Poppy Appeal every year. In addition, there is a benefits, money and debt advice team of qualified debt advisers, providing specialist compensation advice, help with debt and emergency situations and in many cases supporting individuals and families through complex legal and debt processes.

Small Business of the Year

It was an incredible year for us in 2013, so it was a very exciting and proud moment when we won Welsh Small Business of the Year 2013 at the Institute of Welsh Affairs Business Awards event. We had taken a table with ten of the team, so it was a very loud cheer when Connect Assist was announced as the winner. The event was held during Remembrance Week in November, so it was particularly special given what we had achieved with the Royal British Legion.

I have often found it hard to acknowledge our success. It's easy to be focused on day-to-day problems, the constant anxiety of trying to make more sales, worrying about large customers taking their contracts to one of our many and mostly much larger competitors and hoping we will have enough cash to pay the salaries at the end of the month. That awards night was one of the few times where I could gain some perspective and acknowledge our achievements.

In eight years I had taken a risk on a business idea, set up in the Welsh Valleys and created a total of 77 jobs. We had an extraordinary staff team, and all of our managers were people who had started with us in front-line jobs. We were providing world-class services helping hundreds of thousands of people facing serious challenges in their lives.

Rusty and I bounded onto the stage at the Cardiff City Hall and somehow I managed to find the words to express this achievement. I'm sure we got the loudest cheer of the night – but then maybe that was our noisy team table[21].

We were developing a CRM database project for Network Rail

Chapter 44

The First Minister

Around the middle of 2014 we took our one millionth call. And the company kept growing. This didn't happen by itself though.

We had stabilised the Money Advice Service work and stemmed the losses by a combination of improved operational performance and contract price renegotiation. It was still a complicated contract, but it wasn't as business-threatening as it had been.

We had won and implemented the Royal British Legion contact centre and got through the first year to a stable level of performance and size of adviser team. We had a very positive relationship with the Legion, from the senior management to welfare officers and volunteers in their regional offices and pop-in centres.

We had been busy on the new customer front as well. We were providing helplines for seven benevolent funds, having helped create new helplines for the construction and the racing industries. We were delighted to have helped set these up as they are industries that can present a high risk to their employees. We had developed a number of digital services for the children's charity Barnardos and a housing association. We were developing a CRM database project for Network Rail.

I was really impressed with the Welsh government's approach to business support. We had located in one of the poorest areas in the whole of Europe and had done that deliberately. We were encouraged by the business department to apply for funding to encourage employment, and we did.

Over a number of years we were awarded various grants from the Welsh Economic Development Fund. The civil servants were extremely helpful. These grants allowed us to employ for new roles before we had the gross profit to do so. We used this to fill new management, technology and sales positions, as well as safeguard jobs where there was a risk of losing contracts.

It's sometimes been suggested to me by entrepreneurs outside of Wales that we moved there only because of the business grants. I mostly don't rise to this, but it's really insulting. We decided to set up Connect Assist in the Welsh Valleys because we wanted to create jobs there. The fact that we received some financial support for doing so doesn't take away from the need to create jobs there. My answer to those cynical voices became "So why don't you move your business to Wales as well?"

It was a big moment for all of us at Connect Assist when Carwyn Jones, the First Minister of Wales at the time, paid us a visit. He met with some of the staff, and we were especially keen for him to meet those who had started as apprentices and who now had their first permanent employment. He listened in on a phone call from a military veteran, experiencing at first hand the talent and empathy of our advisers. And yes, he cut a cake in the shape of a telephone[22].

Winning and losing

By the end of 2014, Connect Assist was in a good place. The Royal British Legion service was running well and we had completed a very busy Poppy Appeal period very successfully. We had 100 members of staff, and we were delivering helplines for 24 charities and public sector organisations. Three of our customers each delivered over £500,000 a year in income. Our technology team were busy developing CRM systems for 25 customers that year. Turnover was £3.7 million, representing a 24% growth over the previous year.

In the autumn we won the contract to deliver part of a new occupational advice service for the Department for Work and Pensions (DWP). We had been running the NHS Plus occupational health advice service since 2010 and earlier in 2014 we heard that DWP wanted to expand the service to small businesses and general practitioners to include free occupational health assessments for employees and patients. The advice service that we were running would be the first point of contact.

We were cautious about working with such a large a government department particularly after our last experience of public sector procurement with the Money Advice Service. Rusty and I discussed this but in the end we bid and won our part of the tender. It was also the first time that we had worked directly with a government department. They were very demanding and had a huge team of civil servants engaged in the project. On one occasion I was invited to a meeting in Westminster to discuss the website we were building for the advice service. I entered a room with 18 civil servants and was told that we would all stay in the room until the website was designed. I gently explained that a website had never been successfully designed by committee. In the end, the occupational health service staffed by nurses successfully launched on time.

By now Connect Assist had grown to become a significant size, but this comes with challenges of its own. One of these is that every contract you win will ultimately to come up for tender again, typically after three to five years. Inevitably, we would sometimes lose a contract, and in 2015, following an exhaustive process, we lost the tender for the Turn2us contract. We had expected this would be a strong possibility, but it was nonetheless a bitter blow.

There were 25 jobs associated with this contract. We worked intensively to find work for all of the employees and in the end we only made three redundancies. I felt ghastly and that I had let our staff down. So did Rusty. Of course, we had to just keep going. Any growing business has to deal with such moments. There have been many times in my social enterprise career when I have felt a failure, and this was one of them.

The happy postscript is that, following a subsequent tender process in 2021, Turn2us came back to Connect Assist.

Ready for anything

Much of the work of growing an enterprise is a combination of seeking opportunities followed by hard work. Very occasionally an unexpected game-changing event takes place. On Monday 20th July 2015 this happened to us.

I had just arrived at the office around 8am as usual. Monday was my regular day in the office before heading to London for a week of sales and customer relationship activity. But this week turned out to be different. I took a call at 8.30am from someone I knew who worked at the cancer charity Marie Curie. Six months before, we had lost a tender process for the Marie Curie service to our closest competitor, a company named Broadcasting Support Services (BSS).

BSS were based in Manchester, Glasgow and Edinburgh and were seven times larger than us. They had originally been set up by the BBC to offer helpline services at the end of programmes where storylines with challenging situations required that they support affected viewers. They had grown to a £26 million turnover operation providing helpline services to both charity and government customers. We knew many of the people there, including a former employee of ours who had recently taken up a senior management role.

The caller from Marie Curie told me that BSS, their helpline provider, had just emailed them to say that the company had gone into administration and that they had just two weeks to find a new provider. Could we take their helpline on?

It must have been embarrassing to make that call, given that he had recently turned us down after a long and protracted sales process. I took a deep breath and resisted the fleeting temptation to sound superior. "Yes, of course. How can we help?"

As I was speaking, I could see the missed calls piling up on my phone. Still speaking to Marie Curie, I walked over to where Rusty was working and wrote a note saying 'BSS gone bust. Clear your diary'.

I came off the phone and listened to the messages. One of them was from Mind, the mental health charity. We knew that Mind had been one of BSS's largest charity customers. This was getting interesting. I called back and it was the same conversation – could we transfer their helpline by the end of next week? Again, I said yes.

Rusty and I got together with Sharon. It was looking like we would get at least six or seven charity customers by the end of the day. We would need to recruit and transfer members of staff, order more desks, technology and the infrastructure of running helplines. All to be ready to go by the end of the next week.

In classic Connect Assist style, we never even considered not doing this. While it's never a happy moment when a respected company goes into administration, we all knew this was a significant opportunity for us. But the problems were massive.

We had already run out of office space some months ago. We had 100 contact centre staff in our now somewhat crowded building. We had all the sales, technology and support staff working in a building in Caerphilly about 15 minutes away. We had nowhere to put all these new people. And we had less than a week to find them!

Everyone jumped to it. Rusty started recruiting, talking to recruitment agencies, calling staff who had recently left for other jobs to see if they would like to come back (some did). Sharon started ordering additional laptops and associated technology, as well as working out which contact centre staff could work from home. Fortunately we had bought and implemented technology that supported this some years previously for when the office was closed due to severe weather, which came into its own during the Covid-19 lockdowns.

I put in a call to our former employee who worked at BSS. He was in shock. He gave me as much information as he could and set up a call for me to speak with BSS's chief executive. I spoke with her later that afternoon, a call that required some sensitivity. I said how sad I felt for her and the whole company and offered our help. She would have known that many of their customers had been calling us all day, but we had a very sensible talk. She asked me whether we would like to buy some of the assets of the company and put me in touch with the administrators.

The next day I headed to London and met with all the charities who wanted to transfer to us. Despite realistically having no other option, some of them wanted to go through some form of tender process. This was ridiculous as there was no time. I said we would only take on their work by the following week if it was for a minimum one-year fixed fee contract plus a set-up fee for all the work of transferring their service.

I signed a non-disclosure agreement and the administrators sent me the financial data on BSS. I've always been able to read accounts quickly and it was soon clear what had happened. It was also clear that there would be few assets of value. In any case, most of BSS's customers that we would want to work with had already been in touch. In the end, the administrator suggested we just get on with transferring as many of BSS's customers as we could, telling me that we were doing everyone a favour.

Two weeks later we started with five new helplines: Mind, Marie Curie, National Eczema Society, Picker Institute and UKTV. Two further BSS customers came to us soon afterwards. We added £1 million to our annual turnover, and we urgently had to find more premises.

New premises

Finding new office space is always difficult and typically takes months. We needed more space much sooner.

We made some calls to the landlords and agents that we knew. There was a possibility of a floor of 5,200 square feet in a much larger unit on the same estate, a two-minute walk away. I called the agent and agreed a deal the next day. I explained the urgency of getting the lease sorted out to our excellent solicitor, Donald.

I've never known a lawyer move so fast. Very soon we had a lease agreed. Dee, our amazing company secretary, got plans drawn up to set up the internal space, and on the day that we signed the lease the builders moved in.

By autumn we had a large new premises, space for all our staff and a platform for the next stages of growth.

Learning #41: Saying yes before saying no

One of the great strengths of the culture at Connect Assist is that we said yes to opportunities before we said no. This was really visible the day that our largest competitor went into administration and we had to decide whether to take on six or seven charity customers, find another 35 staff and find somewhere for them to work – all in two weeks. There was no debate – everyone just said yes.

Looking back over my career that has been my attitude. Of course there are some occasions where a no is the right thing to say. I have been presented with opportunities that will clearly lose money, are clearly inappropriate or are completely unrelated to the organisation's purpose. In these cases no is an easy answer.

But far more opportunities have been presented where saying yes will be a stretch for the enterprise – and yet it's the right thing to do. So I'm a great believer in saying yes before saying no.

Tobias Ellwood MP came to Cancer Assip to visit the team

Tobias Ellwood MP, came to Connect Assist to visit the team

Chapter 45

Building the future

Every entrepreneur has to think of the future, but all too often we focus on the business and not ourselves. One of the many great qualities of my working relationship with Rusty was our ability to talk about our futures on a regular basis.

By the end of 2015 we had been running Connect Assist for ten years. I would be turning 60 soon and didn't want to keep running the business, any business, into my 60s. Rusty was ready to move on too.

We started a conversation with three of our senior managers. We took them into our confidence and explained that it was our intention to leave at some point in the next couple of years. We offered for them to become directors on the board and run the company. They thought about it and all agreed.

We believed that we had a team that could take the business forward, but what it lacked was a leader who could replace me as chief executive. We had an employee who had some promise a year before, but that had not worked out. For Rusty and me to be able to move on, we needed a suitable successor.

I've often found that all that is needed to solve a problem is to be clear about what you need and then see what happens. Put another way, this means clearly understanding your current reality as well as articulating a very clear vision of the future. This was something I had learned a long time before at Findhorn.

Following a conversation with Rusty about how we would find the right person to lead the business, I received an email out of the blue. Ron used to be the managing director of a company in Cardiff. He ran a contact centre that raised funds for charities over the phone.

We had got to know him some years before and had done some collaborative work together.

Ron's email explained that the company he had been working for had changed ownership and he had left. He wondered if we would like to have a chat. I said yes immediately and arranged for him to meet Rusty and me the next day.

Rusty and I didn't have a chance to discuss this, so we just chatted to him. Within ten minutes we made up a job for him, leading our consulting work. He said yes and started a few weeks later. After a month with us we told him why we had really employed him – we wanted him to consider leading the company after us.

Ron was up for it, but he was very aware that he had newly joined the business, while the other senior leaders had been there since the beginning or early days. He carefully started to build the team, meeting with them for dinner once a week.

We had started building the future of Connect Assist.

Responding to opportunities

Meanwhile, Ron wasted no time and started to develop a number of new business opportunities. During 2015 there had been some negative press articles about telephone fundraising and the pressure sometimes put on older and vulnerable people to give money. A number of the companies fundraising on behalf of household name charities were criticised for their practices and one had gone bankrupt.

I received a call from the fundraising director of the British Red Cross. They had terminated their relationship with their telephone fundraising company and were facing a significant loss of vital donations. Could we help?

We could. First Ron did an analysis of their telephone fundraising and what had given rise to complaints. He created options for them to restart telephone fundraising, with a focus on a values-led operation. The result of this was that we created a dedicated fundraising operation for them at Connect Assist.

This was followed by the Veterans' Gateway. There was a lot of talk in government circles suggesting that there were too many military and veteran charities. A report suggested a requirement for military charities to work closer together. The Ministry of Defence took this on and there was talk of a one-stop shop for veterans seeking help from charities. And then suddenly there was talk of a budget and a tender.

We had been working with the Royal British Legion for three years by now and had a good relationship with their leadership. We had been a key player in the transformation of their services, making the charity more accessible to a much larger number of veterans and military families. I spoke to them about my concern that the Veterans' Gateway service could be outsourced to a large company, with the Royal British Legion and other military charities left out.

As a result we put together a consortium of five organisations. Royal British Legion led, with SSAFA, Combat Stress, Poppy Scotland and Connect Assist. With similar principles to those we had used with the Legion, we designed a service with some incredibly talented veterans to ensure that it really worked well. As we had set up for the Legion, it was a multi-channel service with 24/7 telephone, email, web chat and online information, plus the addition of excellent new mapping software to log every support service for veterans across the UK. It was a very talented team from all the charities and Connect Assist that put this together, and I'm very proud to have been a part of it.

We won the tender and it was a great moment when the then UK Minister for Veterans, Tobias Ellwood MP, came to Connect Assist to visit the team in summer 2017[23]. It has been a really successful service.

During 2016 we also took on a wide range of other customers. These included the veterans' mental health charity Combat Stress, eating disorder charity Beat, fraud prevention organisation Cifas, offenders' charity St Giles Trust and an educational insurance venture. In all of these and others, we won the work because of our collaborative approach to innovation. Connect Assist never had a 'one size fits all' approach to customers. We always went the extra mile to co-create a service that really worked for the customer that we worked for. Although this often created complexity for our own operations team, it was a key part of our success.

By the end of 2016 we had created 135 full-time jobs and had a turnover of £5.4 million. We had a wide range of really interesting customers, talented staff, with the majority of managers having started in front-line jobs, and healthy reserves. The company was making a decent profit and we could invest in our growth.

Most importantly, we had a leadership team getting ready to take on the business.

Learning #42: Reality and vision

I've often found that all that is needed to solve a problem is to be clear about what you need and then see what happens. Put another way, this means clearly understanding your current reality as well as articulating a very clear vision of the future. There is then a dynamic tension between the two that creates the journey from current reality to vision.

Much effort is given to defining a strategy that creates and details this journey, and this is of course important. But my experience is that, more often than not, the detail of the strategy changes along the way, often many times. I have found that the heart of a great enterprise is being honest about reality and clear about vision.

Learning #43: Collaboration with customers

Another great element of the culture at Connect Assist was our approach to collaboration. Rusty and I enjoyed working with our new and existing customers to design their services. Over time our managers and leadership team did the same.

There were so many examples of great collaboration. Among those that stand out were The Royal British Legion who were keen collaborators. Our relationship was so strong that when the opportunity to develop the Veteran's Gateway emerged, both organisations jumped at it.

Collaboration took time, but it's true to say that the better the customer/ outsourcer collaboration, the more successful the service was long term.

Sadly there were some organisations that wanted to issue a tender, sign the contract and then tell us, the outsourcer, how to provide the service. In my experience this never worked and these typically become problem contracts for both parties.

I live in Pembrokeshire with my wife, Amanda

Chapter 46

Moving on

In 2016 Rusty and I started planning our exit from Connect Assist. We explored a number of options for restructuring the business, but at the heart of this was a desire to support the leadership team led by Ron to take on the running of the company. We sought some professional help to make this work and by the following spring we had a plan in place. Rusty and I would remain as non-executive directors and at least for a while would be in a position to exercise control in the event that things went wrong.

The good news is that things did not go wrong. Of course, the new leadership operated differently. But that is what the company needed as the business had reached a scale where it could not be run in the way that Rusty and I had done it. I like to think that we both managed to maintain a good balance of being supportive while not getting in the way of progress. I suspect we were not perfect at this, but I believe we were good enough.

In May 2017 I won the Wales Director of the Year for Corporate Responsibility award at the Institute of Directors. We took the whole leadership team to the event in Cardiff and other members of the company, along with some of our local suppliers. We were in the final stages of a re-tender of one of our largest customers and during the lunch we got a message that we had won the contract. After lunch I won the award, which was a genuine surprise. It felt like a turning point for the company, and I left this event feeling ready to move on. I subsequently won the UK Director of the Year for Corporate Responsibility award.

On 22nd June 2017 the existing directors and new leadership team of Connect Assist gathered to agree the change of leadership. The event felt really important, but it took a long time for it to sink in. The next day we held meetings and told the staff about the changes. There were some tears. Rusty and I had shot a little video for our customers explaining the changes and introducing Ron and the new leadership team. We dropped out of day-to-day leadership as gracefully as we could, but of course we still went back for board meetings monthly. I stayed working part-time to manage the finances until a finance director was appointed in January 2018.

What happened next at Connect Assist

The company did really well. Although very different to me, Ron turned out to be a brilliant chief executive and really enjoyed the job. Almost immediately the company won a large contract with The Princes Trust, the charity that helps 11–30-year-olds to find the tools and confidence to start careers. In 2019 the then Prince of Wales (now King Charles III) visited Connect Assist to meet 'his' team, and he was thrilled to also see the work done on behalf of other charities such as the Royal British Legion.

Other significant new customers included two new initiatives supporting people to stop gambling by self-excluding themselves from access to online sites and shops.

In 2019 the company won its largest ever contract, the Advice, Issue Reporting and Eligibility assistance service (AIRE), a single integrated and national support service for asylum seekers. This was won in a Home Office tender in partnership with the charity Migrant Help. This is a significant and growing contract and, as I understand it, now employs 130 people.

During the Covid-19 pandemic, Connect Assist stayed fully operational making good use of the investment we had previously made in work-from-home technology. As well as carrying on with increased demand from a number of helplines, especially those with a mental health component, it supported some NHS services.

Most importantly, the new leadership team maintains the values and ethos of the original company.

Rusty and I finally left the board of directors in September 2021. The company was turning over in excess of £14 million and employed 327 staff. We had started 15 years earlier with ten employees on a mission to create jobs in the Welsh Valleys. We had a vision of creating helpline services fit for the digital era. We became the UK's leading outsourcer of charity helplines and a specialist in supporting members of the public facing challenging circumstances in their lives. Connect Assist is still going strong and remains a significant success story in the Welsh business landscape.

It is the most successful of all the enterprises I was privileged to start up and lead.

What happened next for me

After I stepped down as chief executive of Connect Assist in 2017, I established a small consulting and coaching company called Enterprise Values. I've been a consultant for various social enterprises and charities, helping them launch new initiatives, lead mergers, raise finance and more. I enjoy coaching leaders of social enterprises and have taught and lectured.

I'm non-executive chair of AAW Group, a global strategy, fundraising and executive search consultancy working with not-for-profits in the UK and around the world.

I'm a trustee of the Money and Mental Health Policy Institute set up by Martin Lewis, and I helped Martin distribute over £3 million to voluntary groups at the beginning of the Covid-19 pandemic.

I live in Pembrokeshire with my wife, Amanda. We are heavily involved in voluntary projects here. I am a trustee and organiser of the Solva Edge Festival and in 2022 launched the St. David's Festival of Ideas, with speakers including Eluned Morgan, Sophie Howe, Rowan Williams, Paul Mason, Sir Michael Marmot, Liz Saville-Roberts and others.

Learning #44: Moving on when it's time to leave

One of the great skills of leadership and entrepreneurship is the ability to move on when it's time to leave. In my experience, it is better to spot the moment yourself than have it forced upon you. I would rather choose the time of my departure. The trick is to spot it in good time.

I have had to move on a few times in my life. I've got better at it, although it doesn't always feel like that. Sometimes I have planned for it. Other times I have spotted a change coming that I didn't want to be part of or I was not the right person for.

But the best occasion was when I decided that I no longer wanted to stay in leadership in my 60s and so actively planned for the handover, leaving the enterprise to the management team.

Learnings from Connect Assist

Although I had been a social entrepreneur for 25 years by the time I started Connect Assist there was inevitably a lot more to learn. Here are some of my key learnings from this time.

Learning #33: Side projects

Many people start up their enterprise while doing another full-time job. It is typically a needs-must situation and gets called a 'side project'. A side project is something you do alongside your day job.

Many side projects have become extremely successful. Twitter and Instagram started as side projects. Interestingly, I found this quote from technology entrepreneur Paul Graham, who said, "The best way to come up with start-up ideas is to ask yourself the question: What do you wish someone would make for you?" This is exactly how Connect Assist started.

If I was in government, I would create some form of tax relief or grant incentive to support company employees to pursue side projects. I'm convinced this would unlock a lot of energy, creativity and enterprise.

Learning #34: Ask someone to set up a business with you, not with you

I had completely assumed that Rusty would come to work with me at Teacher Support Network, and when she couldn't, I made a huge error. I felt under pressure and panicked, making a decision that I soon realised was wrong. I had someone working for me rather than with me to set up the new venture. When it didn't go well, I felt that he was the wrong person. But it was me who made the mistake of appointing him to do this, and that was the greater error.

I was conflicted between my intuition that all was not well and wanting to support the person I had appointed and the team he had assembled. It's always been my view that it's best to support managers to do their job. But on this occasion I neither read the signals nor trusted my intuition.

Learning #35: Consulting as a means to win work

Early on at Connect Assist we used consulting as a means of winning what turned out to be a significant customer, Turn2us (see Chapter 38). While we did not win the consultancy work, the charity discovered who we were.

We quickly found that in order to win a sale of a service to most charities, we needed to spend time with them listening to what their challenges were, dialoguing with them about solutions and ultimately co-designing a new service with them. In most cases, the main challenge was that the charity struggled to reach enough of the people who needed the support that they provided, and with our background we were well placed to help. We acted as consultants through the process of engaging with a new potential customer.

It was a good approach, and it became a key part of the process of winning a number of our larger customers, such as Turn2us and the Royal British Legion, as well as many other charities.

Eventually we realised that we were giving too much free consultancy to prospective organisations, many of who never then contracted with us. We started charging for consultancy work and it became another service of the company. Where we thought that there was a potential for future work with the organisation we would be up front about this in advance.

Learning #36: Be up front with customers

When we pitched for the Turn2us consulting work we had to be up front about a potential conflict of interest. How could we recommend outsourcing their helpline when we were a helpline outsourcer? We decided to give Turn2us the opportunity to decide for themselves whether they saw it as a conflict.

We continued this approach after that. My experience is that customers appreciate straightforward discussion rather than a traditional sales pitch that might fudge difficult issues such as conflicts of interest.

Learning #37: Understand the finances

I'm not an accountant but come from a family of accountants. As a young and slightly alternative person growing up in the 1970s, I rebelled against the notion of training as an accountant. Early on in my career financial management was forced upon me when my business partner went off sick for some time, and I learned one of the most important skills of my working life: how to manage the finances of a small and growing business.

For all the enterprises that I have set up, and for most of the other organisations I have run, I have been the financial manager alongside the day job. We grew Connect Assist with me as finance director as well as chief executive and it served us well.

In some organisations I have experienced a disconnect between the financial management and the rest of the organisation, operations, sales, fundraising and more. By doing it myself I avoided this problem.

I am not suggesting that every social entrepreneur should be their own finance director. The truth is that I enjoy working with numbers and am always happy building a spreadsheet. But I do recommend developing a good understanding of the enterprise's finances. Understanding the profit and loss, balance sheet, cashflow and sales pipeline on a monthly basis is vital. I have always needed a strong understanding of these to make good financial decisions, in order to react appropriately to challenging situations and to convince banks, investors, customers and other external stakeholders that I have a grip on the finances.

This last one is important. I always recommend to social entrepreneurs that I meet that they can answer financial questions immediately with a current knowledge of their financial position. This gives people confidence like little else.

Learning #38: Empathy is a leadership superpower

The definition of empathy is the ability to understand and share the feelings of another. This is incredibly important in leadership. It means that in every circumstance I learned to really listen to what people are saying, sense what they are feeling and try at all times to have a clear understanding of their lived reality, what they are experiencing in that moment or in their lives as a whole.

Empathy involves understanding another person's thoughts and feelings from their point of view, rather than your own. It is not the same as sympathy, where we may be moved by someone's thoughts and feelings while nonetheless maintaining emotional distance.

Empathy with staff and work colleagues is important as it builds trust. As a social entrepreneur, the team looked to me for leadership and reassurance, but most of all understanding and empathy. If I could offer that most of the time, it helped build a team that people wanted to be part of.

The same applied across all parts of the business. The success of the Connect Assist leadership team was down to our empathy for prospects, customers, employees, suppliers, colleagues and even departing customers.

388

When we were meeting a prospective new customer, we didn't pitch what we could do. Rather, we actively listened to what their challenges were, what problems they needed to solve, entering into a co-creative dialogue to find solutions. This was exactly what most of our customers were looking for. When we were pursuing the work with the Royal British Legion, I spent two years doing this with them before we got near a tender process.

The core of our work was supporting people in sometimes really challenging circumstances, and that required a high degree of empathy on the part of the advisers on the phone. We didn't use scripts, as many contact centres do. We expected, trained and coached our advisers to empathise with the callers, gain their trust and gently but with purpose lead them to a place where they could receive support, guidance and the beginning of a way out of the challenges they faced.

We found that this quality of empathy was in the heart of so many people of the Welsh Valleys. And that's why setting up in the Valleys was probably the best business decision of my career.

Empathy was a core behaviour of Connect Assist across the business and what we looked for when recruiting, which was not difficult in South Wales. Customers, suppliers and even departing customers commented on the empathy that they felt from the business as a whole.

Learning #39: Find a higher-margin product or service

Most social entrepreneurs are looking to grow and scale their enterprise. The challenge is how to do this. Growth requires investment and investment requires profitability.

Many social enterprises are categorised as 'not-for-profit' organisations. This technical definition can be misleading, as what it actually means is no distribution of profits to individuals. I have sometimes heard people being shocked that a social enterprise 'makes a profit'.

That's the wrong way of looking at it. Profits are essential in any enterprise, and here are some of the reasons why:

- Growth requires investment. If we didn't make reasonable profits, we would not have had the money to invest in capital assets needed for growth. At Nova Wholefoods this included vertical storage pallet racking when we outgrew the floor space in our warehouse. At Connect Assist it included technology software and hardware, more workspaces and quality systems.

- Paying your people better. A consistently profit-making enterprise is one that can pay employees better, ensuring they can have a better quality of life. I have strived to used profits to pay people an annual bonus as well as increasing salaries.

- Profits allow you to borrow. I needed money to start up most of the enterprises but often needed more when moving from the start-up phase to the scale-up phase. At this point the enterprise rarely had the cash available so needed to borrow. Nova Wholefoods was no exception and our lack of sufficient profits meant that the bank would not lend to us in the early days. As my career developed I realised that I needed to show year-on-year profitability in order to prove to banks and other lenders that we could service the debt.

- Profits allow enterprises to invest in or fund social and environmental causes that are not necessarily part of their core business.

Very early in my career I discovered the value of the high-margin product. At Nova Wholefoods, trail mix was our highest gross margin product. We could mark up the ingredients at a higher price than selling them individually. I'm convinced that without this additional profit we would have struggled to finance the growth of the business.

Ever since then I have looked for the high-margin product or service to support business growth, and when I have found it, up have gone the profit and the cash balances.

At the Ecovillage our building product sponsorship (which you can read about at 'Sponsorship succeeds' in Chapter 18) was a key part of our financial success and in that regard was a high-margin product, contributing some 25% of the product costs of the eco-houses.

And at Connect Assist we found a higher-margin service in our digital services development, as featured at 'The digital business takes off' in Chapter 41.

The procurement process forces enterprises to push down the gross margin percentage, particularly when you are a small or medium enterprise competing against larger companies, so there is a real need to find a service or product that delivers a higher profit margin as a counterbalance. I recommend this approach which has always worked for me.

Learning #40: Stay on top of digital and IT projects

Today the majority of social entrepreneurs have grown up in the era of digital technology, mobile phones and easy-to-use software and applications. Despite this, I still hear of time and money wasted on failed technology procurements and implementations.

I did not grow up in that era so had to learn the hard way, when my first computerised business process failed (which you can read about in Chapter 9). Ever since then I have made sure that I understand any technology, software and hardware that my enterprise has to design, purchase, implement or operate. Not to the level of code writing, but in all cases to use and many cases to configure to meet the needs of the business.

I am not mistrustful of technology and digital experts, but I'm told that I can be tough on them. I insist that they explain what they are doing and deciding in great detail and in normal, jargon-free language. I have no tolerance for the word 'should' and instead look for realistic expectations of performance and timelines. I want to be able to use the systems to a reasonable level so that I can have a personal, kinaesthetic learning experience.

Although I can be the type of social entrepreneur that IT and digital people find frustrating, with all the questions I fire at them, I have generally found that they come to respect me because I make the effort to speak their language and understand what they are telling me. I also make the effort to learn how to use the systems that they have implemented. Digital empathy.

It was a big day when I got this feedback from a digital consultant who had helped us implement a customer relationship management (CRM) system.

> *In a world of talkers, Patrick is a doer. He is extremely innovative, pioneering and loves technology. How many CEOs do you know who hands-on manage and use their CRM? That's Patrick.*

Learning #41: Saying yes before saying no

One of the great strengths of the culture at Connect Assist is that we said yes to opportunities before we said no. This was really visible the day that our largest competitor went into administration and we had to decide whether to take on six or seven charity customers, find another 35 staff and find somewhere for them to work – all in two weeks. There was no debate – everyone just said yes.

Looking back over my career that has always been my attitude. Of course there are some occasions where a no is the right thing to say. I have been presented with opportunities that will clearly lose money, are clearly inappropriate or are completely unrelated to the organisation's purpose. In these cases no is an easy answer.

But far more opportunities have been presented where saying yes will be a stretch for the enterprise – and yet it's the right thing to do. So I'm a great believer in saying yes before saying no.

Learning #42: Reality and vision

I've often found that all that is needed to solve a problem is to be clear about what you need and then see what happens. Put another way, this means clearly understanding your current reality as well as articulating a very clear vision of the future. There is then a dynamic tension between the two that creates the journey from current reality to vision.

Much effort is given to defining a strategy that creates and details this journey, and this is of course important. But my experience is that, more often than not, the detail of the strategy changes along the way, often many times. I have found that the heart of a great enterprise is being honest about reality and clear about vision.

Learning #43: Collaboration with customers

Another great element of the culture at Connect Assist was our approach to collaboration. Rusty and I enjoyed working with our new and existing customers to design their services. Over time our managers and leadership team did the same. As the company grew, we created jobs which were entirely about working with customers to design their helpline, digital platforms, databases and impact reporting.

There were so many examples of great collaboration. Among those that stand out were The Royal British Legion who were keen collaborators. Our relationship was so strong that when the opportunity to develop the Veteran's Gateway emerged, both organisations jumped at it. There were many others where the collaboration between the customer and Connect Assist was outstanding.

We received a lot of positive feedback for our ability to collaborate on innovation. Collaboration took time, but it's true to say that the better the customer/outsourcer collaboration, the more successful the service was long term.

Sadly there were some organisations that wanted to issue a tender, sign the contract and then tell us, the outsourcer, how to provide the service, paying lip service to collaboration and innovation. In my experience this never worked and these typically become problem contracts for both parties.

Learning #44: Moving on when it's time to leave

One of the great skills of leadership and entrepreneurship is the ability to move on when it's time to leave.

We all have to move on at times in our careers. In my experience, it is better to spot the moment yourself than have it forced upon you. I have had many friends over the years who have been made redundant from jobs and received a payment. I confess to having been a little jealous, but always on reflection I would rather choose the time and manner of my departure. The trick is to spot it in good time.

When I left Nova Wholefoods it was a sudden decision after the computer stock control system crashed, which you can read more about in Chapter 10, 'A big decision'. It was an impulsive decision as I really didn't know myself well enough to realise that I was burnt out and needed to stop. It's possible that, if I had stayed much longer, I would have got sick or worse. In this case something intervened that jolted me into moving on. Helpful though that was at the time, it is not an approach that I would recommend.

The next time was leaving the Ecovillage. The Community had made it clear that my latest project was not going to happen. On that occasion my low mood was the signal to move on (see Chapter 25, 'Time to Leave').

I have had to move on a few more times since. I've got better at it, although it doesn't always feel like that. Sometimes I have planned for it. Once I set up my next enterprise while I was still in my existing job, a common start-up story known as creating a side project.

Other times I have spotted a change coming that I didn't want to be part of or was not the right person for.

But the best time (see Chapter 46, 'Moving on') was when I decided that I no longer wanted to stay in leadership in my 60s and so actively planned for the handover and left the enterprise to the management team.

12 great qualities of social entrepreneurs

In 40 years of working life I have set up 12 organisations, social enterprises, companies and charities.

Some of these were small and some of them were subsidiaries. Four of them did not successfully get off the ground, although they made some positive impact along the way. Four of them scaled up to various degrees and are still operating successfully today.

Before finishing this book, I've reflected on what I have come to see as great qualities of a social entrepreneur. These are by no means the only qualities. There are many more, but these are ones I worked at myself and have observed in others. They are in no particular order.

1. They look for inspiration close by

A social entrepreneur will be an innovator. Being innovative means doing things differently or doing things that have never been done before. There is a lot written about inspiration, enterprise and innovation. But how does innovation occur?

My experience is that the best ideas are already close by. Sometimes looking at something in an inquisitive way helps you to see the previously unseen. Sometimes successful innovations are completely original, although in my experience more often they're not.

The best innovations I have been involved in making happen are ideas that were 'just around the corner'. Such ideas are typically neither original nor do they stare you in the face. They are somewhere in between. They are ideas that are close by but not yet quite visible.

Often the idea is hinted at in a conversation. Or they may be an extension of what is already happening, just doing it slightly differently. They exist in a sort of mental and spiritual peripheral vision.

Three of the most successful enterprises I have grown were initially hinted at in a snippet of a conversation. All I had to do was to listen, discuss and then act.

Often the role of the innovator is less having the idea than listening for it and making it happen. It was Thomas Edison the great inventor who said, "Genius is one per cent inspiration, ninety-nine per cent perspiration." He was right.

2. They reject the notion of 'heroic leadership'

When I started working in the early 1980s, the 'heroic leader' was a dominant leadership model. Heroic leaders are charismatic, make decisions unilaterally, are courageous and challenge the status quo. Heroic leaders have a tendency to undermine employee engagement by being inspiring rather than by involving them in making decisions. And they are almost exclusively men.

The financial crisis of 2008 probably put a temporary end to the era of the heroic leader in financial services, but there is plenty of evidence that this is alive and well in certain industries today.

I've always rejected the heroic leader model. And I certainly don't think it works for social enterprise. I started out by co-founding a workers' cooperative, which is the antithesis of heroic leadership, being based on a co-ownership business model.

In all my enterprises I have had a great business partner, and the success of each enterprise has always been in direct proportion to the strength of that partnership. My most successful enterprise was due to the extraordinarily strong partnership that my colleague and I built. I have been fortunate to have great partners in the other enterprises.

Every entrepreneur is different, but I know for me that when it comes to building a successful social enterprise, two is better than one. I need a business partner to bounce ideas, to share the responsibility, to plan and dream with, to make better decisions, to challenge each other, to support each other through the tough times, to celebrate our successes and always to have each other's back.

I reject the notion of the heroic leader. I'm a dialogic leader who needs people to discuss, co-create and work together with.

3. They surround themselves with great people

I have worked with a large number of quite extraordinary people. Perhaps because I have set up and worked in so many different enterprises, I've had an opportunity to encounter many people with different qualities, knowledge and experience.

The benefit of having a lot of minds on a challenge is something that I have learned over the years. For me, the best innovations and enterprises are ones that have involved plenty of dialogue in their implementation.

For the most part I have been privileged to work with a fantastic group of people who were highly aligned with the work and the clients we served. At my first enterprise in my 20s we were all passionate about vegetarian food and its impact on the environment. Building an ecovillage drew architects, engineers, builders, plumbers and others who were inspired to create a new type of housing and a new way of living. At my final enterprise the people I worked with were quite outstanding, speaking on the phone all day to people facing challenging and sometimes traumatic circumstances in their lives.

And then there were those on the outside who were key advisers and supporters of the enterprises.

I've learned over the years to build a network of experts who I know and trust. These are people whose experience and wisdom lie in areas where my skills and experience end and who I know will be available to help at any time. Many of them were there to help at moments of risk.

They include:

- An outstanding crisis communications expert who helped with reputation management when we were in the media for perhaps the wrong reasons.

- Lawyers, quite a few of them, covering employment, commercial, property and other legal issues. I have worked with my employment lawyer for 20 years and made it through a few challenging situations as a result.

- For the last 11 years, I had an IT infrastructure adviser and data security consultant as the enterprise managed confidential data.

- I worked with two excellent corporate finance experts who helped me find investment and finance that I didn't know existed. They both gave me confidence to take sensible risks when borrowing and raising funds.

- I have always had a few trusted industry experts. I started at the Ecovillage with a corporate sponsorship adviser who knew the building trade. At Teacher Support Network I formalised this into an advisory group that meant all the key stakeholder organisations were 'inside the tent'.

- I have always had a great accountant, who has advised on a range of financial and commercial issues.

These people were happy for me to call their mobiles almost any time of day or night, and in some cases I worked with them for over 25 years and across multiple organisations.

4. They are straightforward

Entrepreneurs typically spend a lot of their time communicating with other people. Early on I learned the art of communicating in a straightforward manner.

Being straightforward is about effectively communicating information that both you and the other person should find useful, important or worth conveying. It is polite rather than abrupt but does not avoid the point of the communication. Straightforward is not the same as blunt. It is certainly not rude, because that is likely to provoke unhelpful emotional responses. A polite yet straightforward communication is easy for other people to hear or read.

Difficult conversations are best had in a straightforward manner, such as tackling poor performance by discussing what success would look like or sharing bad news by being honest about the situation and how to turn it around.

When any of my enterprises has gone through inevitable difficult times, I have always been honest and straightforward with the staff. Even when the message has been uncomfortable, I've received feedback that people appreciated the manner of the communication.

5. They grow with the business

One of the challenges of starting up more than one social enterprise was that for a while I found it hard to be anything other than a start-up entrepreneur. I'm by no means the only person who has had this problem. I just don't do corporate behaviour. If I'm not careful, I can get in the way of our colleagues who are trying to do what is necessary to scale up the enterprise.

A key element of success as a social entrepreneur is to grow with the business. I have found that the best way to do this is to empower others and get out of their way as much as possible.

Early in my career I received feedback that I was getting in the way of capable managers and interfering with their ability to do their jobs. I responded by backing off and paying little attention to what they were doing. This wasn't a good response as some of them complained about a lack of support.

Over time, I developed the ability to grow with the enterprise. It took me a while, but I changed my approach to leadership. I was probably a bit interfering from time to time, but I learned to stay out of things that I didn't need to get involved in.

But the main reason for growing with the business is that there are different skills required at each stage of growth. Early on I learned how to fundraise and do a great TV or radio interview. Later I needed to engage with government ministers and became an adept networker despite my inherent shyness. One of the great gifts of setting up and running a social enterprise is that you get to do new things, learn new skills, push yourself into previously uncomfortable situations and gain confidence.

Growing with the business is vital and comes with great benefits.

6. They are empathic

When I started out I was not great at hiring staff. I was horribly impatient and expected our newly hired employees to work as hard and be as adaptable as me. Without anyone to coach my leadership style, I was ruthless and decisive but lacking in relationship skills and sometimes basic compassion. My mindset was typically that I could do most people's jobs better than they could – a classic entrepreneur failure for which my only excuse was that I was young and naïve.

Empathy is the ability to understand another person's thoughts and feelings in any situation from their point of view, rather than your own. It is not the same as sympathy, where we may be moved by someone's thoughts and feelings while nonetheless maintaining emotional distance.

This is important with work colleagues, as it builds trust. My teams looked to me for leadership and reassurance, but most of all understanding and empathy. I sought to offer that most of the time and know of no better way to build a team that people want to be part of.

The same applies across all stakeholders. The success of my most successful enterprise was down to our empathy for prospects, customers, employees, suppliers, colleagues and even departing customers. We extended that to our relationship with the environment by setting ourselves standards.

When we were meeting a prospective new customer, we didn't pitch what we could do. Rather, we actively listened to what their challenges were, what problems they needed to solve, entering into a co-creative dialogue to find solutions. This was exactly what most of our customers were looking for.

Empathy was a core behaviour of the enterprise culture and what we looked for when recruiting. Customers, suppliers and even departing customers commented on the empathy that they felt from the business as a whole

Empathy is a leadership superpower.

7. They continuously develop themselves, personally and professionally

After slightly less than three years, I impulsively left my first enterprise, one that I was passionate about. At the time, my decision to leave just felt instinctive. It had been triggered by a massive computer disaster the night before. On reflection, I was burnt out.

402

This is not the first time this has happened to me and typically there is a signal that I just need to slow down or stop for a while and regroup. I didn't recognise this at the time, but I now understand that I needed to do some personal and professional development to become more self-aware as a person and more mature as an entrepreneur and leader. Announcing my departure that morning was a first step on that journey, although I did not know that at the time.

I've been on that journey of self-development ever since. In my mid-20s I worked in an environment where personal development was a core value. In my early 30s I started seeing a psychotherapist. This continues to play a significant part of my life. I have become more compassionate, reflective, insightful and hopefully a nicer person to be around.

I have also taken the time to develop myself professionally, particularly in the area of leadership. While I have not gone down the route of qualifications in this area (although I do respect those who have), I have been fortunate to have done some really excellent leadership development in conflict resolution, innovation and much more. I received coaching for the last 20 years of my working life and additionally had some incredible mentors who led me through challenging situations, helping me learn much along the way. Eventually I trained as a coach.

Most social entrepreneurs and charity leaders I know take professional development very seriously. Perhaps fewer of them take personal development as seriously. If you don't, I encourage you to do so.

8. They have a coach

I have had a leadership coach since the late 1990s. Since then coaching has been at the heart of my professional development. I typically had a coaching session about every six weeks or so.

403

I worked with a small number of coaches to help me to improve my performance and that of the enterprise. They were all focused on the 'here and now' rather than on the distant past or future. I got feedback, challenge, support and a place to share the un-shareable.

One of the things that I most liked about my coaches is that they believed that I had the answers to my own problems. Their skill was to help me to find the solutions to my challenges myself, which means that I was far more focused on and capable of implementing those solutions successfully.

All of my coaches were people who at some point in their careers had worked with organisations with social values. I don't actually think that is essential, but it was just the way that I found them. I did like that there were times when they understood the issues I was dealing with.

If you don't have a coach, please get one. I can't imagine being a leader without this.

9. They can sell

Social enterprises are businesses with a social purpose. They sell their services and products, sometimes to individual customers, sometimes to other companies and charities, sometimes to government, local or national bodies. Sometimes they have to raise grants or loans. Whatever the enterprise, a social entrepreneur has to be able to sell.

This can be a challenge, particularly if you have previously only worked in charities or public services, which is often the case and where much of the recent growth in social enterprise has come from.

One of the challenges can be moving from a fundraising or grant-funding mindset to a sales mindset. Actually, I don't think it's that different, but I am forever meeting people, including experienced fundraisers, who say that they 'don't like to do sales work' or feel intimidated by the prospect of 'selling'.

404

In my career I have sold products and services, raised funds for charities and submitted endless grant applications. In my experience, selling products and services is very much like fundraising. It's about building great relationships with people. It's about the ability to communicate clearly, in person, on paper and online. The part of my job I most enjoyed was meeting customers and potential customers, finding out about them, their customers or service users and their organisations.

At my first enterprise our customers were mostly small shops run by people and collectives with whom we shared the same passion for vegetarian food. We never really felt like we were selling. But we were.

Later on my customers were teachers, headteachers and local authority managers. They were typically socially motivated people who were dedicating their lives to the education of young people. They were people who I generally shared values with. I wanted to find out about them, why they did what they did, what their challenges were and, most importantly, what made them passionate about education. What was 'sales work' felt like an opportunity to have really interesting conversations rather than selling something.

I spent the last 12 years of my career selling services to charities, and I loved it. I got to visit between three to five charities a week. I got to understand what their challenges were, I got to understand about their service users, and in many cases the people I met along the way have become colleagues and friends, regardless of whether they purchased from me or not.

If you believe in what you have to offer, you like meeting new people, are interested in learning about other people and organisations and can articulate the value you can bring to them, you'll be great at sales.

10. They have a strong handle on the finances

Since responsibility for the company finances was thrust upon me
when I was in my early 20s, I have mostly taken responsibility for the
finances the enterprise I've worked in.

The one exception was when I was a charity chief executive where,
like most charities of a certain size, there was a finance director. Don't
get me wrong, I have a great respect for accountants, but one of my
complaints about some of the finance directors I worked with is that it
could be a tussle about who was ultimately responsible for the financial
and commercial strategy.

Financial and commercial strategy go hand in hand. Whoever is
making the important commercial decisions for a social enterprise
needs to have a keen understanding of the financial position and
future forecasts. Decisions such as pricing of services and products,
investment in technology and assets, setting salaries and the like
require a strong financial understanding.

In the early days of any social enterprise, it is likely that the financial
management will be undertaken by a founder. As the enterprise grows,
you may need someone else to manage the finances, but never lose a
good and very current understanding of the financial position. This is
particularly important when either growing or shrinking the enterprise,
where quick but sensible financial decisions are vital.

I enjoyed managing the finances of all the enterprises I set up. As they
got larger, I had a bookkeeper to do the day-to-day jobs of managing
invoices, making payments and so on. I kept a detailed forecast on a
line-by-line spreadsheet that showed the income per customer, costs
by item, salary by individual and every other financial item month by
month for the year. Even when staff numbers were into the hundreds I
operated at this level of detail.

I compared this against each month's profit and loss line by line. I made changes to the forecast for the month just completed and readjusted the year's forecast on the basis of that information.

Even with an enterprise turning over £5 million and with 150 employees, this would only take two to three hours per month. Not a great investment of time given that I would then know everything there was to know financially about the business.

This detailed knowledge helped me keep all the enterprises on a steady and sustainable track, as well as know immediately what to do when there was a need to invest, the loss of a contract or another financial surprise.

11. They take sensible risks

A lot is said about entrepreneurs being people who take risks. Much of it is true and it's as true for social entrepreneurs. But the real quality of a good entrepreneur is the ability to take sensible or measured risks.

Borrowing money is always an area of risk, and one that in my experience many social entrepreneurs find difficult. Will the enterprise be able to borrow in the first place? And then repay the interest and loan?

I first met a corporate financier when I first pitched for commercial funding. When I didn't secure funding, he approached me and helped me to put together a loan funding application. I went to see him with a three-year forecast with an investment requirement of £500,000. We went through the numbers in detail and he asked questions about every row on the spreadsheet. Then he gave one of the best pieces of business advice that I have ever had:

"Find a way of doing everything you need to do for half the money, and I guarantee you'll get the investment."

We raised £250,000. It was enough. The enterprise took off and we managed the repayments easily. Sensible risk-taking.

12. They focus on the work

As a social entrepreneur it's important to focus on the work and its impact, rather than all the logistics of doing it.

Too much time can easily be spent on strategy, management and governance. While this is important, it does not on its own get the work done.

A focus on the work is not the same as doing the work. It probably will be at the start, but if you are successful and grow it won't be. You will soon need to spend your time working on the business, not in the business.

A focus on the work is about making sure that you and everyone else are clear what the work of the enterprise is. The clearer the work is defined, and the simpler it is, the more successful you are likely to be.

In business strategy language this is often called the vision or the mission, but I prefer to call it simply 'the work'. This feels more down to earth, more something everyone working for an enterprise can relate to.

At my first enterprise the work was changing the world by getting vegetarian food to more people. Our work was rooted in what we now call green politics and was clearly growth orientated.

My next involved building an ecovillage. That was both a massive undertaking but also a political statement about how humans can live more lightly on the planet. That was also growth orientated.

In my early 40s and running a charity I set up a counselling service to support teachers in their vital task. The charity's work had always been about supporting teachers, but it had lost its way and by the time I arrived it was only helping 700 teachers a year, most of them retired, and in the process it had become disconnected from the teaching profession.

My job was to turn that around, which we did, both with huge numbers of teachers seeking our support and our reconnection with the profession as a whole. And again, given that there were over 500,000 teachers in the UK, growth was required to do the work.

At my last enterprise we had a clear vision of what the work was. We had started with ten employees on a mission to create jobs in the Welsh Valleys. We had a vision of creating helpline services fit for the digital era. We became the UK's leading outsourcer of charity helplines and a specialist in supporting members of the public facing challenging circumstances in their lives. It is still going strong and remains a significant success story in the Welsh business landscape. We did this by focusing on the work.

Focusing on the work makes the work happen. And happen well. And at scale.

References

1. Paul Hawken was the managing director of Erewhon Foods, the founders of Sunwheel Foods who were a significant supplier to Nova in the early days. Paul was a leading light in the wholefoods industry in the USA. I did not realise this when I first read the book, but perhaps should not be surprised about a wholefoods/ Findhorn Community connection.

2. Sir Michael Joughin, former chairman of Hydro Electric and farmer; born April 26, 1926, died April 11, 1996. Herald Scotland, April 1996. https://www.heraldscotland.com/news/12047632.sir-michael-joughin/

3. Lois Graessle obituary. Marieke Bosman, The Guardian, April 2016. https://www.theguardian.com/world/2016/apr/06/lois-graessle-obituary

4. Steve Sinnott obituary. Francis Beckett, The Guardian, April 2008. https://www.theguardian.com/education/obituary/story/0,,2271494,00.html

5. Doug McAvoy obituary. Richard Garner, The Guardian, May 2019. https://www.theguardian.com/politics/2019/may/17/doug-mcavoy-obituary

6. NASUWT is the second largest teacher trade union in the UK. https://www.nasuwt.org.uk

7. The Association of Teachers and Lecturers (ATL) merged with the National Union of Teachers (NUT) in 2017 to become the National Education Union (NEU). https://neu.org.uk/press-releases/atl-and-nut-form-national-education-union

8. NAHT represents school leaders working across the school and education sector. https://www.naht.org.uk

9. The Secondary Heads Association (SHA) became the Association of School and College Leaders (ASCL). https://www.ascl.org.uk

10. Voice, formerly the Professional Association of Teachers (PAT), became a section of the trade union Community. https://community-tu.org/who-we-are/our-sectors/education-and-early-years/

11. Teacher Training Agency (TTA) became The Training and Development Agency for Schools (TDA) responsible for the initial and in-service training of teachers and other school staff in England. TDA was subsequently closed down.

12. OFSTED the schools inspectorate remains to this day. https://www.gov.uk/government/organisations/ofsted

13. Local Government Association are the national organisation for local government in England. https://www.local.gov.uk

14. Childline is a free, private and confidential service where children and young people can talk about anything. The charity was established by broadcaster Esther Rantzen and is now a service provided by NSPCC. https://www.childline.org.uk https://www.nspcc.org.uk

15. Stress on happiness. Stephanie Northern. TES, October 2020. https://www.tes.com/magazine/archive/stress-happiness

16. Stephen Lloyd obituary. David Brindle. The Guardian, August 2014. https://www.theguardian.com/society/2014/aug/29/stephen-lloyd. Following Stephen's death, a group of colleagues set up the Stephen Lloyd Awards to support up and coming social entrepreneurs and for a few years I was a trustee. http://www.stephenlloydawards.org

17. The Small Firms Loan Guarantee Scheme became the Enterprise Finance Guarantee Scheme. As of 2019 it was still operating and run by the British Business Bank but I am not altogether sure whether it is still available. I very much hope so. https://www. british-business-bank.co.uk/wp-content/uploads/2019/03/Enterprise-Finance-Guarantee-Brochure-March-2019.pdf

18. Professor Rob Briner and Dr Chris Dewberry. (2007). Staff wellbeing is key to school success: A research study into the links between staff wellbeing and school performance. Department of Organizational Psychology, Birkbeck College, University of London, in partnership with Worklife Support. http://www3.lancashire.gov.uk/corporate/web/viewdoc.asp?id=44615

19. Department for Work and Pensions. https://www.gov.uk/government/organisations/department-for-work-pensions

20. NHS Direct became NHS 111 in England https://www.england.nhs.uk/urgent-emergency-care/nhs-111/ and NHS 111 Wales in Wales. https://111.wales.nhs.uk

21. Winners of Welsh Small Business of the Year 2013 at the Institute of Welsh Affairs Business Awards. http://bit.ly/3iDvdeX

22. First Minister visits Nantgarw contact centre on its ninth birthday. https://www.commercialnewsmedia.com/archives/31751 Commercial News Media December 2014.

23. The Veterans' Gateway records over 10,000 enquiries as it celebrates its first year in service. http://bit.ly/3iFjA7d Gov.UK July 2018.

Further reading

Books

Part One: Nova Wholefoods

Carson R (1962, 2020 edition) *Silent Spring*. Penguin Modern Classics

Eyton, A (1982) *The F-plan Diet*. Penguin

Iacobbo K (2004). *Vegetarian America: A History*. Praeger Publishers Inc.

Powell. T. *Jeans and Beans and a Tub of Miso, Memories of Community Foods 1976 to 2006*.

Part Two: Ecovillage

Belbin, Dr M (2010). *Management Teams: Why They Succeed or Fail*. Routledge.

The Erraid Family. Erraid. *The story of an Island*. Isle of Erraid. https://www.erraid.com/erraid-book/

Hawken, P. (1979). *The Magic of Findhorn*. Fontana.

Talbott, J. (1997). *Simply Build Green*. Findhorn Press.

Tinsley, S. and George, H. (2006). *Ecological Footprint of the Findhorn Foundation and Community*. Moray Sustainable Development Research Centre, UHI Millennium Institute.

Tzu, S., & Giles, L. (2021). *The Art of War*. Duke Classics.

Walker, A. (1994). *The Kingdom Within*. Findhorn Press.

Part Three: Teacher Support Network

Holmes, E (2018). *A Practical Guide to Teacher Wellbeing*. Learning Matters.

Norman, A (2020). *The Dalai Lama: The Biography*. Harper Collins India.

Reffo, G and Wark, V (2014) *Leadership PQ: How Political Intelligence Sets Successful Leaders Apart.* Kogan Page.

Thom, J (2020). *Teacher Resilience: Managing stress and anxiety to thrive in the classroom*. John Catt Educational Ltd.

Part Four: Connect Assist

The Do Lectures. *The Side Project Report.* The Do Lectures.

Summers, J (2021). *We Are The Legion: The Royal British Legion at 100*. Profile Editions.

Websites

Here is a list of websites that I may have referenced in the book or have found helpful or interesting. As is the way of the internet, addresses were correct at the time of writing but may have changed by the time you read this.

Chapter	Information	Website
14	Learning styles. This has a short questionnaire where you can learn about your own learning style.	https://learning-styles-online.com/overview/
17	Belbin team roles.	https://www.belbin.com/about/belbin-team-roles
25	Sustainable living case studies.	https://www.bioregional.com/one-planet-living
40	Empathy. This is a useful article.	https://takealtus.com/2020/06/empathy-1/
40	Connect Assist provides values-based contact centre service	http://bit.ly/3HwLPP4

Organisations

I have mentioned many charities, social enterprises, businesses and other organisations in this book. Here are links to some of them that you may find useful to read more about. As is the way of the internet, addresses were correct at the time of writing but may have changed by the time you read this.

Chapter	Organisation	Websites
Intro	Schumacher Society	https://schumachersociety.net/governance/history-and-mission/
Intro	Greenpeace	https://www.greenpeace.org.uk
Intro	Friends of the Earth	https://foe.org
Intro	Social Enterprise UK	https://www.socialenterprise.org.uk
1	Totterdown Community Centre	https://www.bristolpost.co.uk/news/bristol-news/future-landmark-totterdown-centre-doubt-1123877
1	Green City Wholefoods	https://www.greencity.coop/about-us
1	Harmony Foods	https://www.gregorysams.com/chaosworks/natural-food-history/
1	Whole Earth Foods	https://www.wholeearthfoods.com/our-story/
1	Community Foods	https://www.communityfoods.co.uk/about/who-we-are
2	Doves Farm	https://www.dovesfarm.co.uk/about/our-story
2	Wild Oats	https://woats.co.uk/pages/our-story
4	Suma Wholefoods	https://www.sumawholesale.com

Chapter	Organisation	Websites
6	Katsouris Brothers	https://www.cypressa.co.uk/about
6	Rowse Honey	https://www.rowsehoney.co.uk/heritage
7	Cauldron Foods	https://www.cauldronfoods.co.uk/about
10	Essential Trading	https://www.essential-trading.coop/about-us/founders-interviews/
10	Alara Wholefoods	https://www.alarashop.com/our-story/
12	Isle of Erraid	https://www.erraid.com
13	Findhorn Foundation	https://www.findhorn.org
15	Findhorn Ecovillage	https://www.ecovillagefindhorn.com
16	Community Shares	https://communityshares.org.uk/find-out-more/what-are-community-shares
17	Habitat for Humanity	https://www.habitat.org https://www.youtube.com/user/HabitatForHumanity
17	Belbin	https://www.belbin.com
23	Centre for Alternative Technology	https://cat.org.uk
24	Living Machine	https://www.ecovillagefindhorn.com/index.php/water
24	Biomatrix	https://www.biomatrixwater.com/

Chapter	Organisation	Websites
26	Tibet Relief Fund	https://tibetrelieffund.co.uk/history/
26	His Holiness The 14th Dalai Lama	https://www.dalailama.com
27	NUT is now the National Education Union (NEU)	https://neu.org.uk
29	Association of Chief Executives of Voluntary Organisations (ACEVO)	https://www.acevo.org.uk
32	Centre for Stress Management	https://www.managingstress.com/pioneers-of-cognitive-stress-management
34	Fundraising UK	https://fundraising.co.uk/about/
34	Think Digital	https://thinkds.org/about/
35	Employee Assistance Professionals Association	https://eapassn.org/page/Aboutus
36	Welsh Development Agency became part of Welsh Government in 2006.	https://businesswales.gov.wales/businessfinance/featured-finance-scheme
37	RightNow was sold to Oracle in 2012	https://www.oracle.com/uk/cx/service/

Chapter	Organisation	Websites
37	NATFHE and AUT merged to become University and College Union (UCU)	https://www.ucu.org.uk
37	SMARTCymru	https://businesswales.gov.wales/expertisewales/support-and-funding-businesses/smartcymru
38	Turn2us	https://www.turn2us.org.uk
38	Bipolar UK	https://www.bipolaruk.org
39	Connect Assist	https://connectassist.co.uk
41	NCVO	https://www.ncvo.org.uk/#/
41	Money Advice Service is now part of MoneyHelper	https://www.moneyhelper.org.uk/en/about-us/who-we-are
41	CABA	https://www.caba.org.uk
41	Licensed Trade Charity	https://www.licensedtradecharity.org.uk
42	Save the Children	https://www.savethechildren.org.uk/what-we-do/child-poverty/uk-child-poverty
43	The Royal British Legion	https://www.britishlegion.org.uk
43	Institute of Welsh Affairs	https://www.iwa.wales
44	Mind	https://www.mind.org.uk/information-support/helplines/

Chapter	Organisation	Websites
45	Veterans Gateway	https://www.veteransgateway.org.uk
46	Enterprise Values	https://www.enterprisevalues.co.uk/about/
47	AAW Group	https://www.aawpartnership.com
48	Money and Mental Health	https://www.moneyandmentalhealth.org
48	Solva Edge Festival	https://www.edgefestival.co.uk
48	St Davids Festival of Ideas	https://www.stdavidsideas.co.uk